Hate and the Jewish Science

Also by Stephen Frosh

AFTER WORDS: The Personal in Gender, Culture and Psychotherapy

CHILD SEXUAL ABUSE (*Second Edition*) (*with Danya Glaser*)

CRITICAL NARRATIVE ANALYSIS IN PSYCHOLOGY: A Guide to Practice (*with Peter Emerson*)

FOR AND AGAINST PSYCHOANALYSIS

KEY CONCEPTS IN PSYCHOANALYSIS

IDENTITY CRISIS: Modernity, Psychoanalysis and the Self

PSYCHOANALYSIS AND PSYCHOLOGY: Minding the Gap

THE POLITICS OF MENTAL HEALTH (*with Ragnhild Banton and others*)

THE POLITICS OF PSYCHOANALYSIS: An Introduction to Freudian and Post-Freudian Theory (*Second Edition*)

PSYCHOANALYSIS IN CONTEXTS (*with Anthony Elliot*)

SEXUAL DIFFERENCE: Masculinity and Psychoanalysis

YOUNG MASCULINITIES: Understanding Boys in Contemporary Society (*with Ann Phoenix and Rob Pattman*)

Hate and the Jewish Science

Anti-Semitism, Nazism and Psychoanalysis

Revised Edition

Stephen Frosh
Birkbeck College, University of London, UK

First published in hardback 2005
First published in paperback 2009 by
PALGRAVE MACMILLAN

Palgrave Macmillan in the UK is an imprint of Macmillan Publishers Limited,
registered in England, company number 785998, of Houndmills, Basingstoke,
Hampshire RG21 6XS.

Palgrave Macmillan in the US is a division of St Martin's Press LLC,
175 Fifth Avenue, New York, NY 10010.

Palgrave Macmillan is the global academic imprint of the above companies
and has companies and representatives throughout the world.

Palgrave® and Macmillan® are registered trademarks in the United States,
the United Kingdom, Europe and other countries.

ISBN-13: 978–1–4039–2170–3   hardback
ISBN-13: 978–0–230–22952–5   paperback

This book is printed on paper suitable for recycling and made from fully
managed and sustained forest sources. Logging, pulping and manufacturing
processes are expected to conform to the environmental regulations of the
country of origin.

A catalogue record for this book is available from the British Library.

A catalog record for this book is available from the Library of Congress.

10   9   8   7   6   5   4   3   2   1
18   17   16   15   14   13   12   11   10   09

Printed and bound in Great Britain by
CPI Antony Rowe, Chippenham and Eastbourne

Contents

Acknowledgements

I would like to thank the *Limmud* organisation for stimulating my thoughts on Freud and Jewish identity, with which the project that turned into this book began. I am grateful to the Leverhulme Trust for providing me with a Research Fellowship in 2003–4 to support the writing of the book.

Some parts of this book have appeared in earlier and shorter versions in the following journal articles.

Freud, Psychoanalysis and Anti-Semitism. *The Psychoanalytic Review, 91* (2004), 309–330 (Permission for reprinting granted by *The Psychoanalytic Review* and the National Psychological Association for Psychoanalysis.)

Psychoanalysis, Nazism and 'Jewish Science'. *International Journal of Psychoanalysis, 84* (2003), 1315–1332.

The Other *American Imago, 59* (2002), 389–407.

Preface to the Paperback Edition

Hate and the Jewish Science represents a coming-together of some of my longstanding interests, which now seem obviously to be linked but in the past have been held separately in my mind and in some of my publications. The core intellectual concern of my writing over a couple of decades has been with the social and cultural sources and impact of psychoanalysis, in which I have been less focused on psychoanalysis as a clinical practice than on the theoretical and practical leverage it has given to attempts to understand 'politics', viewed broadly as the play of, and investment in, power relations. This has meant studies of psychoanalysis from the perspective of its implications for social change, for gender, sexual and 'race' politics, and more generally in terms of its place in contemporary (post-)modern society (Frosh, 1999, 2002, 2006a). It has also meant the use of psychoanalysis as a social theory, particularly in the fraught arena of understanding 'subjectivities' and 'identities' (Frosh, 1991; Frosh and Baraitser, 2003), as well as in the construction of a new disciplinary space that is coming to be called 'psychosocial studies' (Frosh and Baraitser, 2008). Amongst other issues, I have been particularly interested in how the concepts of psychoanalysis allow us to think about the perpetuation of discourses that fix identities in certain rigid ways (for example, as racist identities) and more broadly in how subjectivities are constructed in, through and against the workings of the social sphere.

Alongside these concerns, my engagement with the Jewish community in the UK and my immersion in Jewish cultural issues almost automatically led to an interest both in Jewish identities and in psychoanalysis as a 'Jewish' discipline. This is obviously a fraught idea, as the pages of the current book will make clear; but there is no doubt that psychoanalysis – including especially Freud himself – continues to generate great interest within the Jewish community, so that once one is identified as having something to say on both issues (psychoanalysis and Jewish identity), it is hard not to be drawn into teaching, writing and discussion about the two of them together. As it happens, I wrote very little about psychoanalysis and Jewish identity prior to the work that led up to this book; but around its publication and subsequently I ended up producing a series of articles on Freud and Jewish identity, as well as some broader work either drawn from the book itself, or from more general investigations in the area (e.g. Frosh, 2003, 2004, 2005a, 2005b, 2006b, 2008). The continuing liveliness of debates on Jewish identity (including tensions over Jewish responses to the Israel–Palestine conflict) and the propensity of the Jewish community to invite its academics to do teaching and other forms of speaking once one has appeared in print on a Jewish-relevant topic, has meant that my interest in these issues has expanded rather than been excised by the writing of this book. In addition, questions of the relationship of psychoanalysis to *Judaism* (as opposed to Jewish identity) have surfaced, perhaps reflecting a change in the traditional antagonism of psychoanalysts to religious commitment (Frosh, 2006c), and the expansion of interest in *ethics* amongst social theorists has also led to more concern with how 'Jewish ethics' plays out in the wider social sphere.

Amongst all this self-referentialism, this book remains relevant not just in terms of the developments I have described in my own work, but also for the wider scholarly environment. There has been continuing expansion in psychoanalytically-oriented publications on Freud's Jewish identity (Geller's 2007 book, *Freud's Jewish Body* being just one of the more distinguished recent examples) and on Jewish ethics and Zionism (e.g. Rose, 2007), although less on the psychoanalysis of anti-Semitism. There have also been important developments in practical work on the legacy of the engagement of psychoanalysis with Nazism, particularly sparked by the location of the 2007 International Psychoanalytic Association Congress in Berlin – only the second time since the Second World War that the Congress has been held in Germany. Aspects of the programme of that Congress, including the holding of an open 'large group' on 'Being in Berlin', reveal a renewed attempt on the part of psychoanalysts to 'work through' the troubling issues left over from Nazism that are still circulating. Material relating to this forms a large part of the current book, as does the idea that the histories of Jewish and anti-Semitic influences continue to live today both as a 'trace' in contemporary psychoanalysis and as a spur to broader analytic attempts to embrace attitudes and approaches antagonistic to racism. Indeed, this remains the main purpose of the current book: not just to examine the Jewish heritage in psychoanalysis and its effects, but also to provoke renewed efforts to use psychoanalysis as a theory and practical method to oppose racial and ethnic hatred.

References

Frosh, S. (1991) *Identity Crisis: Modernity, Psychoanalysis and the Self*. London: MacMillan; New York: Routledge.

Frosh, S. (1999) *The Politics of Psychoanalysis: An Introduction to Freudian and Post-Freudian Theory – Second Edition*. London: Macmillan.

Frosh, S. (2002) *After Words: The Personal in Gender, Culture and Psychotherapy*. London: Palgrave.

Frosh, S. (2003) Psychoanalysis, Nazism and 'Jewish Science'. *International Journal of Psychoanalysis, 84*, 1315–1332.

Frosh, S. (2004) Freud, Psychoanalysis and Anti-Semitism. *The Psychoanalytic Review, 91*, 309–330.

Frosh, S. (2005a) Fragments of Jewish Identity. *American Imago, 62*, 179–192.

Frosh, S. (2005b) Jung and the Nazis: Some Implications for Psychoanalysis. *Psychoanalysis and History, 7*, 253–271.

Frosh, S. (2006a) *For and Against Psychoanalysis – Second Edition*. London: Routledge.

Frosh, S. (2006b) The Burden of 'Jewish Genius': Einstein and Freud. *Jewish Quarterly, 201*, 51–56.

Frosh, S. (2006c) Psychoanalysis and Judaism. In D. Black (ed.) *Psychoanalysis and Religion in the Twenty-First Century*. London: Routledge.

Frosh, S. (2008) Freud and Jewish Identity. *Theory and Psychology, 18*, 167–178.

Frosh, S. and Baraitser, L. (2003) Thinking, Recognition and Otherness. *The Psychoanalytic Review, 90*, 771–789.

Frosh, S. and Baraitser, L. (2008) Psychoanalysis and Psychosocial Studies. *Psychoanalysis, Culture and Society, 13*, 346–365.

Geller, J. (2007) *On Freud's Jewish Body: Mitigating Circumcisions*. New Jersey: Fordham University Press.

Rose, J. (2007) *The Last Resistance*. London: Verso.

Introduction

It has sometimes been suggested that books on psychoanalysis, rather than being shelved in psychology sections in bookshops and libraries, should instead be listed under 'Jewish Studies'. This is not quite as whimsical as it might seem: not only have psychoanalysts often been Jewish, but those who are not Jewish are frequently thought of as if they were. In addition, it can be argued that psychoanalysis is heavily indebted to, and informed by, 'Jewish' perspectives, attitudes, ethics and methodological approaches. Starting as it did with Freud, its origins were deeply embedded in the secular Jewish culture of the late nineteenth century, at a time in Europe when Jewish and other identities were being debated and were undergoing radical change. Anti-Semitism was a powerful political and cultural force, science was struggling with religion, romanticism was having its nostalgic last gasp, and the revolutionary movements of the twentieth century – in politics, science and the arts – were being born. The Jews were both inside and outside Western society: newly 'emancipated' and able to claim influential positions, yet still victims of social exclusion, anti-Semitic populism and new forms of 'racial' anti-Semitism that were gradually replacing the old Christian anti-Judaism.

Psychoanalysis emerged from this background as one significant expression of the 'Jewish mind', reflecting and analysing Western civilisation, revealing its irrational and intense underside. Subsequently, psychoanalysis has become broader in its appeal and its personnel, yet there is still an irresistible pull towards associating it with Jews and Jewish culture, due partly to an inward-lookingness and fascination with psychological 'depths' that is often thought of as characteristically Jewish. In some ways this has been to psychoanalysis' advantage, giving it energy and a ready-made sense of collective and cultural

1

identity; in other ways, the association between psychoanalysis and Jewishness has been costly. In particular, anti-Semitism has infiltrated attitudes towards psychoanalysis, and there have been times when the denigration of psychoanalysis as 'Jewish science' has been murderously dangerous.

This book explores the intimate relationship between Jewish identity, psychoanalysis and anti-Semitism through what might be thought of as three 'case studies'. The first of these, as is common in books on psychoanalysis, is concerned with Freud himself. Freud was absolutely antagonistic to religion, including Judaism, and at times ambivalent towards Jews. However, he not only acknowledged the influence of his Jewish background on his work, but he also asserted or even celebrated the significance of his Jewish identity and his continuing links with the Jewish people – arguably, increasingly so as he got older. Much of psychoanalysis was first outlined to Jewish audiences; the brilliant examples of dreams and jokes peppering Freud's early psychoanalytic writings were largely Jewish in content and context; and in old age he wrote a major study on the theme of the origins of Judaism. His friends and colleagues were Jews; his way of thinking was Jewish, albeit heavily inflected with European cultural values; and in the end his fate – to be exiled from his homeland as a refugee from Nazism – was Jewish.

As many historians of culture have shown, Freud's Jewish connections were neither artificial nor trivial. Freud's own account of the meaning of his Jewish identity centred on three things: an emotional but somewhat inexplicable attachment to, and identification with, Jews and (to a lesser extent) Judaism; a sense of the value of being sufficiently 'outside' Western culture to gain analytic distance from it; and an appreciation of the extensive nature and effects of anti-Semitism. These three aspects of Jewish identity are discussed in Part I of this book, with the first chapter focusing on establishing the significance to Freud of his Jewishness and on his understanding of its emotional hold, whilst the second looks at his ideas on anti-Semitism, particularly as formulated in the book *Moses and Monotheism*. What emerges from this material is a view of psychoanalysis as founded on both a positive valuation of the critical vision that comes from being slightly outside the host culture, and as a response to – yet also a 'carrier' of – the hostility of that culture towards its outsiders, notably embodied in the figure of the Jew.

If the Jewish heritage of psychoanalysis was something towards which Freud himself felt ambivalence, it is not surprising that this feeling was shared by other early psychoanalysts, Jewish and non-Jewish alike. Psychoanalysis strove to be a neutral science yet patently demonstrated that its origins lay in a very specific set of historical and social circumstances, and that these had a continuing impact on its theories and practices. For Jewish analysts, living in a context in which anti-Semitism was one of the most powerful political ideologies, and in which assimilation to the surrounding culture was a tempting aspiration for Jews as a way to escape it, this meant having to deal with professional investments in something they might have been trying to leave behind. For non-Jewish analysts, the situation was even more stark: in a society in which to be a Jew was to be heavily derogated, they chose to identify themselves with a discipline invented by a Jew and dominated by Jews; they found themselves being analysed and trained by Jews; and they discovered that they were seen more-or-less as Jews by much of the surrounding culture. For them, being adherents of 'Jewish science' would always have some uncomfortable aspects; but once the external situation became one in which it could endanger their careers and possibly their lives, they were faced with a set of very difficult moral and practical choices.

The second 'case study', in Part II of this book, explores what happened when the psychoanalytic movement was brutally faced with the requirement to defend or repudiate its Jewish identity. Psychoanalysis grew up in German-speaking Europe and it was there that it met its great political adversary, Nazism. After the Second World War, the story of what happened was largely buried for about forty years, until a succession of historical 'recoveries' and a new generation of German analysts re-examined it. Historical work on the fate of psychoanalysis in the Third Reich has continued to reveal important information, without resolving all the controversies about the significance of the events in question for psychoanalysis itself and for a broader understanding of what can happen when organisations are faced with the demand to collaborate or die – a demand that, of course, is all-too-often made of individuals in such circumstances as well. In Germany, it is now clear, the decision was made to collaborate, but how and why this happened and the impact of this decision after the war is a complicated tale. Chapters 3, 4 and 5 draw on this historical work to offer a psychosocial account of the collaborationist tendency in psychoanalysis at that time, in particular how it expressed not only personal fears and ambitions and misguided strategies, but also something about anti-Semitism on a psychological and political level. What becomes apparent from this material is that the way German psychoanalysis shed its Jewish identity and then hid its history after the war was not simply a failure to resist political oppression; it also reflected the ambivalence towards that Jewish identity that is embedded in the psychoanalytic movement itself, and has always been there. That is, as part and parcel of being a 'Jewish science' in the various senses outlined in Part I, psychoanalysis has its own anti-Semitic dimension, and this can be seen in operation in the way it capitulated before the Nazi menace. Whether this specific occurrence can be generalised as a statement about the seeds of self-hate lying within any progressive movement even without any Jewish dimension is a moot point; the evidence from history suggests that to some extent that might be so.

The third 'case study' asks a different but related question. If psychoanalysis is so Jewish and has such an experience of anti-Semitism, and if it is so clever at analysing complex, irrational phenomena, how is it that it has offered so little insight into anti-Semitism itself? As several commentators have noticed, there has been a strong tendency to neglect or play down anti-Semitism as a clinical and psychodynamic phenomenon, suggesting that something troubling is being avoided. To put this a little more cautiously, the first two chapters of Part III review the work carried out within psychoanalysis on anti-Semitism, finding a number of interesting observations, speculations and theoretical formulations, but also arguing that these theories fail adequately to address the psychosocial nature of anti-Semitism. What is meant here is that the theories tend to see anti-Semitism as the product of disturbing psychological processes within individuals that are expressed externally through being channelled into historically validated, and therefore ready-made, cultural beliefs and behaviours about and towards Jews. However, it can more powerfully be argued that the direction of effect is better thought of the other way around: that anti-Semitism is a fundamental element of Western culture and is so pervasive and resilient that every individual member of that culture is constructed around it. That is, the Jew, and more generally the figure of the 'other', is a constitutive feature of Western consciousness, an element out of which subjectivity is made. Chapter 8, the final chapter of Part III and of the book, expands on this idea with an examination of what the 'other' of anti-Semitic and racist discourse might be, and ends with a deliberately extreme account of the links between the Western figure of the Jew and the psychoanalytic unconscious.

This book, then, draws on historical and psychoanalytic work to examine the significance of psychoanalysis' Jewish identity and what that can tell us about political and psychological resistance, anti-

Semitism and racism. It is not in itself an historical work – it relies, for example, on the scholarship of others in outlining what happened in Germany in the 1930s and 1940s. It is also not purely psychoanalytic, though the general premise does include acceptance of the idea that unconscious processes are powerfully significant in determining how individuals and organisations respond to the circumstances in which they find themselves. It is, rather, *psychosocial*, arguing that it is artificial to separate psychological from social processes, and that they have to be understood as entwined with one another, so that the deep feelings which people often take to be aspects of their 'identities' are connected in innumerable ways with the social and cultural forces out of which they arise. It is also a polemical book, based on the belief that there is nothing more dangerous in contemporary society than racism, and that studies of racist ideas and actions – here, in the specific guise of anti-Semitism – continue to be necessary as part of the essential task of combating racism wherever it is found.

Part I
Freud, Jews and Anti-Semitism

1
Freud's Jewish Identity

In 1977, whilst inaugurating the Sigmund Freud Professorship at the Hebrew University in Jerusalem, Anna Freud created a stir by returning to an issue which had troubled the psychoanalytic movement throughout its history: the idea that psychoanalysis is a 'Jewish science'. For her father Sigmund, the Jewish connections of psychoanalysis were a source of very mixed feelings, ranging from pride in the idea that psychoanalysis might be an extension of Jewish intellectualism, through anxiety over what this might mean for the safety of his creation, to discomfort due to the belief that psychoanalysis could not belong to any one people or share any ideology other than that of science itself, meaning, in his mind, the disinterested pursuit of truth. As time went on, and particularly in the context of ever more extreme anti-Semitism, Freud became more assertive over his own Jewish identity, even though he never accepted the 'Jewish science' label for psychoanalysis as a whole. This label became increasingly negative once the Nazis came to power in Europe: 'Jewish' science came to mean something corrupt and corrupting, a lying ideology directed at poisoning the health of the Aryan nations. In the post-Second World War period, considerable effort went into maintaining the independence and non-ideological nature of psychoanalysis, based both on opposition to any 'racialised' claims in the wake of Nazism, and a liberal antagonism to the idea that any 'race' or creed could own any properly academic or professional discipline. Anna Freud, however, responding to the powerful symbolism of a psychoanalytic Congress held on 'Jewish' soil as well as the founding of a Freud professorship in

Jerusalem, reclaimed the Jewishness of psychoanalysis, making it acceptable to speak not just of persecution, but also of pride.

> During the era of its existence, psychoanalysis has entered into connexion with various academic institutions, not always with satisfactory results... It has also, repeatedly, experienced rejection by them, being criticised for its methods being imprecise, its findings not open to proof by experiment, for being unscientific, even for being a 'Jewish science'. However the other derogatory comments may be evaluated, it is, I believe, the last-mentioned connotation which, under present circumstances, can serve as a title of honour.   (A. Freud, 1978, p. 148)

The claim of 'honour' here is a direct riposte to those who would hide behind a screen of neutrality; it is a statement of origins and commitment, as well as an emotional reconnection between a troubled discipline and the equally troubled people who had given it life. Interestingly, it also reflects a cultural moment in which identity politics became potent. Jewishness is one of many criticisms levelled against psychoanalysis and was previously a term of opprobrium; here – like feminine, black or gay identity in other movements of about the same time – it is reclaimed as a strength.

The notion of psychoanalysis as a 'Jewish science' depends only partly on the fact that most of its originators in Europe were Jews, although this was certainly the case: as Klein (1985, p. 93) points out, 'Until March 6, 1907, when Carl Jung and... Ludwig Binswanger, attended their first meeting in Vienna, every member of the [psychoanalytic] circle – by this time, there were about 20 – was Jewish.' That there were social reasons for this Jewish dominance is attested to not only by the circumstances in Vienna at the time during which psychoanalysis emerged, but also by its rather different history in places where different conditions prevailed – notably in Britain, where the most significant early analysts were intellectual and literary non-Jews (Frosh, 2003). More significantly, the claim that psychoanalysis should be considered a 'Jewish science' relates to the idea that Jewish thought, Jewish philosophy and Jewish history flooded its foundations, investing it with the specific inward-consciousness of the Jews, who were newly released in the nineteenth century from their ghettoes and at least some of their traditions. That is, the claim is based on the idea of cultural inheritance: that however atheistic these early psychoanalytic Jews were, they *could not but* pursue a way of looking at things which was 'Jewish'. What this 'Jewishness' consisted in was not a religious perspective – not *Judaism* – but an approach to argument and interpretation established over centuries in which debates over the meanings of texts were the main expression of cultural achievement. The claim is therefore not just a sociological one, that Jews became psychoanalysts because they felt comfortable and familiar in this role, but also an argument about intellectual history: the *reason* they felt so comfortable was that the psychoanalytic world-view was so much like the Jewish one.

Much of this argument is focused on Freud himself, who is evoked as not just the founder of psychoanalysis, but its mainstay – something still true today to some degree, but very much the case during his lifetime, which ended only in 1939. Freud is seen as epitomising the kind of secular Jew who played such a powerful role in revolutionising western culture at the turn of the twentieth century, and his 'science' as completely infused with 'Jewish' perceptions. This evocation does not depend on the assertion that Freud himself was committed to his Jewish identity, although there is now not much doubt that he was. In a famous exploration of the impact of psychoanalysis, Philip Rieff (1959) credits it with the invention of what he calls (in gender-blind language) 'Psychological Man'. 'Psychological Man' already sounds stereotypically Jewish, characterised as he is with a tendency to be reflexive, introspective, anxious and depressed; for Rieff, this is the nature of the western human subject throughout the first half of the twentieth century, when the influence of psychoanalysis was at its greatest. Yosef Hayim Yerushalmi (1991), in what is possibly the most influential book on Freud's Jewish identity, quoted and contested by both Jacques Derrida (1995) and Edward Said (2003), makes this link between the 'Psychological Man' and the Jew explicit. For Yerushalmi, behind the Psychological Man is the 'Psychological Jew', with psychoanalysis being a branch of the general cultural explosion that was to a large extent dependent on, and carried forward by, the progressive secularism that arose in the wake of Jewish emancipation.

> The Psychological Jew was born before Freud. If, for all secular Jews, Judaism has become 'Jewishness' of one kind or another, the Jewishness of the Psychological Jew seems, at least to the outsider, devoid of all but the most vestigial content; it has become almost pure subjectivity. Content is replaced by character. Alienated from classical Jewish texts, Psychological Jews tend to insist on inalienable Jewish traits. Intellectuality and independence of mind, the

highest ethical and moral standards, concern for social justice, tenacity in the face of persecution – these are among the qualities they will claim, if called upon, as quintessentially Jewish. It is therefore no accident that the first great culture-hero of modern secular Jews was Spinoza (to be joined later by Marx and eventually by Freud himself).   (p. 10)

The attributes of the Psychological Jew summarised by Yerushalmi neatly define the ideal mentally healthy character proposed by classical psychoanalysis and in many respects embodied by Freud (at least as remembered and idealised by his followers), although post Freudian analysts have added a less obviously 'Jewish' emphasis on fulfilling interpersonal relationships. The ideal person of early psychoanalysis is less worried about how he or she gets on with others, than with living an intellectually coherent and ethical life in the face of the immense instinctual and external pressures towards corruption – a rather neat parallel to the secular Jew balancing between inner doubts and external pressures to convert or assimilate. Yerushalmi, reflecting on secular Jews themselves, adds to this list of positive attributes a sensitivity to anti-Semitism of a very specific kind, far removed from the acceptance of ethnic antagonism that was more characteristic of pre-emancipation eras.

> Floating in their undefined yet somehow real Jewishness, they will doubly resent and fiercely resist any attempt on the part of the surrounding society to define them against their own wishes. The worst moments are those in which, as a result of anti-Semitism, they are forced to realize that vital aspects of their lives are still determined by ancestral choices they may no longer understand and which, in any case, they feel they have transcended or repudiated.   (Ibid.)

One might argue that the post-war shift from secular humanism to Jewish identity politics was partly in response to the discovery that 'ancestral choices' still had the power absolutely to determine one's fate.

The secular Jew's combination of commitment to intellectual goals and ethical achievement, alongside resentment at the demeaning effects of anti-Semitism, is very much the story of Freud, although as Yerushalmi notes there are also ways in which Freud deviates from it. It is also a characterisation of an interior way of being, hovering around questions of belonging and otherness, of historical determination and freedom, which demonstrably influences modern Jewish identities, and perhaps modern identities in general. This 'Psychological Jew' is not a Freudian creation, but it is deeply inflected by, as well as reflected in, Freudianism, with its unsettled, constantly searching, ever-analysing hunt for some elusive truth. Taking this further, what arises is the question of *marginality*, of whether seeing things from the sides, 'looking awry' in Slavoj Žižek's (1991) words, is a necessary condition for the emergence and influence of psychoanalysis. Could someone who was surrounded by the comfort of social acceptance, rather than subjected to the ambivalent love/loathe dynamic characteristic of anti-Semitism as of all racism, have stood far enough outside that culture to offer the devastatingly ironic critique that Freud offered? Does one have to be an outsider to see *in*? This relates to many aspects of Jewish culture emphasising its analytic dimension: Talmudic patterns of exegesis, free thinking within a heavily structured pattern of rules, fascination with words, with reading, with critical commentary, a relentless and unending search for another way of looking at things. Also, it can be asserted, it relates to a reluctance to be one of the crowd, of a kind dramatised in a story from Freud's early (1905) psycho-analytic book, *Jokes and their Relation to the Unconscious*; as usual, the story is a Jewish one (and still in circulation).

> Itzig had been declared fit for service in the artillery. He was clearly an intelligent lad, but intractable and without any interest in the service. One of his superior officers, who was friendlily disposed to him, took him on one side and said to him: 'Itzig, you're no use to us. I'll give you a piece of advice: buy yourself a cannon and make yourself independent!'   (p. 56)

Making himself independent is, of course, precisely what Freud did, and the phallic symbolism of the cannon blasting its own way in the world is clearly no accident, given that Freud thought accidents never happen. Sharing something here with the Protestant, and certainly the capitalist, consciousness in their focus on individual self-determination, but ethnically still embedded in the Jewish *difference*, its 'plague on both your houses', psychoanalysis, at least in its own mythology, stands outside orthodoxies, offering a radical alternative, a language of understanding which is 'independent'. This new language, neither religious nor scientific, whatever Freud's cravings in the latter direction, is best called deeply *critical*: there is nothing that can stand outside analysis, no 'bedrock' (to use Freud's phrase about sexual difference, which he did think was basic), no final resting place for the questing intelligence. 'Almost pure subjectivity,' writes Yerushalmi, 'Intellectuality and independence of mind, the highest ethical and moral standards, concern for social justice, tenacity in the face of persecution': both Jews and psychoanalysts have needed these attributes, and sometimes they have possessed them.

Denials, smokescreens and anti-Semitism

Freud's relationship with his Jewish identity was notoriously ambivalent and has been the subject of a great deal of historical, psychoanalytic and frankly speculative scholarship. For Edward Said (2003, pp. 35–6), 'To say of Freud's relationship with Judaism that it was conflicted is to venture an understatement. At times he was proud of his belonging, even though he was irremediably anti-religious; at other times he expressed annoyance with and unmistakable disapproval of Zionism.' Indeed, Freud worked hard to present himself as someone alienated from even vestigial relationships with a Jewish *religious* identity. In a famous letter of 1930 to A.A. Roback, he comments,

> It may interest you to know that my father did indeed come from a Chassidic background. He was 41 when I was born and had been estranged from his native environment for almost 20 years. My education was so un-Jewish that today I cannot even read your dedication, which is evidently written in Hebrew. In later life I have often regretted this lack in my education.   (Freud, 1961, p. 394)

Noting the force of Freud's repudiation of Judaism, and his aggressive critique of all religion, which he saw as 'illusion', Halpern (1999) suggests that it might reflect an antagonism towards his father that was projected onto the religion itself. In this view Freud, disappointed in his father, refuted the claims of all father-religions to authority: 'He believed that God and religion had no right to demand submission because they had not lived up to their promise. God, far for being idealizable, was seen as the opposite – merely an illusion... For Freud, God represents the disappointing father whose demands were nonetheless still felt, and which Freud needed vehemently to reject' (p. 1200). In contrast, Halpern argues, Freud sought out the 'maternal' warmth of Jewish life through its cultural heritage. Even when, as in his famous letter to the B'nai Brith organisation on the occasion of his seventieth birthday (discussed at length later), he is at his most explicit in acknowledging his continuing links with Jews and Jewish identity, Freud distances himself from its most characteristic outward forms – religion and Zionism.

> What tied me to Jewry was – I have to admit it – not the faith not even the national pride, for I was always an unbeliever, have been brought up without religion, but not without respect for the so-called 'ethical' demands of human civilisation.   (Freud, 1961, p. 367)

Despite these clear disavowals, Yerushalmi (1991) rather persuasively documents evidence suggesting not only that Freud's father remained knowledgeable about, and to some degree at least committed to, Judaism throughout his life (contrary to Freud's assertion about his 'estrangement'), but also that Freud retained at least some knowledge of Judaism. The claim, for instance, that he barely even recognised Hebrew when he saw it seems unlikely, especially given the trouble that his father took to assemble a 'melitza' (a compendium of Biblical quotations) in Hebrew to write into the flyleaf of his gift of the rebound family Bible on the occasion of Freud's thirty-fifth birthday (Yerushalmi, 1991, pp. 71ff). Freud himself, taught religion by the inspirational Samuel Hammerschlag, may have focused on Judaism's ethical principles, but is unlikely never to have come into contact with its forms or its language. Indeed, even though the Freud family 'spoke German and ignored such observances as kashrut and the Sabbath' once they had moved to Vienna when Freud was three years old, they still recognised some major Jewish holidays and some scholars claim that Freud would still have heard his father's 'adept... Hebrew recitation of the Passover service' (Klein, 1985, p. 42).

On the issue of Zionism, as Said notes, there is considerable evidence of Freud's negativity towards the attempts to build a Jewish homeland in Palestine. However, this did not stop him actively supporting Zionist ideas at other times, nor being involved with the fledgling Hebrew University. Diller (1991) describes how Freud's sons Martin and Ernst were both Zionists and belonged to Zionist organisations while they were students at the University of Vienna. According to Diller (pp. 100–101),

> Freud fully approved of their participation and was in fact himself made an honorary member of Kadimah in 1936. In the 1920s he made several 'substantial' contributions to Hechalutz, another

Zionist organisation, and for a number of years he followed quite closely the happenings in the Middle East.... When the Hebrew University was founded, he willingly agreed to serve on its board and even dreamed, for a short while anyway, of establishing there a chair in psychoanalysis for Max Eitingon, who had settled in Palestine in 1933.

One wonders, at times, whether Freud's intellect, which pushed him towards universalism and a mode of ethical humanism imbued with secularism and non-sectarianism, was so at odds with his emotions and his experiences that even he – the founder of the science of psychological conflict – could only take refuge behind a smokescreen of ambiguity and misrepresentation. The 'hidden Jew', one might note, is a recurrent figure in both Jewish and anti-Semitic mythology, and perhaps there was an element in Freud that was not averse to making use of it.

It is clear, however, from the voluminous work on Freud, that he was not really 'hidden' as a Jew at all, even though his rejection of religion was more or less total. Freud explicitly identified himself as a Jew throughout his life, ever more openly as anti-Semitism became increasingly rife in Europe, and in Germany and Austria in particular. Early on, this identification was rather clearly ambivalent: like many 'cultured' Western European Jews, Freud was disparaging towards Jews from Eastern Europe whom he regarded as racial throwbacks and degenerates (Gilman, 1993). One can see this as a kind of internalised anti-Semitism, as the Eastern Jews served as emblems of an enclosed, impoverished and ignorant people played on in anti-Semitic stereotypes. This is Freud in 1872, aged 16, writing to a friend about two Jews he met on a train:

> Now this Jew talked the same way as I had heard thousands of others talk before, even in Freiberg. His face seemed familiar – he was typical. So was the boy with whom he discussed religion. He was cut from the cloth from which fate makes swindlers when the time is ripe: cunning, mendacious, kept by his adoring relatives in the belief that he is a great talent, but unprincipled and without character... I have enough of this lot. In the course of the conversation I learned that Madame Jewess and family hailed from Meseritsch: the proper compost-heap for this sort of weed.   (Gilman, 1993, p. 13)

This is the language of personal revulsion but also of cultural and political anti-Semitism: Jews were (and are) automatically associated with 'unprincipled swindlers', and a 'weed', after all, is something that causes havoc in well-ordered and 'cultured' gardens, and has to be rooted out. Amongst other things, what is conveyed here is the boyish Freud's absorption of these anti-Semitic ideas and his wish to remove himself absolutely from 'this lot'.

These Eastern European Jews remained a source of distanced disgust for Freud for a long time, although later the feeling seems to have been tempered by a kind of amusement. In *Jokes and their Relation to the Unconscious*, for example, Freud (1905) tells a series of jokes against poor and uncivilised Jews, all implicitly at least Eastern European in origin.

> Two Jews were discussing baths. 'I have a bath every year,' said one of them, 'whether I need one or not.' (p. 72)

And now once again two Jews outside the bath-house:

> One of them sighed: 'Another year gone by already!' (p. 78)

Sometimes, however, the humour is of a gentler kind, mixed with family feeling, as in the following joke about how Jews immediately relax in the company of their co-religionists.

> A Galician Jew was travelling in a train. He had made himself really comfortable, had unbuttoned his coat, and put his feet up on the seat. Just then a gentleman in modern dress entered the compartment. The Jew promptly pulled himself together and took up a proper pose. The stranger fingered through the pages of a notebook, made some calculations, reflected for a moment and then asked the Jew: 'Excuse me, when is Yom Kippur?' 'Oho!' said the Jew, and put his feet back on the seat again before answering. (pp. 80–1)

In a related vein, Freud gives considerable attention to schnorrer (beggar) jokes, in which the insouciance of the beggar is not treated as abhorrent, but rather as something recognisable as a manifestation of Jewish intelligence.

> A schnorrer, who was allowed as a guest into the same house every Sunday, appeared one day in the company of an unknown young man who gave signs of being about to sit down to table. 'Who is this?' asked the householder. 'He's been my son-in-law,' was the

reply, 'since last week. I've promised him his board for the first year.'   (p. 112)

Rich, westernised Jews share exactly in this recognisable mode of Jewish wit; their relationship with the Jewish beggar is again a family one, in which there is a kind of contest born out of recognition of the other's similarity.

> The Baron, deeply moved by the schnorrer's tale of woe, rang for his servants: 'Throw him out! he's breaking my heart!'   (p. 113)

If Freud exemplified the way many assimilated Jews tried to put a boundary between themselves and the Eastern Europeans, the frequency with which he quotes disparaging jokes of this kind suggests that he never quite managed it; it is as if he keeps having to remind himself and his readers that he is not a Jew of that type. His occasional outbursts against Jews at various times in his life also shows how deeply anti-Semitic stereotypes can take root in Jews themselves. Gilman (1993) makes something similar of Freud's wishful search to establish a Jewish heritage separate from the East Europeans in his brief analysis of an autobiographical note Freud wrote in 1925.

> I was born on May 6th 1856, at Freiberg in Moravia, a small town in what is now Czechoslovakia. My parents were Jews, I have remained a Jew myself. I have reason to believe that my father's family were settled for a long time on the Rhine (at Cologne), that, as a result of persecution of the Jews during the fourteenth or fifteenth century, they fled eastwards, and that they migrated back from Lithuania through Galicia into German Austria.   (p. 14)

This passage characteristically acknowledges Freud's Jewish origins and asserts his continued Jewish allegiance – unlike others, he never converted or abandoned his Jewish identity. On the other hand, as Gilman notes, Freud subtly introduces into this account the suggestion that he is both an Eastern Jew and *not* an Eastern Jew: they may seem to have come from Lithuania and Galicia, but originally they were from the Rhine.

> Just as Theodor Herzl imagined his ancestors coming from an idealised medieval Spain, so too Freud saw his family moving from one cultural landscape (Germany) through the barbaric East and return-

ing eventually to another cultural sphere (Austria). This tension between the perception of belonging and not belonging to any given culture mirrors the position of the acculturated Jew in late-nineteenth-century Europe.   (ibid.)

Gilman further argues that Freud also participated in a turn-of-the century consensus that the Jewish mind-set was inherently (and inheritedly) pathological, a view shared by many other Jews as well. (Gilman [p. 26] quotes Wittgenstein here, 'even the greatest of Jewish thinkers is no more than talented. (Myself, for instance.) I think there is some truth to my idea that I really only think reproductively.') Nevertheless, throughout these early writings of Freud (and 'early' here means up until his late forties), there is evidence of a considerable amount of fascination with Jewishness mixed in with a distancing strategy laced with the received anti-Semitic tastes of Viennese society. Some of this is amusing – many of the anti-Jewish jokes quoted by Freud continue to circulate in the 'amongst ourselves' context of Jewish society – but it also reveals the discomfort of the cultural marginal, the one aware of being 'other'.

Whatever the strength of Freud's internalised anti-Semitism, however, the external world's actual anti-Semitism ensured that he kept a strong positive identification with his Jewish identity. This was in no way a religious identification: as noted above, he always declared he was of no religion, he kept no festivals or customs, visited no synagogues, and did everything he could to deconstruct religion in general and (in *Moses and Monotheism*) Judaism in particular. He was always wry about the adulation he received from some Jews at least; for example, in a 1926 letter to Marie Bonaparte describing the celebration on his seventieth birthday, he wrote:

> The Jewish societies in Vienna and the University in Jerusalem (of which I am a trustee), in short the Jews altogether, have celebrated me like a national hero, although my service to the Jewish cause is confined to the single point that I have never denied my Jewishness.   (Freud, 1961, p. 369)

But this 'single point' was no simple point. As Peter Gay (1988, p. 507), in a rather sober and slightly desultory analysis of Freud's Jewishness, describes, Freud's trajectory 'in the poisonous atmosphere of the late 1920s and early 1930s' was to do more than simply refuse to deny his Jewish origins: 'He trumpeted them.' Gay argues that this was a consistent attitude taken by Freud throughout his life, from his refusal to see himself as second-class when he was a student at university, right through to the Nazi period. The key moment of self-assertion seems to have come quite early, in the mid-1880s, evidenced by his response to a query about where he stood on the tension between France and Germany: 'I am a Jew, adhering neither to Germany nor to Austria' (Klein, 1985, p. 57). This line was not simply one of keeping out of trouble, but rather of recognising and opposing the anti-Semitism to be found throughout western culture, but especially – and tragically for Freud, schooled and devoted as he was to its high ethical aspirations – German culture. By 1926, speaking to a nationalistic and somewhat anti-Semitic journalist, Freud commented famously,

> My language is German. My culture, my attainments are German. I considered myself German intellectually, until I noticed the growth of antisemitic prejudice in Germany and German Austria. Since that time, I prefer to call myself a Jew.   (Gay, 1988, p. 448)

As anti-Semitism became more widespread and brutal (once again, one might add, rather than for the first time, even in Freud's lifetime), so he became both more assertive about his Jewish identity and more scathing about others. By 1938, in the face of Nazism, he was not only cynical, but also combative and retaliatory, however puny his resources might have been. Writing, whilst still in Vienna, to Max Eitingon, he asks, 'Have you read that Jews in Germany are to be forbidden to give their children German names? They can only retaliate by demanding that the Nazis refrain from using the popular names of John, Joseph and Mary' (Freud, 1961, p. 437) – neatly pointing to the Jewish origins of Christian culture. As will be seen in the next chapter, suggesting Jewish superiority seems to have been one favourite ploy of Freud's when faced with anti-Semitism, particularly that perpetrated by the Nazis. Even in the iconoclastic *Moses and Monotheism*, written during the Nazi period and making the foremost Jewish prophet, Moses, an Egyptian, Judaism is celebrated for its primacy as an intellectual religion devoid of reliance on images and sensual mystification. Jewish civilisation has sustained itself for thousands of years; German civilisation seems by contrast to have been a transient thing.

> In a letter to Wilhelm Reich... [Freud] remarked about Hitler that many people had wondered how in *A Midsummer Night's Dream* Shakespeare could make a lady fall in love with a donkey. 'And

now think of it,' he added, 'that a nation of sixty-five million have...'   (Diller, 1991, p. 119)

Freud should probably not have been so surprised, given that the primary discovery of psychoanalysis is the appeal of irrationality and the fragility of reason. Even in himself, as he knew well, there was much that could not be worked out – specifically, ambitious, wishes and identifications that were not reducible to rational responses to external circumstances. Some of the most powerful of these mysterious patterns, it turns out, circulated around his Jewish identity.

Dark, emotional powers

Not only did Freud define his Jewish identity in relation to anti-Semitism; he also expressed, increasingly as he got older, a strong positive emotional attachment to his Jewishness. Some of this was nostalgic, expressing gratitude for the sense of community and 'home' that his Jewish identity could give him in a hostile world. The most significant element here was Freud's involvement with the Vienna B'nai Brith, a society of Jewish professional men who met together in order to promote Jewish values in the context of lectures on culture and science. Knoepfmacher (1979, pp. 441–22) describes the meetings of the Vienna society as 'solemn affairs [requiring] formal attire, which meant changing into a frock coat at the end of the day. The business transactions were followed by a lecture or discussion and a formal dinner.' For several years in the late 1890s and early 1900s, this group of intelligent secular Jews was Freud's main platform for the presentation of his ideas – and it seems always to have been positive towards him even when these ideas were proving too radical for the medical establishment. Klein (1985) and Diller (1991) both devote considerable attention to Freud's time with the B'nai Brith. Klein makes a claim for its significance for Freud in meeting his 'need for Jewish companionship' (p. 72), and it certainly did provide Freud with companionship free from anxiety in a city governed by the anti-Semitic party of the day (and it should be noted that, according to his son Martin, Freud barely ever had a non-Jewish guest in his home at that time [ibid.]). In addition, however, it was a genuine source of intellectual advancement. Freud gave a startlingly demanding series of lectures to his comrades in the lodge, in particular during 1896 and 1897 offering lectures that became the basis for his ground-breaking work, *The Interpretation of Dreams*. Knoepfmacher (1979, pp. 442–3) describes how the first lecture Freud gave to the members, on December 7, 1897, was 'On Dream Interpretation'. 'The minutes of that meeting... read: "The high-spirited lecture, involving general human interest, and the masterful presentation which, in spite of the difficulty of the subject, was well adapted to lay understanding, made for a most rewarding evening. The audience showed its gratitude by frantic applause."' Freud was actively involved too in the general work of the lodge, he 'attended meetings regularly, was active in recruiting new members and establishing a second Vienna chapter, led discussions on the mission of the order, and delivered twenty-one lectures to the group between 1897 and 1917, mostly before 1902. With the exception of [his friend Wilhelm] Fliess and two talks given to the Judische Akademische Lesehalle in 1896 and 1897, the B'nai Brith was his exclusive audience during this period' (Diller, 1991, p. 169). Indeed, as Klein comments (p. 74), 'The Jewish society became an active intellectual forum for his metapsychological views during the productive five-year period 1897–1902, and, in this respect, was a precursor of the movement of psychoanalysis.' Freud continued his relationship with the B'nai Brith until the end of the First World War, lecturing to them in April 1915 on 'We and Death' and, for the last time, in 1917 on 'Imagination and Art' (Knoepfmacher, 1979, p. 444).

Whilst the lack of an alternative platform was a major reason for Freud's engagement with the B'nai Brith, so that this engagement withered away once he formed the (also initially totally Jewish) Wednesday meeting group that became the Psychoanalytic Society, there was also a set of active reasons for Freud's identification with the lodge that bears on the positive side of his Jewish identity. In a very famous letter to the B'nai Brith written in 1926 in response to its greetings on the occasion of his seventieth birthday, Freud takes care to list both the general and the specific reason why he found this Jewish group so congenial. The letter (Freud, 1961, pp. 367–8) is worth quoting at length.

It happened that in the years after 1895 two strong impressions coincided to produce the same effect on me. On the one hand, I had gained the first insight into the depths of human instinct, had seen many things which were sobering, at first even frightening; on the other hand the disclosure of my unpopular discoveries led to my losing most of my personal relationships at that time; I felt as though outlawed, shunned by all. This isolation aroused in me the longing for a circle of excellent men with high ideals who would accept me in friendship despite my temerity. Your Lodge was described to me as the place where I could find such men.

That you were Jews could only be welcome to me, for I was myself a Jew, and it has always appeared to me not only undignified, but outright foolish to deny it. What tied me to Jewry was – I have to admit it – not the faith, not even the national pride, for I was always an unbeliever, have been brought up without religion, but not without respect for the so-called 'ethical' demands of human civilisation. Whenever I have experienced feelings of national exaltation, I have tried to suppress them as disastrous and unfair, frightened by the warning example of those nations among which we Jews live. But there remained enough to make the attraction of Judaism and the Jews irresistible, many dark emotional powers all the stronger the less they could be expressed in words, as well as the clear consciousness of an inner identity, the familiarity of the same psychological structure. And before long there followed the realisation that it was only to my Jewish nature that I owed the two qualities that have become indispensable to me throughout my difficult life. Because I was a Jew, I found myself free of many prejudices which restrict others in the use of the intellect; as a Jew I was prepared to be in the opposition and to renounce agreement with the 'compact majority'.

This letter offers as full an account of Freud's conscious identification with Jewish life as can be found anywhere in his writings. He first locates his situation in the period after 1895 as one of isolation due to the 'temerity' with which he had begun to uncover the 'sobering... even frightening' nature of the 'depths of human instinct'. Using a standard trope for the prophet who speaks the unpopular truth, Freud thus presents himself as one cast out of society ('outlawed, shunned by all') because of the nature of his 'discoveries'. (The 'compact majority' referred to by Freud in this letter is a quotation from Ibsen's play, *An Enemy of the People*.) Unlike the Biblical prophets, however, Freud was not happy to be so isolated, but 'longed for' contact with others, 'for a circle of excellent men with high ideals who would accept me in friendship.' The fact that what he found was a Jewish group is presented as accidental – there is no mention of actively *seeking* it – but nevertheless 'welcome'. This is for a number of key reasons, which Freud consistently held to throughout the latter part of his life. First, 'I was myself a Jew, and it has always appeared to me not only undignified, but outright foolish to deny it.' The nod here is towards the impact of anti-Semitism, which led many Jews seeking social acceptance to deny their Jewish identity, often going as far as to convert. As noted earlier, Freud always asserted his Jewishness and indeed developed a nice line in ironic superiority claims, making Judaism the source of intellectual monotheism and hence superior to Christianity. (Arriving in England in 1938, he told the representatives of the Jewish community, 'We Jews have always known how to respect spiritual values. We preserved our unity through ideas, and because of them we have survived to this day' (Diller, 1991, p. 122.) More relevantly, he could genuinely never see any sense in hiding or denying his Jewishness when it was thrust at him so relentlessly by the anti-Semitic world, and indeed this anti-Semitism, which affronted rather than frightened him, made him more rather than less assertive of his rights. However, it was also the case that anti-Semitism threw Freud himself, like many other secular and intellectual Jews, back onto his own people when it came to seeking out a safe and welcoming forum for thought and debate.

Secondly, in the letter to B'nai Brith Freud distances himself from religion – which would not have scandalised any members of that secular society – and from Zionism, noting that 'Whenever I have experienced feelings of national exaltation, I have tried to suppress them as disastrous and unfair.' Indeed, although Freud expressed, in a letter to Einstein in 1930, pride in 'our' University of Jerusalem and took pleasure in the flourishing of 'our' settlements, he did not believe Palestine would become a Jewish state and regretted the 'unrealistic fanaticism' of Zionist Jews. However, what 'ties' him to Jewry are two somewhat contradictory feelings: an (intellectual) 'respect for the so-called "ethical" demands' of what Freud calls 'human civilisation' but which seems to be particularly associated with Jewish values, and something else, rather unfathomable, 'many dark emotional powers all the stronger the less they could be expressed in words, as well as the clear consciousness of an inner identity, the familiarity of the same psychological structure.' The *ethical* side of this is again absolutely central to the mission of the B'nai Brith, whose members saw in Judaism a source for humanitarian values that were universal in their application – another plank for feelings of superiority over the bigotry of anti-Semites. This seems to have been the reason why the B'nai Brith members saw Freud's ideas as congruent with their wider aims. Diller (1991, p. 170) quotes in this respect the stirring testimony from Ludwig Braun to which Freud's letter was a response: Braun, defining psychoanalysis as 'genuinely Jewish', 'went on to define the meaning of Jewishness as being comprised of an independence of spirit, the willingness to do battle with an unjust society, and a vision of the whole of nature and humanity. All, he suggested, were intimate aspects of Freud's personality and liberally infused in his work.' Freud himself, later (in 1935) claimed that he had always felt linked to the B'nai Brith over this issue of ethical ideals, even though he had ceased to work actively with the organisation decades before: 'The total agreement of our cultural and humanitarian ideals, as well as the same joyful acknowledgement of Jewish descent and Jewish existence, have vividly sustained this feeling' (Klein, 1985, p. 86). The ideals of Jewish ethics – a life of service, integrity and honesty, intellectual clarity and balanced respect for others, alongside a capacity for clear recognition of differences and of the competing capacities for construction and destructiveness endemic to the human condition – are so close to those of Freudian psychoanalysis as to make it obvious why the latter might have been born out of the former. The sense of Jewish cultural superiority, which Freud seems always to have held, was also consistent with the claims of the B'nai Brith that Jews had particularly high standards, again making it more than a matter of convenience (or inconvenience, as Freud felt it to be later) that all the founders of psychoanalysis were Jews.

The other component of the 'tie' to Jewry mentioned in Freud's letter, the 'dark emotional powers', is more surprising, expressing his attachment to his Jewish identity in mystical terms, as if it was a kind of phylogenetic throwback. Some of this, which Freud calls the 'clear consciousness of an inner identity, the familiarity of the same psychological structure' relates to the ease with which Freud thought he and his Jewish followers could understand one another, and conversely the difficulty non-Jews had in understanding his work, something which became acutely apparent in the struggles around Carl Jung. Jung caused trouble from the start with some of Freud's Jewish followers, perhaps particularly the loyal and talented Karl Abraham, whose capacity to see Jung's anti-Semitism at work was not clouded by the same kind of wish to 'save' psychoanalysis from being deemed a 'Jewish national affair' as was Freud's. As it happens, Freud does seem to have been worried by Jung from early in their relationship, but his concern to universalise psychoanalysis away from its Jewish origins was such that he consistently exhorted his colleagues to tolerate Jung's defects for the greater good. Writing in 1908 to Abraham, for instance, he was clear about the political need to overlook Jung's anti-

Semitism, which he could see in operation if not yet directed consciously at himself.

> I surmise that the repressed anti-Semitism of the Swiss, from which I am to be spared, has been directed against you in increased force. But my opinion is that we must as Jews if we want to cooperate with other people, develop a little masochism and be prepared to endure a little injustice... Why cannot I harness Jung and you together, your keenness and his *élan*?'   (Abraham and Freud, 1965, p. 46)

Freud's pessimism about anti-Semitism is clear here, but so is his assumption that he can talk openly to Abraham, from the position of insider because of their shared Jewishness: the language is consistently that of 'we'. The idea of brotherhood – 'racial kinship' is even more explicit in the following passage:

> Please be tolerant and do not forget that it is really easier for you than it is for Jung to follow my ideas, for in the first place you are completely independent, and then you are closer to my intellectual constitution because of racial kinship, while he as a Christian and a pastor's son finds his way to me only against great inner resistances.   (Abraham and Freud, 1965, p. 34)

This 'racial kinship' determines a way of thinking and reasoning, and non-Jews struggle to keep up with it. Abraham himself thought that this was because of a Talmudic strand in psychoanalysis, something that could only have crept in unconsciously given that Freud never studied the Talmud. Replying to Freud, Abraham wrote,

> I find it easier to go along with you rather than with Jung. I, too, have always felt this intellectual kinship. After all, our Talmudic way of thinking cannot disappear just like that. Some days ago a small paragraph in *Jokes* strangely attracted me. When I looked at it more closely, I found that, in the technique of apposition and in its whole structure, it was completely Talmudic.   (Gilman, 1993, p. 34)

This at least has the virtue of suggesting a cultural explanation for the affinity between Jewish thinkers and psychoanalysis: that the deeply ingrained modes of thought and reasoning which have characterised Jewish intellectual life across centuries should, once allowed to burst out of the confines of solely religious scholarship, infiltrate the wider intellectual and cultural scene, including psychoanalysis.

If the idea of Jewish kinship – 'the familiarity of the same psychological structure' – loomed large in Freud's thinking, there are also times when the mystical element in his Jewish affiliation is more pronounced and less easily reducible. Gilman (1993, p. 35) describes Freud's response to the greetings of the chief rabbi of Vienna on the occasion of Freud's seventy-fifth birthday, in which he stressed the communal, psychological identity of the Jew.

> Your words aroused a special echo in me, which I do not need to explain to you. In some place in my soul, in a very hidden corner, I am a fanatical Jew. I am very much astonished to discover myself as such in spite of all efforts to be unprejudiced and impartial. What can I do against my age?

The 'age' referred to here might be Freud's own age, so he is indexing something emotional or sentimental; but it is at least as likely to refer to the historical period, in which being a 'fanatical Jew' is a response to opprobrium. A marginally later comment to Arnold Zweig (quoted in Gay, 1988, p. 610) bears this out:

> An anxious premonition tells us that we, oh the poor Austrian Jews, will have to pay a part of the bill. It is sad that we even judge world events from the Jewish point of view, but how could we do it any other way?

At that time, how indeed, even for a purely secular Jew; once again positioned by anti-Semitism, Freud has to think Jewishly. However, this is not all that makes him do so: here is the most famous and expressive of the 'mystical' references to Jewish identity, from the preface to the Hebrew edition of *Totem and Taboo*.

> No reader of the Hebrew version of this book will find it easy to put himself in the emotional position of an author who is ignorant of the language of holy writ, who is completely estranged from the religion of his fathers – as well as from every other religion – and who cannot take a share in nationalist ideals, but who has yet never repudiated his people, who feels that he is in his essential nature a Jew and who has no desire to alter that nature. If the question were put to him: 'Since you have abandoned all these common characteristics

of your countrymen, what is left to you that is Jewish?' he would reply: 'A very great deal, and probably its very essence.' He could not express that essence in words, but some day, no doubt, it will become accessible to the scientific mind.   (Freud, 1930a, p. xv)

Jacqueline Rose (2003, p. 71) comments on this that 'Freud offers here one of the most striking self-definitions of the modern secular Jew – that is, the Jew for whom shedding the trappings of linguistic, religious and national identity – paradoxically, by stripping away its untenable and, one might say, most politically dangerous elements – does not make him less Jewish, but more.' Moreover, in a context in which Freud could have had few hopes that anti-Semitism would wither away, it is noticeable that his earlier attempt to divorce psychoanalysis from its identification with Jewry seems to have been abandoned. It is as if he decided that this identification would be made anyway, that psychoanalysis as 'Jewish science' was inescapable, so he might as well do what he always did in the face of anti-Semitism, come out fighting. The tone of the *Totem and Taboo* remarks is that the mysterious link with Jewish identity is deep and a matter of pride; let anyone challenge that who will. Freud's reference to his *essentially* Jewish nature can thus be read both as an act of the deepest political resistance and as an attestation to the limits of psychoanalytic knowledge – an assertion that when all is said and done, something else still remains, not susceptible, or at least not yet susceptible, to psychoanalytic scrutiny. This idea pervades Freud's late writing on his Jewish identity, and is perhaps one source for *Moses and Monotheism*: in the 1926 letter, the 1930 Preface and elsewhere, Jewish identity is inscribed as something mysterious yet profound. By the end of his life, this was one of the few lights in Freud's pessimism about the state of the world. His 1936 letter to Barbara Low on the death of her brother-in-law David Eder expresses this movingly (Freud, 1961, p. 424), with its mixture of despair, solidarity and identification:

The world is becoming so sad that it is destined to speedy destruction – that is the only palliative for me. I can easily imagine how he, too, must have suffered under the bitterness of these times. We were both Jews and knew of each other that we carried that miraculous thing in common which – inaccessible to any analysis so far – makes the Jew.

The paradox here, in which one of the sharpest and most unrelenting rational minds of the twentieth century stands back from uncovering one of its deepest emotional attachments, is expressive of the psycho-analytic conundrum as a whole: that whatever it turns up from under a stone, there is always something else to find.

A spur to achievement

The final element in Freud's letter to the B'nai Brith was also a consistent strand in his thinking about the benefits of his Jewish identity.

> And before long there followed the realisation that it was only to my Jewish nature that I owed the two qualities that have become indispensable to me throughout my difficult life. Because I was a Jew, I found myself free of many prejudices which restrict others in the use of the intellect; as a Jew I was prepared to be in the opposition and to renounce agreement with the 'compact majority'. (Freud, 1961, p. 368)

The difficulties surrounding being Jewish in Europe throughout Freud's lifetime were real and profound, with anti-Semitism never quiet at either the 'high culture' or the violent mass level of society. Nevertheless, despite this anti-Semitism and hence the maintenance of many ideological ghettoes, the Jews flooding out of the physical and theocratic ghettoes of Europe became the embodiment of the modernist revolution. They watered the ground, they carried the ideas; in the specific case of psychoanalysis, they knitted together modernism and emancipation in their forward-looking, tradition-breaking aspects. For Freud, this was no accident: it was rather the specific if uncomfortable virtue of the marginality imposed on Jews that it would make them struggle to achieve greatness and have their voices heard. In a 1907 letter to Karl Abraham who was worrying about beginning work as an analyst in Berlin, Freud advised,

> To a youthful man like yourself it doesn't do any harm to be forcibly turned loose into the world, 'au grand air', and the fact that as a Jew it will be more difficult for you may, as with all of us, have the effect of stimulating your productivity. (Freud, 1961, p. 227)

Freud counselled in similar terms against Max Graf's idea of considering converting his son ('Little Hans') to Christianity: 'If you do not let your son grow up a Jew, you will deprive him of those sources of energy which cannot be replaced by anything else. He will have to struggle as a Jew, and ought to develop in him energy that he will need for that struggle' (Diller, 1991, p. 117). This idea even reached Freud's scientific writings, in a comment to be found in 'Resistances to Psychoanalysis', written at a similar time to his B'nai Brith letter. Thinking about the resistances blocking more widespread acceptance of the psychoanalytic approach, Freud suggests that they may have to do with his ethnicity:

> the question may be raised whether the personality of the present writer as a Jew who has never sought to disguise the fact that he is a Jew may not have had a share in provoking the antipathy of his environment to psychoanalysis[1]... Nor is it perhaps entirely a matter of chance that the first advocate of psychoanalysis was a Jew. To profess belief in this new theory called for a certain degree of readiness to accept a situation of solitary opposition – a situation with which no one is more familiar than a Jew.   (Freud, 1925, p. 222)

What is stressed here is the resilience in the face of adversity that comes from being a Jew, but there is also an undercurrent suggesting superior vision: perhaps, implies Freud, one does not *have* to be Jewish to see the truth in psychoanalysis, but being a Jew certainly helped.

Even Peter Gay (1988), resistant to special pleading, goes along with Freud's claim that his status as a 'marginal man' might have given him an intellectual advantage. Discussing some other creative critical analysts, for example Darwin, Gay is not convinced of the specificity of Freud's suggestion of an inherent link between Jewish marginality and the creation of psychoanalysis, but he nevertheless concedes Freud's point in part.

> While it does not follow that only a marginal man – in particular, a marginal Jew – could have done Freud's lifework, the precarious status of Jews in Austrian society did probably underlie the notorious fact that nearly all the first psychoanalysts in Vienna were Jewish. Their society permitted them to train as physicians but did not let them feel particularly welcome among the medical

---

[1] Freud had written similarly to Abraham nearly twenty years earlier, 'You may be sure that if my name were Oberhuber my new ideas would, despite all the other factors, have met with far less resistance.' (Abraham and Freud, 1965, p. 46)

elite... In the face of social conservatism compounded by bigotry, the early psychoanalysts found a measure of toughness to be a highly adaptive quality.   (p. 603)

Freud certainly had that 'measure of toughness', that capacity to hold to his own thoughts and articulate what might have been half-known, but was also severely repressed. Seizing the modernist moment, Freud could adapt the Jewish penchant for finding hidden meanings and apply it to the state of humanity itself. Being 'modern' here means thinking previously unthinkable thoughts, recognising reason's underside in the workings of the unconscious and of irrational impulses, but also seeking to theorise it, to incorporate it in what can legitimately be considered the arena of scientific activity. Secular Jews, like modernists, cannot hide from the realities of the world, cannot make it all straightforward, clear or acceptable; but their self-perceived task is to wrest the confusions of real life into some symbolisable form, some way in which they can be understood, even if this goes against traditional ideas. Relentlessly interior and self-reflexive, Jewish thought continually examines and interprets, playfully sometimes, with anguish at others; this too is part of the psychoanalytic response to the terrors and thrills of modernity: with revolutionary change occurring everywhere, there is no place of refuge from restless thought. Freud claimed that his Jewish identity freed him from restrictions of the intellect, and in the end he was grateful for it, whatever the costs. The crucial point is that just as post-emancipation Jewish identity is built on the knife-edged awareness of the potential and dangers of the modern experience, so is psychoanalysis: each informs the other, each is the product of the same underlying socio-historical process.

A final point to be made here concerns what Freud himself thought might have been the heritage he passed on. Identifying himself with Moses, he had dreamt in the 1890s of seeing the 'promised land from afar': he would liberate his people from their enslavement to pre-scientific ideas, but others would have to actually lead them to security. By the end of his life, however, without relinquishing this Moses-identification, he was more pessimistic but also more precise: what must be preserved, for psychoanalysis as well as for culture as a whole, was the primacy of reason and truth-seeking, the tradition of scholarship and thought. Faced with the physical brutality of the Nazis, it was an essential task, in which the survival of psychoanalysis was bound up, to hold on to intellectual and ethical values. Characteristically, Freud couched this endorsement of the scholarly tradition when confronted with barbarism in terms from Jewish history. In 1938, at the age of 82 and faced with flight from Vienna after the Anschluss, Freud made the same point in several different places. One is to be found near the close of *Moses and Monotheism* (Freud, 1939, p. 115): 'Immediately after the destruction of the Temple in Jerusalem by Titus, the Rabbi Yochanan ben Zakkai asked permission to open the first Torah school in Yavneh. From that time on, the Holy Writ and intellectual concern with it were what held the scattered people together.' Even more movingly, Freud used this episode as an analogy with the fate of psychoanalysis itself. In his last speech to the Vienna Psychoanalytic Society, on 13 March 1938, he said,

> After the destruction of the Temple in Jerusalem by Titus, Rabbi Yochanan ben Zakkai asked for permission to open a school at Yavneh for the study of Torah. We are going to do the same. We are, after all, used to persecution by our history, tradition and some of us by personal experience. (Diller, 1991, p. 206)

Here, the identification between psychoanalysis and Jewish thought is absolutely explicit, as is the link between the psychoanalytic movement and the Jews. It is as if Jewish history has translated directly into psychoanalytic history, the latter being the continuation of the former. As with many things, not least the repressed elements in the human psyche, this continuation also has the form of a return. Working his way through the gamut of his Biblical and Jewish identifications – Joseph, Moses, Yochanan ben Zakkai – Freud uncovers another one, in what one might note is his father's name. Writing to his son Ernst in May 1938, when Ernst was in London but Freud not yet there, he draws on one of the most poignant of Biblical images to express his state of mind.

> In these dark days there are two prospects to cheer us: to rejoin you all and – to die in freedom. I sometimes compare myself with the old Jacob who, in his old age, his children brought to Egypt. It is to be hoped that the result will not be the same, an exodus from Egypt. It is time for Ahasverus to come to rest somewhere. (Freud, 1965, p. 442)

2
A Hostile World: Facing Anti-Semitism

Sigmund Freud was affected by anti-Semitism throughout his life, and had a rather wry attitude towards it, seeing it as in some ways strengthening of his character, or at least of his capacity to see things clearly – the attribute that he valued above all others. This was consistent with his general view that the Jews had been hardened by their experience of being subject to the opprobrium of others. In 1923, writing to Romain Rolland, he commented,

> I of course belong to a race which in the Middle Ages was held responsible for all epidemics and which today is blamed for the disintegration of the Austrian Empire and the German defeat. Such experiences have a sobering effect and are not conducive to make one believe in illusions. A great part of my life's work... has been spent trying to destroy illusions of my own and those of mankind.   (Freud, 1961, p. 346)

Freud's commitment, both conscious and unconscious, to the continuity between Jewish values and identity and those of psychoanalysis was very deep, with adherence to the rationalist worldview to be found in the Talmudic tradition – the intellectual impulse to 'destroy illusions' – a principle source of this continuity. He was also, however, a proud follower of the Western cultural heritage, specifically that of the German tradition associated with Goethe. However, from the first rude shock of the anti-Semitism he experienced at University until the moment of exile after the Anschluss, Freud was always aware of the profound discrepancy between this 'Germany of the mind' and the reality of the Germanic society in which he actually lived. Yerushalmi (1991, p. 40) notes,

> Certainly a vital part of him lived in a Germanic universe of thought, but this Germany of the mind and the imagination that he, like so many Central European Jews, cherished was that of the German Enlightenment... of literature and philosophy, of nine-teenth-century German science. Unlike so many of his contemporaries, Freud rarely confused this with the real Germany or Austria, even if part of him may have strongly wanted to do so. And this long before Nazism and Hitler.

It may be that Freud's allegiance to his Jewish identity helped him maintain the acerbic and somewhat distant attitude towards the reality of German culture that went along with his admiration for its highest values; that is, not being fully part of it, he could love it without being infatuated by it. Such a capacity for sustained critical distance is arguably a psychoanalytic value in itself: one can admire beauty without being taken in by it; there must always be some space left over for analysis. The Jew outside the beckoning culture might, if he or she is to remain sober and realistically cautious, do well also to retain this ironic stance.

As described in the previous chapter, around the turn of the twentieth century Freud channelled much of his intellectual energy into the Vienna B'nai Brith, turning to it in large part because it was a collection of exactly the same kind of secular, high-minded Jews as he was himself. More to the point, the B'nai Brith offered him a place free from anti-Semitism, a place of brothers in which his creativity could take wing and be admired. Very soon afterwards, this Jewish directed energy, devoted to intellectual searching and ethical practice, was taken over wholesale into the psychoanalytic movement itself, a movement which was in any case entirely Jewish for its first few years, and predominantly Jewish almost everywhere until well after the Second World War. Until 1907 all the members of the Vienna Society were Jews, and with the exception of Ernest Jones (of whom, more below) all members of the 'Committee' created in 1912 to protect the purity of psychoanalysis (and granted rings of symbolic power) were Jews – Ferenczi, Rank, Abraham, Sachs and, later, Eitingon. Klein (1985, p. 140) comments,

> Even after 1908, when Freud attempted to reverse the tendency toward Jewish exclusiveness within the circle, he maintained the

belief in Jewish ethical responsibility. This belief surfaced both in his identification with the Hebrew prophet Moses, and in his communication, to his followers, of the idea that Jews played a crucial pioneering role in disseminating the redemptive insights of psychoanalysis.

These Jewish origins had a very substantial effect on the content of psychoanalysis, particularly in respect of the ethical values to which it committed itself, as well as on its social relations – the intense, family-like bonds with which its adherents have always been characterised, in turn leading to painful schisms and passionate advocacy of belief structures, sometimes irrespective of anything that might resemble evidence. The energy derived from the impulse to make something new and better – to redeploy what were fantasised as traditional Jewish intellectual skills previously committed to taxing religious study – was poured into various cultural projects of the time, including if not especially psychoanalysis. This energy, it might even be argued, was used in a flame that burnt so strongly that it left later generations of analysts enervated, unable to match anything that had come before – not necessarily a healthy state of affairs, but somewhat characteristic of a variety of modernist movements, including contemporary Judaism itself.

In any case, Freud's Jewish identity seems without doubt to have had a massive influence on the form and content of his psychoanalytic discoveries. The passion with which Freud invested psychoanalysis with his Jewish consciousness has been outlined in the previous chapter. As noted there, this had several sources, including a rather mystical sense of some hidden power drawing Freud towards identification with Jews and Judaism (despite his consistent and principled atheism), an explicit recognition of the value of being an 'outsider' to the host Western culture, and an assertive and angry response to anti-Semitism. Freud made a nod towards analysing the first of these, for instance in *Civilisation and its Discontents* (1930b) with its famous opening repudiating the 'oceanic feeling' at the root of many religious experiences; and the second was more or less conscious anyway: it does not take much analysis to understand how being a marginal can help you see clearly, and perhaps inure you to criticism. But the third source, anti-Semitism, to which Freud stood up all through his life, was also subjected to a provocative analysis to which he returned in his last major work, as an old man trying to make sense of the intense investment in hatred of Jews and, by extension if not explicitly, of the 'other' in general. Exploring this hatred is a key element in the current book; this chapter marks a beginning by examining the nature and implications of Freud's own account.

From the start, anti-Semitism marked Jewish identity, both personally for Freud and in the development of psychoanalysis as a whole. Freud became increasingly publicly assertive in response to anti-Semitism as it became more virulent in Europe after the First World War, but both his exposure to it and his refusal to give way to anti-Semitic attacks dates from much earlier, at least to his student days. The most famous instance of Freud's childhood experience of anti-Semitism, however, comes from an earlier memory still, reported in *The Interpretation of Dreams* (1900, pp. 196–7) in the context of an account of the emotional difficulties Freud had in travelling to Rome, something he much desired to do. In this instance, Freud traces this difficulty (which is connected elsewhere to his Moses-identification in dreams representing 'the promised land seen from afar') to his identification with Hannibal, who 'had been the favourite hero of [my] school days.' This identification is linked explicitly with anti-Semitism:

> When in the higher classes I began to understand for the first time what it meant to belong to an alien race, and anti-Semitic feelings amongst the other boys warned me that I must take up a definite position, the figure of the semitic general rose still higher in my esteem. To my youthful mind Hannibal and Rome symbolised the conflict between the tenacity of Jewry and the organisation of the Catholic church. And the increasing importance of the effects of the anti-Semitic movement upon our emotional life helped to fix the thoughts and findings of those early days.

Following this combative stance through, Freud comes up with what he describes as 'the event in my childhood whose power was still being shown in all these emotions and dreams', and which resonated throughout his life. This is the memory of the moment when anti-Semitism brings his father down to size, and Freud takes on the mantle of avenger.

> I may have been ten or twelve years old, when my father began to take me with him on his walks and reveal to me in his talk his views upon things in the world we live in. Thus it was, on one such occasion, that he told me a story to show how much better things were now than they had been in his days. 'When I was a young man,' he

said, ' I went for a walk one Saturday in the streets of your birth-place; I was well dressed and had a new fur cap on my head. A Christian came up to me and with a single blow knocked off my cap into the mud and shouted "Jew! Get off the pavement!"' 'And what did you do?' I asked. 'I went into the roadway and picked up my cap,' was his quiet reply. This struck me as unheroic conduct on the part of the big, strong man who was holding the little boy by the hand. I contrasted this situation with another which fitted my feel-ings better: the scene in which Hannibal's father, Hamilcar Barca, made his boy swear before the household altar to take vengeance on the Romans. Ever since that time Hannibal has had a place in my fantasies.

Psychoanalytically speaking, this memory interestingly connects Freud's resilience in the face of anti-Semitism with the idea of avenging or even surpassing his father – a consistent theme in Freud's writings, and one worked over many times in the *Interpretation of Dreams*, a book which he acknowledged to be a 'portion of my own self-analysis, my reaction to my father's death – that is to say, to the most important event, the most poignant loss, of a man's life' (p. 47). Freud's not infre-quent ambivalence towards Jews, which sometimes was expressed forcefully towards his Jewish fellow-analysts and was not limited to his youthful and culturally reinforced antagonism towards the Eastern European Jews from which his mother's family came, was also presum-ably connected to this sense of his father's weakness, as well as being a direct expression of what is nowadays called 'internalised anti-Semitism'. In this respect, as Boyarin (1997) has pointed out, the gloss Freud puts on this memory also represents an attempt to distance himself from the 'feminised' aspects of Jewish identity, which in Judaism itself actually had considerable credibility – the vision of the ideal Jewish male as scholarly and weak rather than as physical and tough was a valorised version of masculinity in rabbinic Judaism. Freud here, and in much of his writing, seems to be adopting the anti-Semitic view that such 'femininity' is to be despised and that true heroism – true manliness – is to be found in strength. Thus, without reducing Freud's relationship with his Jewish identity to something based solely on unresolved Oedipal issues, it is plausible to argue that part of the emotional investment Freud had in Jewish *achievement*, particularly in the face and context of anti-Semitic attack, might have been connected with his sense of his father as a failed hero, and of Jewish passivity in general as a sign of 'racial' disrepute.

Psychoanalysis as a response to anti-Semitism

At the simplest sociological level, anti-Semitism constructed psycho-analysis through enforcing a collective consciousness amongst the set of Jewish intellectuals and doctors surrounding Freud, pushing them together as a 'movement' rather than allowing them to dissipate their affiliations amongst a number of welcoming groups. There were, it seems, few such welcomes available: if Jews were to work on something new, they would have to do so together.

> The irony of the impact of incipient racial anti-Semitism on Freud, and on German Jews like him, was the influence it had on their dis-covery of a new basis of emotional and ideological support. Though the movement frustrated the aspirations Jews associated with German nationalism, it stimulated, at the same time, a positive Jewish response – the feelings of self-defence, pride and courage, as well as the mutual recognition among Jews of shared beliefs and of strength through unity.   (Klein, 1985, p. 55)

The sense of comfort given by Jewish companionship in the face of a hostile world was undoubtedly translated into the psychoanalytic movement, which has always had more than its fair share of paranoid fantasies as well as always being the object of fascination and abuse – very much like the Jews. As Klein notes, the other side of this is a very positive sense of self-worth, coded amongst Jews as a deep-seated idea of 'chosenness', however this might be interpreted under modern con-ditions (for example, as there being something special about Jewish ethical responsibility, or as an idea about Jewish 'genius' or the 'Jewish mind'). Psychoanalysis too, in direct proportion to the criticism heaped upon it, has always taken pride in its special knowledge, its access to truth: the unconscious exists, it was discovered by Freud, and it can only become available to scientific scrutiny through the methods of psychoanalysis. Everyone who does not understand this is either ignorant or insufficiently analysed; the psychoanalytic ark is the one chosen to carry Freud's tablets of stone.

As well as this relatively straightforward connection between the anti-Semitism of the surrounding society and the clustering together of Jews, either (at the time) as secular Jews or as Zionists or as psychoana-lysts, there is a more specific intellectual response to anti-Semitic per-ceptions to be found in the content of the psychoanalytic world view. Gilman (1993) has documented this most exhaustively, arguing that, throughout the nineteenth century, there was a fascination both in popular and in medical culture with the body and 'difference' of the Jew, and that this particular manifestation of 'othering' focused on sexuality. The Jew was seen as having a kind of rabid yet damaged sexuality, manifested in the male Jew's circumcised state (and, though Gilman discusses this less, the female Jewess' oriental-like sultry sexuality) and through modes of insanity which were basically hysterical in form and were caused by incest and early seduction. The Jew thus becomes the embodiment of feminised masculinity, which turns into madness; indeed, Jewish men, like women but not like non-Jewish men, could even suffer from the feminine disturbance, hysteria. 'For at the close of the nineteenth century,' writes Gilman (1991, p. 333), 'the idea of seeing the hysteric was closely bound to the idea of seeing the Jew – but very specifically the male Jew... The Jew is the hysteric; the Jew is the feminised Other; the Jew is seen as different, as diseased.' There was also a link here with homosexuality, as the feminised Jew could be seen as a kind of 'third sex', fitting in with speculations about the biological origins of homosexual desire. 'This chain of associations,' writes Brickman (2003, p. 164), '([male] Jews-circumcised-feminised-homosexual-hysterical) was understood as biological, evolutionary fact, each of its elements (and many others) taken as inherited dispositions of the Jewish race.' In the popular and medical fantasy, circumcision was equivalent to castration, provoking fear and abhorrence, and not a little fascination. Gilman suggests that if this was the mirror held up to the Jew by the outside, then Jews on the way to emancipation, anxiously scanning the faces around them for traces of acceptance and rejection, would internalise the racist equivalence: Jew equals emasculated man. One response, one might guess, would be repudiation of Jewish identity, and this was certainly taken on by many Jews, including some who converted to Christianity. Another response was to assert the positive value of what, anachronistically, one might term 'non-macho' masculinity, something which has been evident in Jewish culture throughout many centuries, where the image of the ideal man emphasised learning rather than strength, other-worldliness rather than material being (Boyarin, 1997). The attitude adopted by Freud, however, could be seen as a specific strategy of resistance to anti-Semitic stereotyping: this was to take this supposedly peculiar Jewish condition and argue that it was not specific to the Jews, but universal.

According to Freud, feminisation through castration is the key anxiety shared by all men, and the core distress of the female state:

the 'bedrock' condition of human psychology is repudiation of femininity (Freud, 1937, p. 252). However, what marks the human subject as specifically human is precisely the imposition of castration: the Oedipus complex, which forces on the young child the reality of limitations on desire (the boy *must not* sexually possess his mother; the girl *must not* have the father's baby) has its effect because of castration anxiety. It is not, therefore, only the Jew who is marked as castrated, even though it is the Jew's body that displays that mark; rather, all humans, men and women alike (but particularly men in this context) are psychologically organised through castration. Gilman (1991, p. 336) builds up on this basis the claim that Freud's theorising was a direct response to anti-Semitic stereotyping. 'For Freud,' he writes, 'every move concerning the articulation of the nature of human sexuality responds to his desire to resist the charges of his own Jewish specificity by either projecting the sense of his own sexual difference on to other groups such as women or by universalizing the attack on Jewish particularism, mirrored in the particularism of the Jew's body.' That is, one of the central ideas of Freudian psychoanalysis – that human subjectivity is constructed amidst and through castration – can be understood as a universalisation of an anti-Semitic smear. The Jew consequently can no longer be pilloried as deviant; he or she is rather the flag-bearer for the whole of humankind. Only, as Lacan (1972–3) would later say about women, humankind in general does not know this, but is caught up in its fears and neurotic obsessions; only Jews and psychoanalysts know what is what. Perhaps this captures the kernel of truth in Derrida's (1995, p. 46) seemingly bizarre statement that, 'At issue here is nothing less than taking seriously the question whether a science can depend on something like a circumcision.'

Although Freud's possibly unconscious strategy successfully redeploys anti-Semitic ideas about Jewish masculinity in subversive ways, this does not mean that their pejorative elements disappear. Circumcision itself becomes amalgamated with a threatening idea of castration, with the Jewish/non-Jewish distinction being displaced onto a different, similarly socially valorised divide: that between femininity and masculinity. Writing in his 1909 study of 'Little Hans', Freud comments,

> The castration complex is the deepest unconscious root of anti-Semitism; for even in the nursery little boys hear that a Jew has something cut off his penis – a piece of his penis, they think –

and this gives them the right to despise Jews. And there is no stronger unconscious root for the sense of superiority over women.   (p. 36)

For Boyarin (1997), there is plenty of evidence here of Freud's own internalised anti-Semitism, in which the Judaically *valued* state of being circumcised is made into the repugnant state of castration, with tales of horror attached to it: the male Jew here is 'damaged' rather than completed, and is associated with the feminine, the already-castrated, just as he is in anti-Semitic propaganda. Brickman (2003, p. 165) comments on Freud's 'universalising reconfigurations' turning the despised Jewish body into the model for humanity as a whole, that they 'were made at considerable expense, however: the modalities of inferiority previously ascribed to the Jews did not simply disappear but were ambivalently displaced onto a series of abjected others: primitives, women and homosexuals.' The revulsion of both circumcised and non-circumcised males was turned on femininity, seen in psychoanalysis as the real 'abject', that which is always denied and avoided, by males and females (the anti-feminine attitude of women is expressed in 'penis envy') alike. In addition, a different kind of colonising impulse is produced within psychoanalysis, in which the 'other' – in nineteenth century Europe represented above all, but not exclusively, by Jews – is repositioned as the female other, but also as the 'primitive' other of colonialism. Hence Brickman's critique of psychoanalysis' own racial politics:

> The inclusion of the previously excluded Jew within the universal subject position of psychoanalysis not only repudiated femininity and homosexuality, it included Jews in the overarching, dominant cultural/racial category – civilisation – which was defined by its excluded, constitutive opposite, the racialised other as primitive. Categorised as a member of a primitive race, Freud repudiated primitivity, locating himself and his work within European civilisation, with both its scientific and colonising enterprises, and replacing the opposition of Aryan/Jew with the opposition of civilised/primitive.   (p. 167)

Taken together with Gilman's analysis, this suggests that Freud responded to anti-Semitism by producing in psychoanalysis a theory that reconstructed human subjectivity according to the image of the disparaged Jew (we are all circumcised/ castrated now); but in so doing he also preserved the dynamics of racialised discourse, displacing it into his theorising on the 'dark continent' of femininity, and embedding in the idea of the 'primitive' – itself a powerful motif in nineteenth century western thought – the seeds for much of psychoanalysis' later racial blindness. As will be argued, moreover, this overwriting of anti-Semitic ideology with other modes of discriminatory thought did not mean that anti-Semitism disappeared, either in society as a whole (one would not expect this, anyway) or in psychoanalysis itself.

Protecting psychoanalysis: anti-Semitism amongst the analysts

The deep roots of psychoanalysis in Jewish identity and culture had, it is being argued, a massive impact on the development and content of psychoanalysis itself. The effects of this have been very profound, both positively, in giving psychoanalysis a powerful identity and cultural legacy of its own, and negatively, in fostering a sense of siege and an over-reliance on loyalty over the pursuit of critical engagement with differing points of view. However, the prime 'negative' effect of psychoanalysis' Jewish origins lies in the way in which anti-Semitism comes to bear on it, both internally and externally. Freud himself was very aware of what he regarded as the danger that psychoanalysis would be seen merely as a 'Jewish national affair', stirring up anti-Semitic resistance as well as the unavoidable resistance due to psychoanalysis' own unpalatable truths. It was for this reason that he was especially enthusiastic about the presence of Jung in the movement, and optimistic that through Jung the future of psychoanalysis would be preserved in the outside world. In this regard, as noted in the previous chapter, he was out of step with some of his Jewish colleagues from the start. Karl Abraham, for instance, who had studied and suffered with the Swiss as a young doctor, was never much enamoured by Jung, nor taken in by him. In this, Abraham was more prescient than Freud, who was so wishful in his relation to Jung that he could either not see, or decided to overlook, the latter's transparent grandiosity and anti-Semitism. Drawing on one of his favourite Biblical allusions, Freud saw Jung as Joshua to his Moses, the one who would take the movement into the Promised Land when it was his, Freud's, fate only to glimpse this place from afar (Diller, 1991, p. 179). Irritated by Abraham's and others' opposition to Jung's appointment in 1910 as President of the International Psychoanalytic

Association, Freud phrased his views in melodramatically apocalyptic terms, with more than a hint of the anti-Semitic idea that Jews could never be truly creative.

> Most of you are Jews and therefore incompetent to win friends for the new teaching. Jews must be content with the modest role of preparing the ground... I am getting on in years and am weary of being perpetually attacked. We are in danger. They won't leave me a coat on my back. This Swiss will save us – will save me and will save you as well. (ibid., p. 172)

'They won't leave me a coat on my back': this is the classic complaint of the old Jew threatened either by anti-Semites or by the grasping and internecine quarrelling of his ungrateful children. Even when Freud was forced to recognise Abraham's acuity in identifying Jung's anti-Semitism, he thought he should overlook it: 'But my opinion is that we must as Jews if we want to cooperate with other people, develop a little masochism and be prepared to endure a little injustice' (Abraham and Freud, 1965, p. 46). Even though Freud was staunch in standing up to anti-Semitism where he encountered it, the idea that the outside world would always be full of anti-Semites and if one wants to get on with life one has to put up with this was a consistent strain in his thinking. For example, in a letter to Jacob Meitlis in 1938 from England, he wrote, 'Basically all are anti-Semites. They are everywhere. Frequently anti-Semitism is latent and hidden, but it is there. Naturally, there are also exceptions. But the broad masses are anti-Semitic here as everywhere' (Yerushalmi, 1991, p. 54). In the case of Jung, however, he was desperate not on his own account, but out of anxiety over the survival of psychoanalysis itself: if a non-Jewish home for psychoanalysis could not be found, in order to demonstrate its universalism but also simply to protect it from abuse, then the chances of its survival were slim. 'Our Aryan comrades are quite indispensable to us,' Freud wrote to Abraham, 'otherwise psychoanalysis would fall a victim to anti-Semitism' (Diller, 1991, p. 183). Jung himself clearly also saw things in racial terms, complaining to Ernest Jones, for example, when Jones failed to support him against Freud, that 'I thought you were a Christian' (ibid., p. 185). The effects of this racialised dispute on later relationships between Jungians and Freudians, and indeed on the history of the psychodynamic movements, was profound, leaving a bitter taste nearly a hundred years after their split. In particular, once loyalty to

Freud had disappeared Jung seems to have been relatively uninhibited in displaying his racist beliefs, a point which, as will be seen in a later chapter, came to be of considerable importance once the Nazis came to power in Germany. Freud gave up completely on Jung and became deeply embittered over him, including in this a racialised component. Responding to some mediating efforts by Sabina Spielrein in 1913, he wrote, 'I shall not present my compliments to Jung in Munich, as you know perfectly well... We are and remain Jews. The others will only exploit us and will never understand and appreciate us.' (Yerushalmi, 1991, p. 45)

The other central non-Jew in the establishment of the psychoanalytic movement, who again became extremely important during the Nazi era, was Ernest Jones. Unlike Jung, Jones retained a very strong loyalty to Freud throughout his life, yet also showed an independence of mind and spirit and an organisational capacity that was of immense value to the movement as a whole, however ambiguous and ambivalent some of his activities might have been. Whist these ambiguities were in part produced by the complex exigencies of the age, Jones' mixed attitude towards the Jewish domination of psychoanalysis also played its part. On the one hand, there was something about the intellectual alertness and quickness of mind of the European Jewish intelligentsia that attracted Jones and helped him feel less 'English' and more Welsh – and hence more critical and less stuffy. 'Coming myself of an oppressed race,' he wrote, 'it was easy for me to identify myself with the Jewish outlook which years of intimacy enabled me to absorb in a high degree. My knowledge of Jewish anecdotes, wise sayings, and jokes, became under such tutelage so extensive as to create astonishment among other analysts outside this small circle' (Diller, 1991, p. 199). He identified himself as having the position of '*Shabbes-goy* among the Viennese' (Yerushalmi, 1991, p. 53), this being quite a good joke as it conveys the idea that the Jewish analysts needed a non-Jew to carry out tasks which, because of their identity (albeit not their religious beliefs) they found hard to do. Jones certainly seems to have been better at *organisation* than his squabbling comrades, and the usefulness to the movement of this sympathetic non-Jew in a position of institutional power was immense during the dark Nazi night. For Jones, it seems as though his links with Freud and the Jewish Viennese in particular gave him a sense of his own exoticism, as well as a setting in which his qualities of imaginative service could shine and be appreciated.

The negative side of Jones' ambivalence was also strong, however, and was matched in some measure by the ambivalence surrounding him. Klein (1985, p. 143) comments that,

> Jones was especially unhappy about the manifestation of Jewish pride within the circle. He felt that despite the warm welcome Freud extended to Jung and to himself in 1907–8, and despite his genuine interest in attracting non-Jewish followers, Freud maintained a 'certain mistrust' for non-Jews.

There is independent evidence that Freud did indeed express a feeling of 'racial strangeness' towards Jones at this time (ibid., p. 142), so Jones was not being particularly paranoid in thinking that there was some holding back in the warmth of the welcome. Later on, in the wake of the disappointment over Jung, this feeling became even more pronounced. Diller (1991, p. 198) notes that,

> Jones stood steadfastly on the side of the Viennese Jews during the Jung affair. He had even hoped that Freud might consider him as a replacement for Jung in the role of representative and disseminator of psychoanalysis to the non-Jewish world. Unfortunately, this episode had only reinforced Freud's basic mistrust of non-Jews, which in turn made him more susceptible to those amongst the Viennese who continued to be suspicious of Jones, both personally and racially. ... Jones did feel that the Jews on the committee, Freud least of all, showed a rather heightened sensitivity to anti-Semitism and mistrust of non-Jews.

Whilst this suggests that Jones' sense of the Jews sticking together and regarding him with some unease might have been well-founded, it is also apparent that he failed to appreciate the extent to which Jewish identity and what Klein (1985, p. xii) dubs 'the positive value of Jewish pride' was important not only in motivating Freud himself, but also in energising the entire fledgling movement in the early years of its existence. For Jones, it seems that this Jewish foundation – which he saw as a vestige of a racial sense of Jewish superiority – interfered with the establishment of psychoanalysis as a science, as well as being a nuisance in relation to his own position within it. At times, his failure to distinguish between the Jewish analysts' nervous response to anti-Semitism and a sense of personal injury or antagonism, either led him to, or drew out in him, anti-Semitic attitudes at odds with most of his actions and beliefs. In particular, there is some evidence that Jones believed Jews should abandon their separateness and assimilate, indicating a view that their refusal to do so was a source of trouble. Yerushalmi (1991, p. 53) gives the clearest example of Jones' negative side.[1]

> [T]oward the end of World War II, the amiable disciple delivered himself of a disquisition entitled 'The Psychology of the Jewish Question' which advises total assimilation as the solution to anti-Semitism and contains some astonishing passages, including the broad implication that most German-Jewish refugees in England were ungrateful draft-dodgers. Turning to the physical features of the Jews that contribute to unconscious hostility against them, Jones identifies one as circumcision which, according to Freud himself, arouses castration anxieties. The other is Jones' original contribution: 'The second physical feature alluded to is the Hittite nose, so suggestive of deformity, which the Jews unfortunately picked up in their wanderings and which by an unlucky chance, is associated with a dominant gene.'

Some stray comments, and more stray actions, of Jones in the 1930s suggest that the attitude expressed in this 'disquisition' were not isolated aberrations, nor did they lack effects, although this is not to claim that Jones was anti-Semitic in the way that Jung clearly was. Rather, the origins of psychoanalysis lie in a complex network of identity and social processes, within which Jewish identity was a key player, and which thus necessarily evoked the immensely powerful (then even more than now) forces of anti-Semitism. This had some profound effects in mobilising the activities of the Jewish analysts, first and foremost Freud himself, but it also drew along in its wake tempestuous ambivalence towards psychoanalysis by non-Jews, even those who became central to the psychoanalytic movement. Not all non-

---

[1] Yerushalmi (1991, p. 53) also quotes the following 'grotesque encounter' between Jones, James Strachey and Joan Riviere over the translation of the word 'id'. Writing to his wife Alix in 1924, Strachey commented, 'They want to call "das Es" "the Id". I thought everyone would say "the Yidd". So Jones said there was no such word in English: "There's 'Yiddish,'" you know. And in German 'Jude'. But there is no such word as Yidd". – "Pardon me doctor, Yidd is a current word for a Jew." – "Ah! A slang expression. It cannot be in very widespread use then."'

Jews fell into this trap, of course, but the exceptions certainly surprised Freud, as he noted when getting generous greetings from Thomas Mann on his eightieth birthday: 'A noble Goy! It's nice to know that these, too, exist. One is apt to doubt it sometimes' (Diller, 1991, p. 128). Given the circumstances at the time (this was 1936), Freud's comment is not as ungracious as it sounds; more to the point, he was well aware that there were 'noble' non-Jews (he admired many of them and benefited directly from some), but by the end of his life he had ceased to doubt the pervasiveness and deep-rootedness of anti-Semitism as a psychological and socio-political phenomenon. The question that arises from this, for a mind as alert and unforgiving as Freud's, is how to explain this: what is it that makes anti-Semitism so virulent, what irrationality fixes it so firmly in place, and why, amongst all the possible victims of racist hatred, do the Jews figure so large?

Theorising anti-Semitism

Psychoanalysis has produced various accounts of anti-Semitism, which are the subject of later chapters. In the 1930s, faced with inescapable evidence of the virulence and pervasiveness of the anti-Semitic 'repressed' returning, Freud produced his own most sustained and provocative reading of the phenomenon, in the context of his epic meditation on Jewish identity, *Moses and Monotheism*. This book, rightly castigated for its sweeping historical inaccuracies, repetitious-ness and logical inconsistencies, nevertheless continues to give rise to rich interpretations, speculations and responses, the most seductive of which has been Yerushalmi's (1991) *Freud's Moses*. *Moses and Monotheism* is set up as a scholarly exploration of the pre-history of monotheistic Judaism, advancing the radical claim that Moses was an Egyptian who sought out the Hebrew slaves in order to create a monotheistic cult, and whose personality can be glimpsed behind the version of God created in this cult. Exploration of the meaning and madness of these claims has taken up much of the critical commentary on the book from the time it was published. However, one powerful way of reading *Moses and Monotheism*, which leaves behind questions of accuracy concerning the assertions Freud makes about the origins of Judaism, is as Freud's search for some resolution of his lifelong tensions over his Jewish identity. In this reading, the urgency and emotional power of the book is lent it by the context in which it was written: the rise of Nazism in Germany and eventually in Austria. Thus, Diller

(1991, p. 137) argues that Freud's 'great hesitancy and agitation over the work, his return to biblical themes of his childhood, his resurrection of the Oedipal drama and instinct theory, and the fact that although he was gravely ill, near death, and deeply disturbed by the outside world, he could still harness the energy to write such a book – all point to *Moses and Monotheism* as a last and final reckoning for him, a parting opportunity to find emotional peace and quietude, especially in relation to his Jewish identity.' Jacqueline Rose (2003, p. 77), in partial contrast with this, argues that *Moses and Monotheism* reveals Freud's continued state of being torn 'between belonging and not belonging as a Jew'; she thus emphasises not so much the *resolution* of Freud's Jewish identity as its continuing openness, a position which provides more political leverage than Diller's, if less comfort. Both these positions, and many others, imply that the main thrust of the book is a quest to deal with personally insistent identity issues.

Readings of *Moses and Monotheism* as an expression of Freud's personal identity crisis, or at least quandary over his Jewish identity, in the 1930s are legitimised in part by his own successive 'prefaces' to the book, as he worried away about the propriety of publishing it. At the beginning, famously, Freud sets this context of anxiety as relating to the Jewish people and his possible betrayal of them in a time of trouble; significantly, he does not hesitate to remind the reader of his own membership of this disparaged group.

> To deprive a people of a man whom they take pride in as the greatest of their sons is not a thing to be gladly or carelessly undertaken, least of all by someone who is himself one of them.   (Freud, 1939, p. 7)

Freud's defence of his actions, as ever, is in the name of scientific truth, reflecting his deep-rooted if increasingly pessimistic belief that the only viable route to human progress is through the dispelling of illusions and the exercise of rationality.

> But we cannot allow any such reflection to induce us to put the truth aside in favour of what are supposed to be national interests; and, moreover, the clarification of a set of facts may be expected to bring us a gain in knowledge.   (ibid.)

Nothing, in Freud's universe, is more important than a 'gain in knowledge', even the maintenance of Jewish self-esteem – an attitude on his part that is linked at least to some Talmudic traditions, in which everything bows to the power of truth. However, Freud's main cautions about publication were not caused by worry over its effect on the Jews, but by fear that it would call down the wrath of external authorities on psychoanalysis itself. This is clearest in his 'Prefatory Note' to the third part of the book, written in Vienna before the Anschluss of March 1938. Here, Freud expresses anxiety about alienating the Catholic authorities when they might be the only protection against the 'prehistoric barbarism' of Nazism – a hope demonstrating that Freud's reading of political events was not as perspicacious as his reading of psychology. Even whilst holding onto this hope, however, Freud is characteristically ironic and negative in his framing: the old power is to be invested in only because it is less destructive than the new. 'The new enemy,' he notes acerbically, 'to whom we want to avoid being of service, is more dangerous than the old one with which we have already learnt to come to terms' (p. 55). Psychoanalysis, Freud rather proudly claims, will always draw 'the resentment of our ruling powers down upon us' because it 'reduces religion to a neurosis of humanity', so there is not really much chance of finding protection in the Church. However, where there is little hope to be had, that which there is must be preserved, so Freud, uncertain of the impact of his book, chose to withhold it from publication, and clung on to the idea that in so doing he might be helping psychoanalysis retain its home. 'Psychoanalysis,' he wrote, in terms resonant of his state of mind, 'which in the course of my long life has gone everywhere, still possesses no home that could be more valuable for it than the city in which it was born and grew up' (ibid.).

A few months later, however, the Viennese situation and that of Freud had changed: the former was in Nazi hands, the latter in England. Freud wrote, as part of a further 'Prefatory Note', 'In the certainty that I should now be persecuted not only for my line of thought but also for my "race" – accompanied by many of my friends, I left the city which, from my early childhood, had been my home for seventy-eight years' (p. 57). External causes for delaying publication have now gone: England has proved friendly, if rather prone to be a source of Christian attempts to save Freud's poor soul, and there is nothing any more to be hoped for by way of protection for psychoanalysis from the 'broken reed' of Catholicism. The uncertainties now are only internal, Freud's 'lack of the consciousness of unity and belonging together which should exist between an author and his work', his 'critical sense' that 'this book, which takes its start from the man Moses, appears like a dancer balancing on the tip of one toe' (p. 58). But time and energy have run out, and the deep investment Freud has in this final great work is such that he cannot hold it back from its readership. Indeed, thinking psychoanalytically as one must about Freud's work, the very existence of all the uncertainties and anxieties, the breaches with logic and narrative sense, the 'lack of balance' and anxiety that this generates, all suggest that there is a powerful emotional identification and wish at work. It is not hard to see what these might be: the identification is clearly with Moses, the one who – like Freud – brought a benighted people out into the light of order and law; the wish is that psychoanalysis, like Judaism, might survive its dispersion.

Thus, at the very end of his life, ready 'to die in freedom' (Gay, 1988), Freud let loose on the world his meditation on the origins of Judaism, and on the perseverance of Jewish identity. Edward Said (2003), pursuing a view of psychoanalysis as a disruptive discipline, comments on how *Moses and Monotheism* cannot be seen as the summation of Freud's thinking, but rather is another creative move on his part, a lurch further into the unknown, in which the problematics of identity and belonging, and correspondingly of otherness and marginality, are revolved and left hanging. Said codes this, by virtue of a comparison with Beethoven, as a particular kind of 'late style'.

> In Beethoven's case and in Freud's... the intellectual trajectory conveyed by the late work is intransigence and a sort of irascible transgressiveness, as if the author was expected to settle down into a harmonious composure, as befits a person at the end of his life, but preferred instead to be difficult, and to bristle with all sorts of new ideas and provocations.... Freud's *Spätwerk* is obsessed with returning not just to the problem of Moses' identity... but to the very elements of identity itself... Reading the treatise, we feel that Freud wishes us to understand that there are other issues at stake here – other, more pressing problems to expose than ones whose solution might be comforting, or provide a sort of resting-place.   (pp. 29–30)

For Said, the 'other issues at stake' are those of a theory of identity, especially the opposition to be found in Freud's writing to a notion that identity might be formed once and for all, coherent and complete, at either the individual or cultural level.

> Freud's profound exemplification of the insight that even for the most definable, the most identifiable, the most stubborn communal

identity – for him, this was the Jewish identity – there are inherent limits that prevent it from being fully incorporated into one, and only one, Identity.　(p. 53)

Making Moses an Egyptian has the effect of asserting a brokenness within Jewish communal identity: at its source is an outsider, so claims for national or racial purity must always break down, in the specific case of Jews (and Israel), and in the general case of all cultures. Parenthetically, Julia Kristeva (1988) uses the Biblical figure of Ruth to similar effect. Ruth is a Moabite and hence a prohibited outsider to the Jews, a member of a group with which they were not allowed to inter-marry. Yet, her conversion to Judaism and her marriage to a Jewish sage are celebrated, and she becomes the grandmother of King David, the central figure in Jewish nationalism. As with Said's reading of *Moses and Monotheism*, this focus on the otherness at the source of cultural myths is congruent with the general psychoanalytic claim that the unconscious produces a kernel of strangeness at the heart of the human subject; however, what Said and Kristeva both do is write this 'strangeness' into cultural history and hence into politics as well.

Yerushalmi (1991, p. 2) offers a more comprehensive account of what *Moses and Monotheism* might be about.

> If the book can be read as the final chapter in Freud's lifelong case history it is also a public statement about matters of consider-ably wider consequence – the nature of Jewish history, religion and peoplehood, Christianity and anti-Semitism – written at a tragic historical juncture.

In particular, Yerushalmi argues that 'the true axis of the book' is 'the problem of tradition' (p. 29), the question of what perpetuates the past, what, specifically, gives Judaism its continued hold over Jews, even those who, like Freud, have not a trace of religious belief in them. Yerushalmi points to the pervasive Lamarckian assumptions in the book – the idea that specific 'learned' characteristics can be passed down through the generations, so that all Jews share not just a sense of a past history that links them, but the *actual memory trace* of that history, embodied and internalised, and linking them with one another through a mysterious yet material bond.

> Deconstructed into Jewish terms, what is Lamarckianism if not the powerful feeling that, for better or worse, one cannot really cease

being Jewish, and this not merely because of current anti-Semitism or discrimination, and certainly not because of the Chain of Tradition, but because one's fate in being Jewish was determined long ago by the Fathers, and that often what one feels most deeply and obscurely is a trilling wire in the blood.   (p. 31)

Freud's appeal, discussed in the previous chapter, to 'dark emotional powers' inexplicably tying him into his Jewish identity, fits well with this idea: it is as if what was learnt and experienced by the Jews throughout history becomes the emotional as well as the intellectual heritage of each new generation. In particular here, as Freud asserts throughout *Moses and Monotheism*, the reliance of the Jews on intellectual understanding, their appropriation of ideas and words as the domain of their portable material heritage, and the accompanying emphasis on reason rather than emotion or mysticism – these characteristics are both the heritage of all Jews and a sign of cultural or even racial superiority. The 'chosen people' takes new form in Freud's account of Judaism's origins, even though he makes the original instigator of the religion an Egyptian; and once again it is by no means surprising that these same attributes are those valued within the psychoanalytic movement itself.

Moses and Monotheism can undoubtedly be seen as a record of Freud's emotional response to Nazism and his attempt to work out his relationship with his own Jewish identity in that context. It is also, undoubtedly, an exploration of the conditions that have allowed for the survival and reproduction of Judaism in a hostile environment, and hence it does indeed deal, as Yerushalmi claims, with questions of tradition and inheritance, as well as opening out domains of speculation on national and political identity, the aspect of the book that Said draws out. It is thus a moving and complex document at numerous personal and intellectual levels. In the midst of all this, however Freud gives a startling account of anti-Semitism that embodies some of the recurrent themes of psychoanalysis' encounter with otherness, perhaps particularly in terms of its own institutional history. Freud's theory of anti-Semitism, whatever its shortcomings, also offers a way into another area of considerable importance: how psychoanalytic insights might be turned on the phenomenon of racialised hatred.

A good deal of *Moses and Monotheism* is devoted to considering ways in which Judaism offers an intellectually satisfying and rather superior way of engaging with the world, psychologically at least. Much of this is given in the terms outlined above: that in preferring an invisible, abstract God to a set of idols or images, monotheistic Judaism promotes intellectuality over sensuality, with vast gains for the Jews specifically and human culture in general. In developing this argument, as Boyarin (1997) has persuasively shown, Freud was at best exaggerating one trend in Jewish thought over another, and in particular was producing a version of Judaism that explicitly contested the anti-Semitic version of the Jew as feminine, sensual and consequently 'uncivilised'. Freud seems to have shared this vision of the feminine and been disturbed by the strong elements of 'feminine' passivity that he found within himself as well as within his people; hence, his assertion of the masculine 'spirituality' of the Jewish vision was fuelled in part by his own internalisation of anti-Semitic discourse. Freud's assertion of Jewish superiority thus has both psychological and political roots and resonance. His final comment on this at the end of the book is also his most egregious, showing a fine sensibility for polemic in the context of a historical juncture in which Jews and Judaism were being castigated and deplored.

> The pre-eminence given to intellectual labours throughout some two thousand years in the life of the Jewish people has, of course, had its effect. It has helped to check the brutality and the tendency to violence which are apt to appear where the development of muscular strength is the popular ideal. Harmony in the cultivation of intellectual and physical activity, such as was achieved by the Greek people, was denied to the Jews. In this dichotomy their decision was at least in favour of the worthier alternative.   (p. 115)

This beautiful amalgamation of Freud's admiration for the Greeks and his acceptance of at least some aspects of the claim of Jewish superiority must be read, again, in the context of the apparent historical triumph of 'brutality and the tendency to violence' in his own lifetime. For Freud, 'the idea of a single god, as well as the rejection of magically effective ceremonial and the stress upon ethical demands made in his name' (p. 66) was the originating force behind this skew towards intellectuality, and a great achievement it was too. The Jews themselves have always known this, hence their pride in their culture and their refusal to apologise for holding tightly to what is supposed (by Christians as well as atheists) to be an outmoded way of being. Freud, who always sought intellectual superiority and achievement, could see this in his Jewish compatriots, and could not restrain his own approbation of them.

> The Mosaic prohibition [on representation] elevated God to a higher degree of intellectuality... All such advances in intellectuality have as their consequence that the individual's self-esteem is increased, that he is made proud – so that he feels superior to other people who have remained under the spell of sensuality.   (pp. 14–15)

Not only *is* Judaism superior as a religion because it advances intellectual life over sensuality, but the Jews *feel* themselves to be superior because of their advances in intellectuality. They look down on the brutishness of ordinary life and regard themselves as special, not so much because of their supposed peculiar relationship with God, but more because of their power of thought, their capacity to reason and to appreciate the significance of ideas and ethical values. Again, if one wanted to draw a simple parallel between Freud's ideas on the virtues of Judaism and his advocacy of psychoanalytic values, it would be very easy to do so. Just as psychoanalysis promotes the importance of reason in making sense of the irrational, and hence sees itself as an advance over systems promoting physical enactment of emotion, so Judaism is superior to its predecessors and also to its 'successor', Christianity, in stressing the primacy of intellect over emotion, an abstract, invisible God over a material one. This also has its gendered components, reflected in Judaism's patriarchal vision and in the emphasis on *renunciation*. Brickman (2003, p. 151) draws out the parallels here by suggesting that 'Freud valued religious renunciation over religious fulfilment, seeing the former as masculine and characteristic of Judaism and the latter as feminine and characteristic of Christianity.' Moreover, 'The standard of comparison was encoded in raced and gendered terms: masculine renunciation created spiritual and moral advances that contributed to civilization; whereas with religious fulfilment the subject regressed to a pre-oedipal, primitive and feminine compliance with external authority' (ibid.). Christianity is thus a regression, psychologically and perhaps historically, and its feminine components demonstrate that; Judaism – whatever the feminisation of *Jews* – is truly masculine, intellectual, renunciatory and symbolic.

It is from here that the analysis of anti-Semitism begins. Anti-Semitism has numerous sources, of course: 'A phenomenon of such intensity and permanence as the people's hatred of the Jews must of course have more than one ground. It is possible to find a whole number of grounds, some of them clearly derived from reality, which call for no interpretation, and others, lying deeper and derived from hidden sources, which might be regarded as the specific reasons' (p. 90). One of these sources is undoubtedly the claim to superiority of the Jews, the fact that 'they have a particularly high opinion of themselves, that they regard themselves as more distinguished, of higher standing, as superior to other peoples – from whom they are also distinguished by many of their customs' (p. 105). This kind of superiority sense, built out of the deeply-rooted belief that the Jews really are the 'chosen people' of God, is bound to produce envy in others: 'If one is the declared favourite of the dreaded father, one need not be surprised at the jealousy of one's brothers and sisters, and the Jewish legend of Joseph and his brothers shows very well where this jealousy can lead' (p. 106). For the Christians at least, this abhorrent claim might even have seemed confirmed by their own religious history; why else, if not because they were already chosen as special, would the Christian Messiah, Jesus Christ, come from that obscure people? This fact, once again, intensified hatred of the Jews; somehow, it is always they who are selected for the starring role. 'I venture to assert,' writes Freud, 'that jealousy of the people which declared itself the first born, favourite child of God the Father, has not yet been surmounted among other peoples even today: it is as though they had thought there was truth in the claim' (p. 91).

Other sources of anti-Semitism have less to do with the behaviour of the Jews and more to do with their circumstances. Freud notes that the fact that Jews live as minorities amongst others and that they are different 'often in an indefinable way' from the people amongst whom they find themselves, is enough to generate continued hostility, especially as despite centuries of persecution they show no signs of being 'exterminated'; 'on the contrary, they show a capacity for holding their own in commercial life and, where they are admitted, for making valuable contributions for every form of cultural activity' (p. 91). More psychologically, building on Freud's speculative account of the origins of culture both in *Moses and Monotheism* and the earlier *Totem and Taboo* (1914), the Jews are held to be responsible for the murder of the primal father and not to have been willing to acknowledge this. The argument here is complex, and – as Freud himself acknowledged when he referred to his anthropological account in *Totem and Taboo* as a 'just-so story' (Freud, 1921, p. 122) – far-fetched. Paralleling the prehistory of all peoples, the Jews are held by Freud to have murdered their own paternal founder, Moses. However, the historical truth of this was repressed, resurfacing as remorse and an increasing sense of guilt, which in turn 'provided the stimulus for the wishful fantasy of the Messiah, who was to return and lead his people to redemption and the promised world-dominion' (p. 89). Jesus thus represents the return of the murdered primeval father, the return of Moses-the-founder; he also *re-enacts* the murder itself, both in an act of expiation (Jesus on the cross) and as retribution: the son-religion (Christianity) conquers and destroys the father-religion (Judaism). 'Ostensibly aimed at propitiating the father god,' writes Freud (pp. 87–8), 'it ended in his being dethroned and got rid of.' Judaism, both in its refusal to acknowledge and deal with the father-murder and in its *specificity*, its insistence on the mark of difference, becomes the recalcitrance of a past wished away but continuing to return. Christianity, by contrast, celebrates and ritually atones for the murder of the father and extends its wings to all people who choose to participate in it – and, historically, to many whose choice is forced. The Jews, however, are a thorn in Christianity's side, denying not only its truth but also reminding the world that there was once a father and that his shadow looms large, albeit mainly in the unconscious. This unadmitted 'guilt' of the Jewish people, stubbornly holding onto the idea that they are preferred amongst all people, acts as a continual provocation, and in so doing appeases the guilt of other peoples, specifically the Christians, who themselves have primal murder on their hands.

Freud was not much impressed with Christianity, seeing it as a regression barely able to hold onto the monotheistic achievements of Judaism. *Christians* were even less convincing, and Freud turned his ironic vision scathingly on the behaviour and attributes of those who claimed allegiance to the Christian religion, only to show – in Nazism particularly – that barbarous violence was closer to their souls. This is another source of profound anti-Semitism, according to Freud; that is, Christians are themselves ambivalent, and project their hatred of their own religion onto the Jews.

> [W]e must not forget that all those people who excel today in their hatred of Jews became Christians only in late historic times, often driven to it by bloody coercion. It might be said that they are all 'misbaptised'. They have been left, under a thin veneer of Christianity, what their ancestors were, who worshipped a barbarous polytheism. They have not got over a grudge against the new religion which was imposed upon them; but they have displaced the grudge on to the source from which Christianity reached them.

Their hatred of Jews is at bottom a hatred of Christians, and we need not be surprised that in the German National Socialist revolution this intimate relation between the two monotheist religions finds such a clear expression in the hostile treatment of both of them. (pp. 91–2)

There is an interesting uncertainty here about whether hatred of Judaism is fuelled by its refusal to participate in the conscience-cleansing rituals of Christianity, or whether it masks a deeper hatred of Christianity itself held by those who are at heart pagan; but the astute Freudian point is that, whatever their unconscious origins, poisonous feelings are directed at the Jews. The Jews channel, collect and carry hostile projections; anti-Semitism allows all who hate to combine together in their antagonism towards one specific enemy.

Finally, the anxiety-producing mark of bodily difference so important in nineteenth century racial thinking, is a key element in the generation of anti-Semitic feelings.

Further, among the customs by which the Jews made themselves separate, that of circumcision has made a disagreeable, uncanny impression, which is to be explained, no doubt, by its recalling the dreaded castration and along with it a portion of the primaeval past which is gladly forgotten. (p. 91)

This castration is at the hands of the primal father, who was then murdered by the band of brothers whose subsequent guilt and atonement became the founding act of civilisation. Circumcision therefore not only links with the fear of femininity, but also raises the spectre of murder and guilt, reminding the non-Jew of the violence at the root of civilisation. The Jew becomes the recipient of hatred because he literally embodies the mark of castration, visibly presenting to the other nations the reality of the great vulnerability of the human condition, the exercise of power and the enforcement of the law of culture. Perhaps it is understandable that this produces a furious response: while Jews themselves claim that circumcision 'perfects' them, to outsiders it looks like an act of subjugation, hence demanding renunciation of any omnipotent fantasy.

What is one to make of all this? Freud's text is full of telling ambiguities: he debunks religion and, in making the founder of Jewish nationhood, its great redeemer, an Egyptian, he exposes the fragility of Jewish claims to purity and originality. The appropriation of the position of being the 'chosen people' of God is obviously a wish fulfilment, almost certainly born out of the actual powerlessness of the Jews, alongside their stunning assertion of intellectual superiority over others. All this punctures the case for a secure and strong Jewish identity. On the other hand, and at least as forcefully, Freud allows domains of *actual* superiority. Whatever the source of monotheistic Judaism, its creation and perpetuation is a great achievement of the Jews, promoting real intellectual advances and steering them away from the brutal sensuality so evident in Nazism and more generally amongst many other nations. The so-called civilisation of the others, particularly Christianity, which claims to have surpassed Judaism, is mostly a thinly-laid veneer over deep-rooted barbarism, and the hatred of the Jews that results is as much a hatred of all culture and order as it is a specific anti-Semitism. On the other hand again, if a people claims a special place in the eyes of its 'father' God, and indeed seems to have one, it is not surprising that it draws hatred upon itself – jealousy of this kind will always be produced amongst siblings, whether they be individuals or entire nations. Then there is the mere provocative act of survival itself: how *dare* the Jews outlive their oppressors. And finally there is circumcision, a mark of fascination and fear; anti-Semitism sees in it the display of the power of castration, the mark of violence, the allure of sexuality, and the enthralling inescapability of coercive power. All this generates hate: hate of the Jew's religious priority, of the Jew's special position, of the Jew's claim to intellectual and ethical superiority, of the Jew's sexuality, of the Jew's difference, his or her 'otherness'.

Freud's account of anti-Semitism thus revolves a number of themes that recur in considerations of racialised hatred, despite its apparent speculativeness and specificity, and its rather troubling implication that there is a sense in which the Jews themselves, with their excessive confidence in their own superiority, are implicated in the production of anti-Semitism. First, Freud suggests that *jealousy* is a key element, arising from a fantasy that there really is something special about the Jew. This idea has entered into the common armoury of explanations of racism in general: the other group is seen as having some privilege, something special about them, and this envied thing fuels the hostility. Linked to this is the notion that the hated other is an object of fascination as well as hostility: the anti-Semite cannot leave the Jew alone, is stirred and excited by the Jew, and is made real and alive only through this fascination. Likewise, explorations of anti-black racism have also noted that the racist *needs* the hated other, that the racialised opponent holds, in fantasy, repudiated but essential parts of the racist

– in the case of colour racism, this often being the white person's repressed sensuality (Kovel, 1995). Indeed, for the white non-Jew, the circumcised Jew and the black may be classed together as a sexual threat that is also a seduction and an excitement; Jung himself, as one of millions of examples, seems to have been sexually attracted to Jewish women (for instance Sabina Spielrein), as a product of, rather than in opposition to, his anti-Semitic tendencies. The 'exoticism' of the racialised other is thus both a source of attraction and of fear; the one emotion fuels the other in a powder keg of explosive ambivalence.

Freud did not lay out a systematic theory of racism, nor even of anti-Semitism. However, arising from his personal experience as much as, or perhaps more than, from his clinical judgement, he articulated the various sides of the Jewish experience that are related to anti-Semitic phenomena. The Jews are hated partly because they survive, they are forced into difference and this in turn provokes hatred, they are excluded and then seen as holding themselves separate. They are objects of fascination, seen as a kind of yeast for culture in general, but this creates envy; they are allowed only the currency of intellectuality and then their fantasised 'cleverness' is feared. Above all, if psychoanalysis as well as popular culture is to be believed, they are sexualised, with their 'castrated' state provoking anxiety as well as desire. Jews like Freud, as well as psychoanalysts, might think that they are on the side of reason and hence of the advancement of human culture, but they very easily become the bearers of 'unreasonable', irrational projections; that is, they become the carriers and recipients of culture's repressed underside. As will be seen in subsequent chapters, when psychoanalysis, which invokes this underside in its everyday work, comes into conflict with a rampantly irrational social order, its own fantasised 'Jewish identity' as well as its actual Jewish history can become an embarrassment, even an albatross around its neck. When that happens, the temptation to run for cover, dropping ethics and values all the way, can become hard to resist.

Part II

Psychoanalysis, Nazism and Jewish Science

3
Psychoanalysis, Nazism and Jewish Science

Clearly, the idea that psychoanalysis might at least have a strong Jewish connection, even if one might baulk at the idea of it being a Jewish 'science', is not particularly contentious. Sociologically and philosophically, in its membership, its practices and its mind-set, psychoanalysis was constructed out of the energy released from the anti-semitic as well as the theocratic restrictions of the past. With the resurgence of the antisemitic part of this in its newly virulent twentieth century European form, that of Nazism, these issues became key once more: psychoanalysis was to be damned because of its Jewish origins and structure, and if it was going to be rescued, then – so at least some of the thinking went – its Jewishness (including its Jewish membership) would have to be discarded. In Germany, where everything had to be worked out for the first time and where the full extent of the Nazi terror only slowly dawned on people, the ducking and weaving that psychoanalysts became involved in to preserve themselves and their profession adds up to a sorry tale of collaboration with oppressive power and a readiness to relinquish the attachments and commitments of the very recent past. However, this is no simple tale of vindictiveness or of moral and political blindness, even though both tendencies can be found in the activities of at least some German psychoanalysts of the time. Instead, the now well-mined buried history of psychoanalysis in Germany under the Third Reich reveals a complex pattern of conscious and unconscious affiliations and renunciations, whereby genuine if (with hindsight) misguided efforts to preserve psychoanalysis became entwined with powerful destructive impulses capable of using the Nazi whirlwind to achieve their own ends. In particular, as if parodying Freud's writings of exactly that time, the anti-Semitic underside of the analysts' apparent Judeophilia found expression, with the Jewish elements in psychoanalysis – some would say, its Jewish *essence* – being traduced and denied.

There are numerous important elements in this, including questions of institutional and individual culpability. However, the major reason for rehearsing this history here is to examine what it shows about the ways in which a radically subversive and critical discipline, psycho-analysis, can be co-opted into an oppressive, totalitarian system, shedding its ethics and its essential values in the interests of some kind of survival. One issue here is a rather romantic question about whether there is something so violently disruptive about the psychoanalytic 'discovery' of the unconscious that given pressure, well-founded anxiety and half a chance, even those who are attracted to it will not only repudiate the Freudian unconscious, but will also try to take their revenge on its discoverer. In particular, in the light of what has already been claimed here concerning the close links between psychoanalysis and its Jewish origins, infiltration of anti-Semitism into the psychoana-lytic movement can hardly be surprising; what is of interest is how, once the external environment became threatening enough, this anti-Semitic impulse became barely containable, and seems to have spread throughout the organisation, poisoning its ground wells. Perhaps this in itself lends support to Freud's wild ideas about the killing of the primal father – here, the father of psychoanalysis; it certainly seems to offer credence to his tired and bitter observation that, 'Basically all are anti-Semites. They are everywhere' (Yerushalmi, 1991, p. 54).

A ferocious silence

The history of psychoanalysis in Germany during the Nazi period has been a source of some controversy and heart-searching within the ana-lytic community since the end of the 1970s. Prior to that, with the exception of controversy over C.G. Jung's involvement with the Nazis (Bair, 2004) and a rather negative report to Ernest Jones from John Rickman on the immediate post-war German analysts in 1946 (reprinted in Brecht et al, 1985), there had been a ferocious silence over events between 1933 and 1945. The term 'ferocious' is used here because the silence not only covered up a troubled history, but also repressed a set of contradictions and tensions which have relevance both to the social history of psychoanalysis as a profession, and also to its theoretical positions. Both this history and these theories are heavily invested in by psychoanalysts and others committed to the dis-cipline, the benign nature of which is to some extent called into question if one argues – as it is possible to do – that psychoanalysis fell rather easily into Nazi hands. Thus, applying psychoanalysis crudely to itself, 'not speaking' about the Nazi period can be seen as one of those functional defences arising out of a partially unconscious awareness of the problems that could have been caused by speaking too clearly. The silence not only served to create a space to get on with post-war reconstruction; it was also a way of holding together a movement that might easily, faced with its own destructive impulses, fragment.

Since about the mid-1970s, there has been an opening out of work on the Nazi period, with one spur to action being the meeting of the International Psychoanalytic Association in Hamburg in 1985, although this produced disappointment in some Jewish analysts that the issues of the Nazi Holocaust were not fully attended to (Moses and Hrushovski-Moses, 1986). The work includes documentation by Brecht et al (1985) and English-language studies of psychotherapy in Nazi Germany by Cocks (1985, second edition 1997) and of psychoanalysis by Goggin and Goggin (2001). In addition, *Psychoanalytic Review* published a special issue on the topic (Issue 88, 2001) and there have been many substantial papers on various aspects of the historical record (Riccardo Steiner's work based on the correspondence between Anna Freud and Ernest Jones is of special importance – Steiner, 2000). The controversy has been and remains one between those who see the Nazi period as an aberration in which psychoanalysis was destroyed and therefore had to be recreated anew in Germany, and those who argue for 'continuity', that however much it was constrained by its Nazi masters, psychoanalysis continued and possibly – at least as a form of psychotherapy – flourished. As will be described more fully in Chapter 5, this controversy was part of the post-war debate between the two German institutions claiming psychoanalytic legitimacy. The Deutsche Psychoanalytische Gesellschaft (DPG), which was the 'original' group, claimed that psychoanalysis had been 'saved' by its members during the war. The Deutsche Psychoanalytische Vereinigung (DPV) – which split from the DPG largely on issues of the 'purity' of psychoanalytic practice and which was recognised by the IPA in 1951, with Carl Müller–Braunschweig as its leader – argued that psychoanalysis had been destroyed and that a new organisation was needed to resurrect it. Cocks (2001, pp. 230–1) comments,

these rationalizations were true only in small part. The DPG offered a misleading and apologetic gloss on a very complicated relationship between the practice of psychoanalysis and the Nazi regime.

The DPV was equally inaccurate in its dismissal of the work as not having *anything at all* to do with psychoanalysis.

Brecht et al (1985, p. 214), tracing the history, similarly note:

> In the efforts to rebuild the Psychoanalytical Society after 1945 there were now two currents: one apparently continued without a break the evolution toward psychotherapy which had begun under National Socialism, the other tried to free psychoanalysis from other therapeutic trends and to make common cause with the developments which had meanwhile been going on abroad. But in both divergent trends there was little room for reflection on their common past under National Socialism, their collaboration with it, their own susceptibility to its ideology, the advantages they had gained from it, or the fact that representatives of the new psychoanalytical institution had belonged to the NSDAP. If such thoughts emerged, they apparently disappeared again without trace.

The debate on whether or not psychoanalysis 'survived' in Germany has continued, most importantly to include Cocks, whose work proposed that 'the history of psychotherapy in general in the Third Reich displays important institutional *continuities* with preceding and succeeding developments inside and outside the discipline' (ibid., p. 232) and that psychoanalysis participated in this. The Goggins, on the other hand, whose study of psychoanalysis in the Nazi period was prompted by Cocks' work, dispute this. Their response shows something of the emotional investments involved:

> Cocks not only startled us, but also dismayed us by insisting that psychoanalysis not only survived, but it experienced professional growth during the Third Reich. It was this claim that led us to investigate the particular issue of whether or not psychoanalysis survived.   (Goggin and Goggin, 2001, p. 25)

The emotional language here is revealing and also appropriate for a discipline that claims that emotion – especially in the form of unconscious ideas – drives action, including striving for knowledge. It is because they are 'startled' and 'dismayed' that the Goggins seek to find out whether psychoanalysis survived or not. What is at stake is its ethical standing, embodied in a paradox: if it survived, then given what is known about what happened, it must have collaborated, so true survival (or the survival of true psychoanalysis) depends on psychoanalysis having been destroyed during that time of violence. Perhaps not surprisingly, given their starting point of dismay at the idea that psychoanalysis may have survived, tainted by collaboration with the Nazis, the Goggins discover from their own reading of the material that this could not have happened, that the conditions were such that psychoanalysis must have been destroyed. The reasoning here is intriguing and revealing. Goggin and Goggin argue that the conditions under which the remaining psychoanalysts and psychotherapists worked in Germany during the Nazi period were so antipathetic to psychoanalysis that whatever they did could not be called psychoanalysis, even if some of its outward forms just about survived. Instead,

> In assessing the transformations – and continuities – within the psychoanalytic community in Germany during the Third Reich, we have arrived at one central conclusion: namely, the major ideas and world view represented by the psychoanalytic movement did not, and could not, survive in Nazi Germany... the very nature of totalitarianism during the Third Reich renders it highly unlikely, if not impossible, for psychoanalysis to be permitted and practised. Despite the heroic attempts of a few individuals in Nazi Germany to keep psychoanalysis alive, the psychoanalytic movement did not survive during those years. (ibid., pp. 9–10)

This is both an argument *in principle,* that psychoanalysis needs a certain modicum of freedom ('freedom of association' in a political/psychoanalytic pun), and *in practice* – that in fact psychoanalysis was so adulterated by its forced alignment with other therapies, that it lost all its disciplinary integrity. The latter claim is a kind of empirical, or at least historical, one and will be returned to later; specifically, is it actually the case that psychoanalysts ceased to engage in the recognisably distinct elements of their therapeutic practice, for example free association, interpretation (including transference interpretation) and a focus on unconscious conflicts and defences? The Goggins state that 'free association and exploration of transference in a safe setting [are] professional requirements or demand characteristics inherent in the practice of psychoanalysis' (ibid., p. 26), and argue that because the setting was anything but 'safe', then what passed for free association could not really be understood to be the real thing. However, whether the analysts of the time saw their activities in that way might be a relevant question; if they noticed no fundamental change in their professional

behaviour, then who can state that at some point they ceased to practice analytically? More generally, the Goggins espouse a view of psychoanalysis as only possible within a liberal society, and as such
unimaginable within Nazi totalitarianism:

> First, for psychoanalysis to exist, there needs to be scientific and
> political freedom; the revision of the social order abrogated such
> freedom. Second, the Nazis attempted to impose their altered vision
> of what it was to be a healthy human being on psychotherapeutic
> practice. They required that people needed to be in harmonious
> unity with society, their leader, their soul and the soil – health
> equals unity... Freud conceived of the self in part submitting to
> culture and yet at the same time being in opposition to it; the self,
> in a sense, is in a standing quarrel with culture.   (p. 43)

There is much that is accurate in this claim, and the point about
Freud's view being of the self as 'in a standing quarrel with culture' and
hence being incompatible with a totalising social vision is one that will
be returned to later. However, the Goggins' argument here is too slip-
pery, a sleight of hand: defining psychoanalysis as needing 'freedom'
and observing that freedom was 'abrogated' under Nazism, they conclude that psychoanalysis *must have* died. But what if, in fact, it did
not; what if it did continue, was practised in a recognisable form, shed
some of its 'Jewish' attributes and made itself acceptable to its Nazi
masters; dabbled in conformist psychotherapy, but was still there, still
called itself psychoanalysis, still maintained its core commitment to
the unconscious and to a therapeutic method based on free association
and interpretation? Under such circumstances, one can see why the
Goggins and others might be 'dismayed', for their precious ideal
object, that ethically sound psychoanalysis that could not possibly go
along with 'Nazi ideology and the totalitarian system' (p. 46), might be
found to have done exactly that, and therefore no longer to be ideal.
Instead, psychoanalysis itself becomes another embodiment of an
anxious and conflicted social reality, not averse to using racialised
hatred as a means towards its own survival. That this meant assaulting
the source of psychoanalysis' own distinctive creativity – its Jewish
heritage – is, from a psychoanalytic point of view, a not unexpected
turn of the screw.

Not only has this debate between those who posit continuity and
those who claim discontinuity in psychoanalysis from the Nazi period
to the post-war situation had practical ramifications in the structures

and splits in contemporary German psychoanalysis, but it also says a considerable amount about the fundamental assumptions of psycho-analysis, the conditions under which it can survive, those under which it can thrive, and the moral standing of its practitioners. None of these issues has gone unnoticed, although often they become somewhat swamped by the political and transferential realities of the psychoana-lytic scene. In addition, there is the relatively silenced question of psy-choanalysis as a 'Jewish science', which the Goggins have brought back into focus in their book (including in its title – *Death of a 'Jewish Science'*). This was, of course, the way psychoanalysis was catalogued by the Nazis and the notion of it as 'Jewish' therefore has strong anti-Semitic connotations; but as has been argued earlier there is also plenty of evidence of a genuine set of links between psychoanalysis and Jewish identity, making any simple repudiation of the 'Jewish science' idea difficult to sustain. This chapter and those following take up the history of psychoanalysis in Germany in the Nazi period to explore some of these issues. In particular, this history is seen as an example of the tension between the socially critical stance of psychoanalysis and the impulse to repress this criticality; the absorption of psychoanalysis into projects of social adjustment is one manifestation of the repressive impulse, grandiose under the totalitarian conditions of Nazism, but present elsewhere too (see Jacoby, 1975, 1983). However, the thesis here is that something both more specific (because it dealt with the Jews) and more general (because it shows how 'turning against the other' can be used in the interests of institutional as well as individual survival) took place amongst the psychoanalysts in Germany. The essence of the argument is that the collaborationist tendency in psy-choanalysis under the Third Reich expressed not only personal and professional fears and ambitions and misguided strategies, but also something about anti-Semitism on a psychological and political level.

Appeasing the Nazis

By the early 1930s, German psychoanalysis and specifically the Berlin Psychoanalytic Institute (BPI), was a model for how psychoanalysis might be practised and developed in an advanced society. The BPI had been founded by Ernst Simmel and Max Eitingon in 1920 and was bankrolled by Eitingon, who in the early 1930s was also President of the German Psychoanalytic Society (DPG), which itself had been founded in 1910. The BPI was explicitly social reformist in attitude and approach, and had amongst its members some of the stars of the movement to combine socialism or Marxism and psychoanalysis – Wilhelm Reich, Otto Fenichel, Erich Fromm, Edith Jacobson, Ernst Simmel, Siegfried Bernfeld and others – most of them Jews. It also adopted a programme of developing psychoanalysis so that it could be of benefit to working people, with a substantial commitment to low cost psychotherapy. Indeed, this commitment was so strong that every analyst, including analysts in training, 'had to pledge 10 percent of their time and 4 percent of their income for these humanitarian principles' (Goggin and Goggin, 2001, p. 18). Otto Fenichel ran the famous 'Children's Seminar' at the BPI, the 'children' of the title referring to their position in the hierarchy of analysts rather than their focus, for the purpose of this seminar was to study relations between psychoanalysis and politics, particularly socialism (Jacoby, 1983). The BPI thus enacted both a commitment to psychoanalytic practice and education, and an attempt to make psychoanalysis of cultural and political relevance – a serious yet immensely exciting affair. Goggin and Goggin (2001, p. 19) comment, 'it is not too much to say that by 1930 the BPI had established itself as a role model for the profession.' Yet, within a remarkably short time after the accession of the Nazis to power in 1933 all this had gone.

The story of how this happened is quite complex, and its underlying dynamics are even more so. There are continuing uncertainties over the role of certain important protagonists, including Sigmund and Anna Freud themselves. Mixed up in the narrative is the provocative figure of Jung, and a subsidiary plot is provided by the machinations around Wilhelm Reich. Ernest Jones is at times both villain and hero. Three names recur: Matthias Göring, Felix Boehm and Carl Müller–Braunschweig. The first of these was a cousin of the top Nazi politician, Hermann Göring, and as a consequence took over leadership of the psychotherapy movement; the other two were non-Jewish psychoanalysts who were instrumental in the collaboration with Nazism in the 1930s and who survived the war, in Müller-Braunschweig's case going on to head the new psychoanalytic organisation in West Germany. The story is one of failed appeasement and muddled thinking, not especially scarce commodities in the 1930s, with a contributory undertone of self-deception.

The history has been reasonably well documented in recent years, particularly in Brecht et al (1985). Hitler was elected Chancellor of Germany at the end of January 1933 and rapidly consolidated his power. Within months the opposition had been largely defeated, the mechanisms of terror had been put in place, and the writing was on the wall for Jews, communists and other anti-Nazi elements. The psychoanalysts panicked. Max Eitingon, then President of the DPG, went to consult with Freud, leaving Boehm and Müller-Braunschweig in temporary charge. These two immediately began a process of negotiation with the Nazis, which from any vantage point looks like betrayal, hatching a plan for Eitingon to be replaced as leader of the DPG and for the Jewish members to resign. The conscious sources of this behaviour seem to have arisen from Boehm's anxiety to protect psychoanalysis from being dismantled on 'technical' racial grounds before it could mount an attempt to negotiate with the Nazis. Thus, having seen a notice in the *Medical Journal* requiring all medical organisations to 'Aryanise' their directorships, he actively sought confirmation from the Nazis that this applied to the psychoanalysts, effectively drawing their attention to the DPG when it is not clear that they had particularly thought about it (Goggin and Goggin, 2001). This then gave Boehm the ammunition to fire at Eitingon, whose Presidency he saw as a major obstacle to legitimising the DPG under the new rulers of the nation. What the possible *unconscious* sources of Boehm's actions might have been are of necessity a matter of speculation, but it is perhaps obvious that anxiety played a major part, also ambition (the suggestion was that Eitingon should be replaced by Boehm himself); as will be described later, it also looks likely that Boehm and Müller-Braunschweig had some sympathy with the Nazis, and that as a concomitant of this, and for other reasons too, they were not completely devastated by the thought that German psychoanalysis might lose its Jews.

Freud himself, when consulted by Boehm, agreed that he could take over the DPG if he could get a majority to vote for him, apparently hoping that hiding the Jewish culture of psychoanalysis behind the 'Aryan' figure of Boehm might be enough to appease the Nazis. This was also the view of Ernest Jones, President of the International Psychoanalytic Association, who in the early period of the Third Reich was strongly committed to an approach that would protect the interests of German psychoanalysis even at the expense of its individual members – that is, its Jewish members. As late as 1935, Jones was to write, 'I prefer Psycho-Analysis to be practised by Gentiles in Germany than not at all' (Jones to Anna Freud, letter of November 11, 1935; in Goggin and Goggin, 2001, p. 98), and this idea that psychoanalysis should be preserved at all costs was one strand in his thinking throughout the 1930s. Freud, too, whilst not as cavalier in his attitude towards his Jewish colleagues, was in the early days at least over-optimistic about the impact of the Nazis and their capacity to spread; like many others, his faith in the capacity of politicians to act decisively against Hitler would have been touching if it were not so dangerously misplaced.

> We can expect with certainty that the Hitler movement will spread to Austria, is indeed already here, but it is very unlikely that it will present a similar danger as in Germany... We are in transition toward a rightist dictatorship, which means the suppression of social democracy. That will not be an agreeable state of affairs and will not make life pleasant for us Jews, but we all think that legal emergency declarations are impossible in Austria because the terms of our peace treaty expressly provide for rights of minorities, which did not happen in the Versailles treaty... Here legalized persecution of the Jews would immediately result in the intervention of the League of Nations.   (Letter from Freud to Jones, 7 April 1933, in Steiner, 2000, p. 25)

Although Freud wavered on the potential impact of Nazism and the degree to which German psychoanalysis might be protected behind a non-Jewish veneer, he was clear-sighted enough to recognise that Boehm's proposal for the DPG to exclude 'foreigners' from its Board would not prevent attacks on psychoanalysis, and he was also pre-scient enough to believe that some of the changes being proposed had a hidden agenda of changing psychoanalysis itself (Eickhoff, 1995, p. 946). The DPG members actually opposed Boehm's move to displace Eitingon and ethnically cleanse the Board; nevertheless, correctly sensing the way the wind blew, Eitingon resigned at the DPG meeting of 6 May 1933 and shortly afterwards left Germany to live in Palestine. In the previous month, he had commented in a letter to Freud that having Boehm as the 'representative of our German institution... is of course a misfortune' (Steiner, 2000, p. 48); thus, at every stage, from 1933 onwards, the question of whether Boehm and Müller-Braunschweig were saving psychoanalysis or destroying it was a controversial one, actively debated and personally felt.

By the end of 1933 a further twenty or so Jewish analysts had left the country and, in a symbolic act of great significance in bringing home to them the new State's attitudes, Freud's books had been publicly burnt. Simmel, a past chairman of the Association of Socialist Doctors, had also been arrested in the summer of 1933, increasing the anxiety of the DPG leaders about their own future (Brecht et al, 1985, p. 112).

Boehm and Müller-Braunschweig now constituted the entire Executive of the BPI, which as an organisation had been devastated by the exodus of analysts: 'The number of psychoanalysts at the institute had dropped from around 65 to between 12 and 15, the number of candidates from 34 in 1932 to 18 in 1934, and the number of students fell from 222 in 1931 to 138 in 1932 and to 34 by 1934' (Cocks, 1997, pp. 61–2). It is not hard to see why, even without any underhand motives, Boehm and Müller-Braunschweig might feel they needed to do something with regard to the position of psychoanalysis under the Nazis, and indeed they were hard at work, following an appeasing plan that aimed to preserve the organisation of the DPG and with it German psychoanalysis. They had met with the Nazi Ministry of Culture in September 1933 to discuss the conditions under which the DPG could be preserved, and by November 1933 all the offices of the DPG had been taken over by non-Jewish members, while only non-Jewish candidates for membership were approved. Otto Fenichel, for one, noticed this and saw it as motivated by political allegiances and not just caution; previously, he had also commented directly on Boehm's identification with the dictatorial Nazi style.

> Boehm said that he thought that in such difficult times it would be best to have as few board members as possible, so that only a small number should bear the responsibility. I told him that he was already infected with the modern 'Führer principle' and said that in my opinion, in difficult times not as few but as many people as possible should be heard before decisions are made. My suspicion turned out to be justified. In his actions and in his pronouncements Boehm frequently declared himself to be the 'leader' [Führer] of psychoanalysis in Germany, albeit a leader who in many respects trembled with more anxiety than many other leaders. (Fenichel, Rundbriefe 3, 1934, in Eickhoff, 1995, p. 948)

Others have noted that the term 'Führer' was in very wide use at the time, so much so that the Nazis clamped down on it. Nevertheless, Fenichel clearly identified the anti-democratic urge in Boehm, which could hide behind the apparent necessity to do something decisive in order to appease the Nazis, but which did so with such alacrity that one wonders how painful a course of action it actually was. More broadly, there was continued debate between those analysts who remained in Germany and those who left about which was the better course of action, whether to support the continuation of a viable association or whether to take a stand. Fenichel noted, 'Many colleagues who have emigrated are in favour of collective resignation because the conformism is going too far for them' (Rundbriefe of March 1934, in Eickhoff, 1995, p. 949).

Jewish science

To the Nazis, psychoanalysis was a prime example of the corrosive nature of Jewish thought, its degenerate capacity to poison the sources of idealism and feeling for race and nation and, especially, 'to strike the Nordic races at their most vulnerable point, their sexual life' (*Deutsche Volksegesundheit aus Blut und Boden*, 1933, quoted in Brecht et al, 1985, p. 101). Psychoanalysis 'belonged to the overrationalized corruptions of late capitalism, its alleged obsession with sexual drives plaguing primitive peoples like the Jews making it a proper therapeutic method only in rare cases' (Cocks, 1997, p. 60); the practice of psychoanalysis could thus be seen as actively anti-social. Its truths, such as they were, had not even been discovered by Freud, but were rather based on distortions of the work of genuinely Germanic philosophers: 'Freud himself remained a favourite object of scorn, vilified as a major representative of Jewish nihilism and entrepreneurship and accused of perverting the work of the Aryan German creators of "depth psychology" – Novalis, Carus, Schopenhauer, Goethe – by turning it into a business enterprise that thrived on a clientele of rich hysterics' (ibid.). Psychoanalysis, like the Jews themselves and consistent with what would be expected of a Jewish science, was thus parasitic, sucking the life blood out of the Aryan nations and using it to feed the growth of Jewish corruption. Its origins in Freud and his Jewish colleagues, its focus on sex, its critical and ironic stance towards society and the links with socialism of so many of its German adherents all added up to compelling evidence of its perniciousness, and made it a prime candidate for persecution.

Defending psychoanalysis against this onslaught, Boehm and Müller-Braunschweig therefore saw themselves as faced with the task of persuading the Nazis that psychoanalysis was not necessarily 'Jewish', but could be utilised in the service of the state. From Boehm's own account (Brecht et al, 1985, pp. 132–137), a great deal of his energy went into persuading Nazi functionaries that psychoanalysis was not dependent on the fact that Freud, a Jew, had founded it, but rather stood independently of this, on its merits. Moreover, whereas the Nazis were inclined to see it as a 'subversive' discipline, Boehm himself attempted to persuade them that 'I had never known psychoanalysis to have a destructive effect on love of country' (ibid., p. 132). Müller-Braunschweig wrote a famous 'Memorandum' on psychoanalysis for the Nazis, published in a slightly adapted form in October1933, under the title 'Psychoanalysis and *Weltanschauung*' in *Reichswart*, a 'rabid anti-Semitic publication' (Nitzschke, 1999, p. 357). In this article, the basis of psychoanalysis is asserted to be not just the understanding of sexuality, but of ego-instinct conflicts in general; this particular slant (ironically, in a different form, later to become dominant in American ego psychology and hence to incur the wrath of radical critics such as Marcuse (1955) and Jacoby (1975)) allows Müller-Braunschweig to use the language of 'mastery' so resonant with the Nazis – the unconscious can be 'mastered', the patient can achieve 'mastery of himself'. Then comes an infamous passage, taken generally as an example of the slippage in Müller-Braunschweig's thinking between an analytic stance and one in which service to the Third Reich could come to predominate.

> Psychoanalysis works to remodel incapable weaklings into people who can cope with life, the inhibited into confident types, those divorced from reality into human beings who can look reality in the face, those enslaved by their instincts into their masters, loveless, selfish people into people capable of love and sacrifice, those indifferent to the totality of life into those willing to serve the whole. Thus it does outstanding work in education, and is able to give valuable service to the principles, only now mapped out anew, of a heroic, constructive conception of life, attuned to reality.   (Brecht et al, 1985, p. 116)

This last sentence in particular shows the direction of the argument, calling as it does on the ('only now mapped out anew', that is, Nazi) 'heroic' conception of life and advancing the idea that psychoanalysis, despite its past faults, can contribute to this. Interestingly, the key advocate of 'neo-analysis' in the DPG before and after the war, Harald Schultze-Hencke, published a very similar article at about the same time as that by Müller-Braunschweig. In this, he too argued that the goal of psychotherapy should be to 'free the powers of fitness and proficiency within the individual,' and contended 'that the achievement of this kind of psychological health was a duty each individual owed to his community and that its maintenance was the corresponding duty of the psychotherapist' (Cocks, 1997, p. 87). The pervasiveness of this kind of thinking, which could pass for a kind of patriotic idealism, should not be underestimated; what both Schultze-Hencke and Müller-Braunschweig were doing was realigning psychoanalysis to fit a context in which subservience of the individual to the racial and national community was the primary political and psychological virtue.

In Schultze-Hencke's article, psychological health was defined 'in terms of blood, strong will, proficiency, discipline, community, heroic bearing, and physical fitness' (ibid.); from here to the idea of an accommodation with the Nazis' projected 'German psychotherapy', in which service to the state would have priority as the aim of therapy and the measure of mental health and personal worth, was an easily managed step. Importantly, Schultz-Hencke's psychotherapeutic 'deviation' ('neo-analysis') was seen by Freud as a great threat to psychoanalysis before the War, and was a major source of contention within the International Psychoanalytic Association when the Germans sought reacceptance afterwards; yet it was clearly part of a larger urge, reflected in Müller-Braunschweig's writing, to fall in with the Nazi philosophy that saw personal liberation as occurring through overcoming the inhibitions preventing active commitment to, and absorption in, the Reich.

With the support of Jones, who saw this as the best way to ensure the survival of psychoanalysis in Germany and who also later claimed to have been motivated by the need to protect Jewish members of the DPG (Steiner, 2000), Boehm and Müller-Braunschweig thus followed a tactic of negotiating with Nazi officials and penning realignments of psychoanalytic thought in an attempt to persuade the Nazis that psychoanalysis could be divorced from its Jewish origins and its socialist associations. Boehm and Müller-Braunschweig were left in no doubt by the Nazis that the proportion of Jewish analysts in the DPG made it very likely that their organisation would be banned, and that for the sake of the survival of the DPG, the Jewish analysts had to go. Steiner (2000, p. 70) comments on Jones' part in this,

> Once Eitingon had finally departed for Palestine...and Boehm had become President of the Berlin Psychoanalytic Institute, Jones had no hesitation in giving the new President his full support; and his support for Boehm steadily increased as the situation steadily worsened under the pressures of the Nazi regime... it has to be noted that in 1934–35 there still seemed to be some room for manoeuvre as far as the suspicions and the accusations of the Nazis were concerned. Jones' ambivalent attitude, therefore, towards the Jewish

members of the Berlin Psychoanalytic Institute for what he felt to be their excessive personal anxieties, and his growing impatience with those who voiced these anxieties on their behalf, was induced by the damage he feared this mood would cause to the German Psychoanalytic Society... One may perhaps surmise that Jones was worried that the anger, the anxieties and the criticisms of the Jewish members of the German Psychoanalytic Society and the Berlin Institute might have encouraged Boehm to side with the Nazis.

The ambiguities in Jones' behaviour and attitudes will be discussed again briefly below, but at this point it is important not to make use of too clear a hindsight. Jones, like almost everyone else, was uncertain about how serious the Nazis were in their threats, nor was he clear whether the danger to psychoanalysis was really to do with psycho-analysis itself, or whether it was specifically because of the domination of the organisation by Jewish analysts. He seems originally to have been opposed to the plan that the Jewish analysts should resign from the BPI, because that would reveal just how many there were and thus would play into the Nazi claim that psychoanalysis was 'Jewish' (Steiner, 2000, p. 78). On the other hand, writing to Anna Freud in October 1935, Jones expressed the view that, 'About the Jewish members I think that his [Boehm's] suggestion is the only possible one, for it would surely not be sensible to make the gesture (which would impress nobody) of dissolving the whole Society on the ground that the Government makes a foolish racial distinction' (ibid., p. 74). The fact that the psychoanalysts in Germany had been left alone for about two years seemed to confirm that there might be room for manoeuvre, and it may have been this as much as his anxiety over what Boehm would do that eventually persuaded Jones to go along with the idea of making the DPG *Judenrein*. It has to be noted, however, as Steiner (2000) points out, that Anna Freud and Eitingon in their correspon-dence with Jones at the time were rather more exercised by the dangers to their Jewish colleagues than was Jones himself.

Jones seems to have had genuinely mixed feelings and also to have been shocked when he visited Berlin to discover the actual state of terror in which the Jewish analysts were living. Nevertheless, in the interests of preserving the psychoanalytic society, he supported the plan to get the German Jewish analysts to resign their membership 'voluntarily', sending them telegrams in November and December 1935 urging them to do so, and chairing the meeting that finally pro-voked them to go. The DPG was thus 'Aryanised' by the end of 1935.

By 1936, Fenichel could comment that the 'Aryan' members of the DPG 'are avoiding any contact – both the slightest professional contact as well as personal contact – with their non-Aryan colleagues: an almost incredible example of the devil, who will grab your whole hand when you stretch out your little finger' (Eickhoff, 1995, p. 950). Their non-Jewish erstwhile colleagues thus embraced the exclusion of the Jews with some enthusiasm, whether through fear of being associated with the specifically derogated marginality of the Jews, or through active anti-Semitism. Ironically, there was a beneficial outcome of this in that most of the Jewish analysts, deprived of their livelihood, left Germany before the Holocaust, and so were saved (although fifteen did die in the concentration camps, as Jones confirmed at the first post-war International Congress – A. Freud, 1949; according to Hermanns, 2001 [quoted by Kreuzer-Haustein, 2002], twenty-three Jewish psychoanalysts were murdered in all). Jones played a heroic part in getting them out and in finding them places to go; however this was not the motivation at the time. Rather, the vain hope of appeasing the Nazis was the conscious purpose of this collusive strategy. One might wonder, in addition, whether behind this there was a darker strand, a point that will be returned to below.

Excluding politics and Ernest Jones

The pressure to resign 'voluntarily' under which the Jewish analysts were put can be seen as an only slightly more benign version of the famously brusque treatment meted out by the psychoanalytic movement to its errant scion, Wilhelm Reich. Reich had been seen as an analyst of considerable promise in Vienna in the 1920s, where he had conducted a highly regarded seminar on therapy, a seminar that bore fruit in his 1933 classic, *Character Analysis*. Moving to Berlin, he joined the communist party in 1930 and caused dissent within it because of his views on the gravity of the working classes' defeat with the advent of Hitler, as well as because of his promotion of sexual liberation (Sharaf, 1983). From that time on he became increasingly involved both in a theoretical project to link Freudianism with Marxism, and in practical politics surrounding sexual reform, and along with Fenichel was the acknowledged leader of the 'political Freudians' (Jacoby, 1983). Increasingly, however, Reich's ideas diverged from Freudian psychoanalysis, becoming more biological in focus and less interested in the fantasy dimensions of psychic life; this tendency became exaggerated as time went on, despite some very important later work, notably

The Mass Psychology of Fascism (Reich, 1948; Frosh, 1999). More relevantly, his political radicalism was also of concern within the psychoanalytic movement, with Freud himself being demonstrably critical – although some of the problems here concerned Reich's opposition to Freud's theory of the death drive. With the arrival of the Nazis in power, the threat posed by 'political' activity to the safety of psychoanalysis within Germany was seen by Freud as well as by Jones as potentially extremely damaging, with Reich (who in fact left Germany for Vienna in March 1933 and a month later embarked on some hectic to-ing and fro-ing around Scandinavia) as its most flagrant exponent. Anna Freud's letter to Jones of 27 April, 1933 shows the reasoning as well as the emotion:

> Here we are all prepared to take risks for psychoanalysis but not for Reich's ideas, with which nobody is in agreement. My father's opinion on this matter is: If psychoanalysis is to be prohibited, it should be prohibited for what it is, and not for the mixture of politics and psychoanalysis [Nitzschke's (1999, p. 355) translation is 'a hodgepodge of politics and analysis'] which Reich represents. My father can't wait to get rid of him inasmuch as he attaches himself to psychoanalysis; what my father finds offensive in Reich is the fact that he has forced psychoanalysis to become political; psychoanalysis has no part in politics.   (Steiner, 2000, p. 128)

Promotion of the idea that 'psychoanalysis has no part in politics' was a key element in the defence of psychoanalysis against the Nazi critique of its inherently destabilising nature, and was precisely the line taken by Boehm and Müller-Braunschweig in their negotiations with the Nazis. Boehm, for example, noted in 1934 that 'Reich had often come out publicly as a Communist and as a psychoanalyst, presenting his opinions as the results of psychoanalysis... I had to fight against this prejudice' (Brecht et al, 1985, p. 120). Boehm did this explicitly by arguing to the Nazis that there were two kinds of psychoanalysis, one being the genuine form that, as Müller-Braunschweig's article made clear, could be of service to the state, and the other being the distorted, politicised version brandished by Reich. That this paved the way easily for a distinction between 'pure' and 'Jewish' psychoanalysis was not a point made explicitly, but was clearly a move made available by this 'two types of analysis' rhetoric. Freud himself had taken the view that Reich and Fenichel had been using the *International Zeitschrift für Psychoanalyse*, of which Fenichel was editor, for 'Bolshevik propaganda', as a result of which Fenichel lost his position (Nitzschke, 1999, p. 353). As implied in Anna Freud's letter, Freud was actually quite brutal in his view of what should happen to Reich. Writing to Eitingon in 1933, he commented, 'Since Reich is now causing trouble in Vienna, he should be removed from the DPG. I want this done for scientific reasons but have no objection to this being done for political reasons as well and wish him success if he wants to play the martyr' (Nitzschke, 1999, p. 355). Preserving psychoanalysis through getting rid of troublemakers had always been one of Freud's strategies, and has never been alien to the psychoanalytic institutions' way of operating; here this approach was additionally fuelled by the hope that depoliticising psychoanalysis through excluding its wildest radical would convince the German authorities that it should be judged on its 'scientific' merits alone.

As it turned out and as Reich and a few others were prescient enough to see, this 'non-political' attitude effectively paved the way for a partial Nazification of psychoanalysis, while depriving psychoanalysis of its crucial critical role. It also resulted in the 'secret' expulsion of Reich from the DPG and the IPA. Boehm's account of this is instructive:

> At a Board meeting [in the summer of 1933] Simmel proposed that Reich should no longer be included in the list of members (Fenichel was away and was not at this meeting). Besides Simmel himself, his proposal was supported by Müller-Br[aunschweig] and myself; by Eitingon too, in principle, but he asked urgently that this 'purge' should be postponed until the next General Meeting at the beginning of October, when he would have resigned. The decision to inform Reich about this was not carried out, because we did not consider it opportune to have any contact with Reich, who was still abroad. Here I should like to add at once that at a later Board Meeting at the beginning of 1934 we asked Frau Jacobssohn to inform Reich of this decision during the meeting in Oslo, which however she failed to do.   (Brecht et al, 1985, p. 121)

In fact, Reich seems to have known nothing about it until he arrived at the Lucerne Congress of August, 1934, when Müller-Braunschweig informed him that he had been expelled from the DPG a year earlier; over the course of that Congress it became apparent to Reich that the leadership of the IPA endorsed this decision. Jones later claimed that Reich had resigned from the IPA at that Congress, but this, it seems, was never Reich's view (Sharaf, 1983, p. 188).

Jacoby (1983) has discussed some of the complex politics surrounding Reich at this time, pointing out that he did not have the unequivocal support even of the 'political' Freudians, notably Fenichel. However, the key point here is not so much how difficult Reich was even for those who might be seen as potentially aligned with him, but rather that from Freud down, the early period of Nazi rule in Germany was seen as requiring extreme caution about political involvement of any possibly subversive kind – and that the consequence of this was that the politics of the psychoanalytic movement itself came to be played out under the shadow of Nazi demands. In particular, splitting the presentation of psychoanalysis so that it appeared that its political, or at least socially critical, dimension could and should be divorced from its 'scientific' claims, was a strategy employed to make psychoanalysis seem safe and useful to the new German authorities. However, this strategy was not only parallel to, but formed a metaphoric unity with, the splitting of the movement between its 'Jewish' and 'Aryan' components, the former being what marked it out as potentially subversive and parasitic, the latter what made it serviceable. The seeds of psychoanalysis' later absorption in the dejudaicised 'New German Psychotherapy' were very strongly sown here: without its critical dimension, and without its Jewish elements (both people and ideas), it would indeed survive, but as subservient, a technology devoted to making citizens work.

Fear of rocking the boat when there was some hope that psychoanalysis might be saved, and with it the livelihoods of its practitioners, was, however, real and powerfully dictated the activities of many analysts in those desperate times. In addition to the shenanigans over Reich, the other famous instance of psychoanalysts' duplicity arising from this fear was that of the response to the arrest of Edith Jacobson, one of the better known members of the socialist psychoanalytic grouping. Jacobson had been visiting Scandinavia in 1933 but had returned to Berlin to continue her training analysis and specifically to work in the resistance movement there. The form this took was her membership of a group called 'New Beginning', which also contained a politically active patient of hers whom she protected and continued with in therapy even after it became clear that circumstances were becoming dangerous. Rickels (2002, p. 55) comments, 'Jacobson had openly identified with her patient's political associations and had seen no problem in being her patient's analyst and his co-member in the resistance organization New Beginning. She did welcome the group into her apartment for meetings; sometimes she lectured on psychoanalytic topics, which led to long discussions on the merits of Marxism over the politics of fascism.' Jacobson was arrested on October 24th 1935 whilst trying to destroy documents relating to the group and was held in custody for a year before coming to trial. The indictment against her focused on her involvement in the 'New Beginning' group:

> The accused...made her home available for meetings... The accused gave lectures which were supposedly concerned with psychoanalysis, but which according to her own statement ended in political discussions on Marxism and Fascism... It must be regarded as proven that she belonged to the *Miles-Gruppe* from Autumn 1933 to Winter 1934, paid contributions, made her home available and herself gave many talks at these meetings...   (Brecht et al, 1985, p. 128)

Eventually, Jacobson was sentenced to more than two years in prison; however, while on leave from prison in 1938 for an operation, she managed to escape to Prague and thence to New York, where she settled and became a distinguished analyst. Rickels (2002, p. 56) makes the following, characteristically flamboyant, interpretive link:

> She specialised in the treatment and understanding of borderline cases. There must have been some overlaps in her borderline explorations and the borders and boundaries that were in flux in Nazi Germany, where she chose to be trained as an analyst, even while she was opposed to the new state opposed to her survival. The boundary limits came crashing down, completely shut down, when she took political sides within an unexamined transferential relationship to her politically active patient. She was arrested and punished by the Nazi state and abandoned by the psychoanalytic state. Both sides viewed her as traitor.

Rickels' reference to treachery and being 'abandoned by the psychoanalytic state' is quite a precise reproduction of the psychoanalytic response to Jacobson's arrest. Ernest Jones had initially been ready to steam into action, organising a political campaign to gain Jacobson's release, but was gradually persuaded that this might be damaging for the chances of preserving the DPG. Anna Freud's view, as expressed to the Norwegian analyst Nic Hoel, was apparently that 'Edith had been very uncautious and had put the analytical movement in danger'; more precisely, 'Edith had been treacherous towards Boehm as she had not told him both that she had the patient and did let them [the resistance group] meet in her home' (Brecht et al, 1985, p. 129). Hoel herself, writing to Jones after meeting Anna Freud, commented that she thought Jacobson's behaviour 'showed naivety as well analytical as political, but not treason' (ibid.). Still, Anna Freud's initial response is very revealing, being couched in terms of treason versus loyalty, rather than primarily concern for the arrested individual. Additionally, it was still not clear what the risk to Jacobson herself might be; for example, Jones, revealing the ignorance of the nature of the Nazi regime characteristic of the early period of their rule, believed that once Jacobson was sentenced there was 'a considerable probability of the Gestapo educating her in a concentration camp, but a still greater probability that English influence would be able to get her out of it in a few days' (Jones, letter to Anna Freud of 2 December 1935, in Brecht et al, 1985, p. 130).

Boehm was even more frantic, and it was his intervention that really persuaded Jones to hold back from intervening on Jacobson's behalf. Boehm was frightened that the spin-off from the Jacobson case would be that the DPG would be damned as a political organisation and disbanded, and he was convinced that creating an international fuss would only make things worse. Jones seems to have picked up his anxiety very strongly, and to have sided with him not just on strategic grounds but also in response to the sense of turmoil originating with Boehm: 'the essential point ... proceeds psychologically from this case, which has so shattered Boehm's inner self-confidence that he can no longer rely on his judgement' (ibid.). Rely on Boehm's judgement, however, is exactly what Jones went on to do, aborting his planned campaign on Jacobson's behalf not because he did not care about her fate (his letters make it clear that he did), but because of Boehm's worry about the implications of involvement for the DPG. This remained a controversial act. Fenichel, for one, was appalled at the lack of action and eventually managed to get Anna Freud to agree with him; other analysts in Europe could also see that the policy of appeasement towards the Nazis was now getting out of hand. Thus, in mid-1936 another analyst based in Norway, Anne Buchholtz, wrote an appeal to all analysts around the world on Jacobson's behalf, which included the following perspicacious paragraph:

> The Berlin group, under the leadership of Boehm and Müller-Braunschweig, has fallen into line and identified itself with National Socialism, despite the fact that the founder of the psychoanalysis

they represent, and most of their productive collaborators, are Jews. Will the anxiety-ridden atmosphere of the Berlin group become the occasion for Edith Jacobssohn to lose her life and liberty, perhaps for years?   (Brecht et al, 1985, p. 127)

The answer to this was yes, despite an angry response from Jones who argued that 'any attempt at a publicity campaign in the Press would greatly worsen her chance of freedom' (ibid., p. 126), and Buchholtz's characterisation of the German analysts as 'der ängstlichen Berliner Gruppe' was certainly to the point.

It is worth noting a few more of the ambiguities in Ernest Jones' actions at this point. That he followed a policy of appeasement of the Nazis in the early period of the Third Reich is not in doubt, though in the context of the time this was less indefensible than it now seems, and the effort to avoid at all costs a repeat of the carnage of the First World War could be seen as a highly ethical principle. It is also true that Jones' skilfulness and energy in finding routes out for endangered Jewish analysts was exemplary. Goggin and Goggin's (2001, pp. 132–3) overall verdict seems about right:

While we point out some of Jones' idiosyncratic weaknesses under certain circumstances, there is not any question about his leadership skill and determination in saving Jewish analysts' lives. During the period from 1933 to 1938 he was president of the IPA, and in 1938 he was president of the British Psycho-Analytical Society...it is hard to conceive of anyone else in the movement who could have used the authority of his position to carry out his responsibilities more effectively and energetically than Jones... The end result of Jones' policies was quite clear. Among the Jews who were faced with the onslaught of the Nazi blitzkrieg, the relative percent of psychoanalysts who were exterminated during the Holocaust compared to other professions was quite low. Perhaps the most important reason was the exceptional job done by Jones in planning, organising, and implementing the emigration of Jewish analysts.

Reading through the documentation in Steiner's (2000) collection of letters between Jones and Anna Freud is an especially moving experience, particularly if one can project oneself back into the mind of people actually living through the times and only gradually beginning to understand their significance. Anna Freud herself comes over as a protector and campaigner on behalf of the endangered German and

Austrian analysts, with an immense amount of moral courage and integrity. Steiner (p. 19) picks this up in relation to an early letter of the Nazi era, in which Anna Freud drew Jones' attention to the serious financial difficulties facing Simmel and Landauer, two senior German analysts.

> In talking about them, Anna refers to them as '*Sorgenkinder*': 'children in need of care, and who are causing concern'. This expression crops up very frequently in her letters, at least until her departure from Vienna to London some five years after this correspondence began. Her use of this expression would appear to be of particular significance... because it gives the idea of an extended family comprised of infants and children, older brothers and sisters, and parents whose duty it is to provide for them. Indeed, Anna's choice of words becomes all the more significant when one recalls that those to whom she refers were none other than adult psychoanalysts who, in finding themselves in very precarious circumstances, were being forced to regress, so to speak, to a state of dependency on Anna, Jones, and the Americans.

Even though there were times when Anna Freud could not see the wood for the trees, so strongly did she identify with the need to put the survival of the psychoanalytic movement above all other imperatives, her strength of character and her sense of solidarity with, and appreciation of, the terrible situation of her Jewish friends and colleagues (something the gentile Jones seems to have been slower to realise) led her to be the most powerful of advocates for her many needy 'dependants'. Action, however, was much more the province of Jones, safe in England, with contacts at the Foreign Office and more importantly, through his presidency of the IPA, with analytic societies throughout the world. In this role, 'he understood it as his duty to assume overall responsibility to safeguard the general well-being of his colleagues... from the spring of 1933 onwards, there is not one of his letters that does not, in some way or other, reflect his commitment and his responsibility towards his colleagues' (Steiner, 2000, p. 28). What Jones had to juggle with was a very difficult combination of needy and endangered individuals, many of whom seem to have been blessed with exceptionally difficult personalities and an utter conviction of their correctness in all things psychoanalytic (the American Brill wrote to Jones in 1934, 'I often ask myself whether psychoanalysis really gives cognition enough to help in the controlling of emotions. My observation, particularly of the Berlin School, does not seem to show this. It would seem to me they are all on a pregenital level, oral-anal, sadistic' (ibid., pp. 67–8)), plus a fragmented and in many places fragile psychoanalytic movement which could not always cope with an influx of more analysts seeking work. Balancing the well-being of the psychoanalytic movement against the needs of its individual threatened members was a classic but nevertheless unsolvable organisational problem, and while Jones did not solve it, tending to give the former demand priority over the latter and at times dithering and being over-cautious, it is hard to see how he could have managed things better overall. From 1933 onwards he showed flexibility and imagination in placing analysts around the world, particularly in America and in Britain, seemingly considering the needs and attributes of each one of them in the context of what might be available in terms of work, and the orientation and state of stability or instability of any local psychoanalytic society which might accept them. Often there were disputes between the indigenous analysts and the newcomers, which Steiner (p. 44) suggests were produced as much by the immigrants' attitude of 'bei uns war es besser' ('we did it better at home') as by the rivalries and threatened livelihoods of the locals. In America in particular, which insisted on medical qualifications for psychoanalysts, there were additional problems with the European 'lay analysts', some of whom, such as Fenichel, were very senior and influential. In many places there were also immigration quotas, and Jones had to work exceptionally hard and efficiently to manage the bureaucracy these rules imposed. Despite all these difficulties, however, Jones was remarkably successful in finding places for fleeing analysts and thereby not only saving them but also enriching other national societies – notably that of Britain, where the immigrants had an immensely energising, if also conflictual, impact. Steiner (p. 126) summarises that Jones' placement of emigrants was 'a shrewd and very carefully considered plan of action, in that it not only found the emigrants a place of refuge, but it did so by evaluating each individual according to his professional competence, his personal idiosyncrasies, and, when necessary, according to political and ideological criteria that, if not discriminatory, were decidedly "selective".' Whatever the duplicity involved, on the whole this selectiveness seemed to work.

Whilst increasingly appreciating the dire situation of the Jewish analysts, Jones clearly played a double game in regard to the German psychoanalytic society. As described above, Jones played an important role in persuading the German Jewish analysts to resign from the DPG, in the hope that this might preserve the society against Nazi attack. Even before that, however, he had shown some impatience with the cries and complaints that were reaching his ears about the activities of the German psychoanalytic leaders, who were being accused of betrayal and of collaborating with the Nazis from the very start. This seems to have provoked something in Jones that cannot quite be reduced to his decision to make psychoanalytic unity and the preservation of psycho-analysis in Germany his priority. Supporting Boehm, he wrote to him in July 1934 to warn him of what might happen at the forthcoming psychoanalytic Congress in Lucerne, in which his activities in negotiating with the Nazis were bound to come under attack. Revealing both personal prejudices and the acceptable language of the time (which may also have indicated some of his own ambivalence towards the Jewish dominance of psychoanalysis), Jones included in his letter the following piece of gentile solidarity.

> You will know that I myself regard those emotions and ultra-Jewish attitude very unsympathetically, and it is plain to me that you and your colleagues are being made a dumping-ground for much emotion and resentment which belongs elsewhere and has displaced in your direction. My only concern is for the good of psycho-analysis itself, and I shall defend the view, which I confidently hold, that your actions have been actuated only by the same motive. (Brecht et al, 1985, p. 78)

Jones had previously expressed some similar sentiments (without the aside on ultra-Jewish attitudes) to Anna Freud. In a letter of 2nd October 1933, he commented that, 'After the interview [with the DPG leaders during a visit to Berlin] my impression of the Germany situation has slightly altered and I don't feel that the people concerned are quite so villainous as it has been suggested to me here.' Boehm in particular, whose 'initial action was very debatable' was seen as 'having saved Psycho-analysis in Germany from a horrific explosion that threatened early in August... which would have probably ended in the dissolution of the Society and Institute and the internment of most of its members in concentration camps' (Steiner, 2000, pp. 53–4). To the psycho-analyst van Ophuijsen, who consistently worked to alert Jones and others to the reality of the Nazi threat, Jones wrote in September 1933, 'Unless any reason appears to the contrary I think our wisest course is definitely to support Boehm and Müller-Braunschweig in the honest efforts they are undoubtedly making to salvage the situation' (ibid.,

p. 47). In the same letter he expressed the understanding that the German authorities had agreed not to interfere with the work of the psychoanalytic institutions – an understanding that was more-or-less correct for another couple of years.

In his presidential address at the Lucerne congress itself, Jones offered a not-so-subtle critical commentary on the politicising of psychoanalysis, presumably with Reich in his sights, although he also managed to suggest in the course of this that psychoanalysis must be opposed to the racist policies being perpetrated in the political world. Praising Freud for always keeping his 'humanitarian desires for the betterment of human life...strictly apart from his scientific work', he went on to argue that anyone who 'yields to such impulses' becomes so much the less a psychoanalyst, and 'perverts' its true nature (Glover, 1934, p. 487). However, the fault does not all lie with those who muddle up their humanitarian wishes with their psychoanalytic practice:

> Nor unfortunately can it be maintained that our Association is entirely free of the national and even racial prejudice which we so deplore in the world around us, and which have engendered there such dire consequences.... While respecting the social conditions and laws in the particular country in which it is our lot to live, I have urged that our common interests, as those of every body of scientific workers, are strictly international or rather super-national in character, and that the intrusion of local prejudice is in every way to be deprecated.... Emotional influences of just the kind we see acting so balefully in the world of politics seem to infect at times individual analysts or even whole societies.   (ibid.)

The code here is slightly obscure, but seems to be antagonistic to both the political Freudians and those willing to kowtow to Nazi demands for ethnic cleansing; both represent an unwarranted intrusion of political ideology into the scientific purity of psychoanalytic procedures. This might seem as much a critique of Boehm as of Reich, but Jones went on in his business report to single out Boehm for praise:

> No doubt different positions can legitimately be held concerning the wisdom of various steps taken by Dr Boehm, but the value of such opinions must depend on the holder being in possession of the relevant facts. I have known of strong opinions being voiced in ignorance of these facts, which is itself evidence of non-rational factors being at work. I will only add that Dr Boehm first personally

consulted Professor Freud in April, 1933, in anticipation of critical
junctures which did in fact subsequently arise, and that he then
took an early opportunity of giving me, as President, a faithful
report of all that had happened, in personal interviews I had with
him and other colleagues in Holland in the October of the same
year. I have reason to hope that the services Dr Boehm has rendered
to psycho-analysis will survive any temporary criticism he may have
to endure.   (ibid., p. 513)

Jones was a consummate politician and well capable of praising Boehm
simply for strategic reasons, based on a belief that unity was more
important than even well-founded criticism of the DPG leaders at this
time, when the future direction of Nazi policy towards psychoanalysis
was unclear. However, it also seems from his private correspondence
that he was genuinely impressed with the steps Boehm had taken, and
that he thought that if negotiations with the Nazis were not pursued
there could be dire consequences both for psychoanalysis as an institution, and for individual psychoanalysts – those who might indeed end
up 'in concentration camps', perhaps for more than just 'education'.

   On the other hand, public praise of the leaders of German psychoanalysis did not mean that Jones was blind to their possible motives
and actual affiliations and character traits. In the same letter to Anna
Freud in which he credited Boehm with having 'saved' psychoanalysis,
he also noted two somewhat different appeals of Nazism to the two
leading figures in the DPG.

   Müller-Braunschweig was pretty objective. He showed no signs of
   any anti-Semitism, but evidently felt rather German. I suppose his
   leanings towards idealism draw him a little to that somewhat
   neglected aspect of Hitlerism. Boehm, on the other hand, was more
   sceptical about the Government but did show some indications of
   anti-Semitism, possibly associated with the unfortunate discovery of
   his unhappy grandmother.   (Steiner, 2000, pp. 53–4)

This differentiation, between Müller-Braunschweig's tendency towards a
generally nationalist feeling infused with the heritage of German
Romanticism and Boehm's more active, possibly biographically-rooted,
anti-Semitism, was played out in many other spaces in German society,
including the wider psychotherapeutic and psychiatric professions
(Cocks, 1997), with the effect of encouraging collaboration with the
Third Reich. Interestingly, by 1935 Jones had reversed his assessment of

which of the two German analysts showed the more obvious antisemitic tendencies. Writing again to Anna Freud, he portrayed Boehm as a weak and inadequate leader: 'He has neither the personality required to manage a group nor a sufficiently quick grasp of the essentials of the strategic situation' (Brecht et al, 1985, p. 131). Müller-Braunschweig, on the other hand, was infected rather more with the times: 'Müller-Braunschweig is busy coquetting with the idea of combining a philosophy of Psycho-Analysis with a quasi-theological conception of National-Socialist ideology... No doubt he will proceed further along these lines, and he is definitely anti-Semitic, which Boehm is certainly not' (ibid.). Who was, and who was not, and for what reasons, is a complex question, but Jones' acuity in most areas is not to be doubted, and clearly at different moments in the 1930s he was persuaded of the anti-Semitism of each of the two main DPG leaders. In his 1946 report, Rickman confirms the Nazi taint in Müller-Braunschweig: 'I believe his personality has deteriorated during the Nazi regime... and I think he is "dark grey"' – Boehm was seen as possibly 'black', meaning completely corrupted (Brecht et al, 1985, pp. 237–8). Within four years of Rickman's report, however, Müller-Braunschweig was back in favour and Jones acted in his support, making his political judgement more important than any moral scruples he may have had.

In conclusion, the demise of the German psychoanalytic scene was not a simple matter of cowardice or self-serving, though both these elements operated and indeed came more to the fore as time went on, as the next chapter will show. Rather, in the early period of Nazi dominance in Germany, many analysts, including Freud at times, thought that it might be possible to protect psychoanalysis through offering a non-Jewish, conformist front, in which divisions would be made between the kind of psychoanalysis that the Nazis objected to – Jewish, socialist, sexual – and the kind that they might be willing to tolerate as a contribution to the State – gentile or 'Aryan' and adaptationist. Excluding political radicalism and protecting the psychoanalytic institutions also involved excluding Jews, so if anti-Semitism was not the motive it certainly was the effect, laying the movement open to more pernicious patterns of feeling and action later on. From the top down, the psychoanalytic movement enacted a dynamic in which self-preservation was balanced against moral integrity, and in which concern for the well-being of individuals sometimes came into prominence, but at other times was obscured. None of this is unique to the experience in Germany under Nazi rule, but there its consequences were particularly profound, and had effects for decades thereafter.

4
A Non-Jewish Psychoanalysis

C.G. Jung as a Nazi spokesman

Whilst the Deutsche Psychoanalytische Gesellschaft was stumbling towards self-destruction, a parallel development in the General Medical Society for Psychotherapy became the context for another lively piece of controversy, the role of C.G. Jung as a Nazi spokesman. The General Medical Society had been founded in 1926 supposedly to bring together the disparate psychotherapeutic schools to be found in Germany at that time. Its failure to do so is described by Cocks (1997, p. 30):

> Although it was the aim of the General Medical Society to unify the various schools of thought among psychotherapists, there were inevitable factions: Adlerians (including Adler), Jungians (including Jung), Stekelians (including Stekel), and Freudians such as Groddeck, Horney, Wilhelm Reich, and Sando Rado (though not including Freud). The great majority of psychoanalysts who were members of the General Medical Society were revisionists like the neo-Freudian Horney, the almost indefinable Groddeck, the free-love communist Reich, and the intensely intellectual rebel Schultz-Hencke. For its part, the German Psychoanalytic Society did not recognise the General Medical Society and increasingly the two organizations found themselves moving further apart rather than closer together.

Cocks points out that the General Medical Society 'comprised a more or less conservative, nationalist – and largely Protestant – membership at odds with the generally liberal, cosmopolitan – and largely Jewish –

membership of the German Psychoanalytic Society' (p. 31), and that this orientation made it more easily aligned with Nazi ideals as they began to permeate the whole of society. Indeed, according to Cocks psychotherapy benefited under the Nazis partly at least because its philosophical connections with German Romanticism made it susceptible to appropriation by the Nazis' nationalist and holistic 'ideals'. The tension between this 'totalising' approach, in which the achievement of harmony between the individual and society is one component, and the traditional psychoanalytic emphasis on conflict, including that between individuals and society, was a significant theme in the bowdlerising of psychoanalysis during the 1930s, and in the eventual 'triumph' of the movement to embed psychotherapy in the apparatus and culture of the Third Reich.

At the time of Hitler's accession to power, the General Medical Society was functioning as a forum for debate between differing schools of psychotherapy and was headed by Ernst Kretschmer, a distinguished psychiatrist. Kretschmer, however, was regarded as 'politically suspect' by the Nazis; he resigned as Chairman of the General Medical Society on April 6th 1933, 'primarily because he refused to help the Nazis subvert the discipline for propagandistic purposes' (Bair, 2004, p. 436), returning to resume leadership of the organisation after the war. In June, Jung, who was Vice President of the Society, accepted an invitation to become its President, naming as his deputy Gustav Richard Heyer, a Jungian who had already shown especial enthusiasm for the coming of the Nazis and who was the psychotherapist of Rudolph Hess (Cocks, 1997, pp. 84, 101). Jung's acceptance of this position came after a period of considerable uncertainty on his part, and was rather a surprise to many who had assumed that he was aligned with Kretschmer. Bair (2004) and others have shown that Jung was put under considerable pressure by the leaders of the German psychotherapists and probably did believe that only he could 'save' dynamic psychology (including psychoanalysis) from being destroyed in Germany. Kretschemer himself encouraged Jung to stay on within the General Society, arguing that 'Jung, as an independent Swiss, could withstand whatever pressures conformed Nazi officials might exert, thus ensuring a modicum of independence for the society. Jung shared this view and tried to convince "all those who have political misgivings because of the political conditions in Germany" that he stood "on strictly neutral ground"' (Bair, 2004, p. 439). It did not help Jung's reputation, however, that his chosen deputy Heyer had been a Nazi supporter since at least 1930; this choice was but one of a number of at best dubious actions by Jung that have led to continuing debate about his integrity during this period.

Jews were now excluded from the executive, as they were from the executive of any organisation, and as with the DPG there was a substantial exodus from the Society as a whole. By September 1933, following a period of uncertainty and tension about the direction in which it should go, the General Medical Society split in two. One part, which was renamed the German General Medical Society for Psychotherapy, became a clearly national organisation; it was headed by M.H. Göring. The other part, representing the more generic concerns of the old Society, became the *International* General Medical Society for Psychotherapy, led from Zurich by Jung. Each national Society was a member of the International Society; individuals could also be members of the International Society, an issue of some importance for Jung's claims that he maintained a place for Jews who were excluded from membership of the German group. Andrew Samuels (1993), in a thoughtful review of material on Jung and racism, provides some material on this:

> Jung claimed that he took this post [of President of the International General Medical Society for Psychotherapy] expressly to defend the rights of Jewish psychotherapists and he altered the constitution of the GSMP so that it became a fully and formally international body. The former General Society became the German national member group. Membership was by means of national societies with a special category of individual membership.... Jews were already barred from membership of the German national society and so, under Jung's new provision, were enabled to join the Society via membership of the individual section. Jung always maintained that his motives for taking on the presidency were to protect Jewish colleagues in this way and to keep depth psychology alive in Germany.   (p. 291)

Bair (2004, p. 459) provides evidence that Jung acted in support of Jews trying to gain refuge in Switzerland and abroad and that he treated many Jewish patients without charge once they managed to get into Switzerland, while Cocks (1997, p. 134) gives an example of Jung's claim that he acted in the interests of the Jewish members of the international society. 'When Max Guggenheim of Lausanne objected to Jung's role in working with the psychotherapists in Germany, Jung responded that, among other things, he had enabled Allers, a Jew, to stay on as editor of the review section of the *Zentralblatt*. Jung also inserted a circular letter in the December 1934 issue of the *Zentralblatt* which declared that the "international society is neutral as to politics and creed."' This letter did indeed separate membership of the international society from membership of any of the national groups within it, thus enabling Jews to continue in membership even once they were excluded from the German Society – something that happened in 1938. Nevertheless, as Samuels discusses very fully, Jung also used his post to promote his theory as a fully Aryan alternative to the Jewish psychology of Freud and his followers. Indeed, from the time he became President of the International General Medical Society for Psychotherapy until 1939, he seems to have been caught up, albeit ambivalently, in admiration of Nazi philosophy, mystical celebration of the cult of Wotan, anti-Semitic innuendo, and self-aggrandisement at the expense of Freudian psychoanalysis.

Jung clearly hoped that his own brand of depth psychology would become the leading psychology of the Third Reich, and to that end he was ready with pronouncements offering support for Hitlerism and casting Freudianism as 'Jewish psychology', which in the context of Nazi Germany could not have been thought of as a neutral description. There is considerable evidence of Jung's anti-Semitism and, at least during the 1930s, of his admiration for the Nazis as releasers of the German people's potential, evidence which has been thoroughly documented in various places (e.g. Hayman, 1999, Diller, 1991, Cocks, 1997) and sensitively discussed even within the Jungian movement (Samuels, 1993). Even prior to 1933, Jung had praised Mussolini and he was quick to see Hitler as the leader the Germans needed and the S.S. as 'a caste of knights ruling sixty million natives' (Hayman, 1999, p. 313). In a speech delivered in Vienna in November 1932, he had this to say about the aims of 'personality training':

> the great liberating deeds of world history have sprung from leading personalities and never from the inert mass, which is at all times secondary and can only be prodded into activity by the demagogue. The huzzahs of the Italian nation go forth to the personality of the Duce, and the dirges of other nations lament the absence of strong leaders.   (Jung, 1934a, pp. 167–8)

Grossman (1979, p. 232), drawing attention to this passage, continues, 'When publishing the text of this lecture in 1934, Jung added a footnote to the above, eliminating any doubt that Hitler was the kind of leader or personality he meant to indicate in his *Kulturbund* lecture of November 1932. "Since then," he wrote, "Germany too has found its leader".' Jung's admiration for Hitler's leadership qualities seems even more explicit in a radio broadcast in Berlin from 1933.

> Times of mass movement are always times of leadership. Every movement culminates organically in a leader, who embodies in his whole being the meaning and purpose of the popular movement. He is an incarnation of the nation's psyche and its mouthpiece. He is the spearhead of the phalanx of the whole people in motion. (Goggin and Goggin, 2001, pp. 72–3).

Admittedly, it is difficult to recover the exact tone of these comments at this historical distance; Bair (2004), for example, argues that Jung incorporated criticism of Hitler into them, even when apparently praising his strength. Referring to the radio broadcast of June 26th, 1933, she quotes Jung's comment, 'As Hitler said recently, the leader must be able to be alone and must have the courage to go his own way. But if he doesn't know himself, how is he to lead others?' and interprets it as an attack on Hitler (Jung 'trained his sights on Hitler', she writes) that was quickly covered over by the interviewer. This reading is clearly possible, but one can just as easily interpret Jung to be suggesting that, whatever the price to be paid in violence or demagogy, there is something attractive in the idea of the leader 'possessed', embodying and expressing the will of the people, 'the meaning and purpose of the popular movement'. This would also be consistent with other evidence that Jung's anti-democratic and anti-rationalist tendencies were such that he might see the leader who could be the 'incarnation of the nation's psyche' and could express its will as a more appealing and worthy leader than one who might simply appeal to reason, a line that had obvious political consequences: 'The state of disorder called democratic freedom or liberalism brings its own reactions – enforced order... the dictatorships may not be the best form of government, but they are the only possible form of government at the moment.' (Jung in Grossman, 1979, p. 245).

Even after the war, Jung still argued that looking back there was much to be admired in the leadership of Hitler and Mussolini, centring on the energy and cleansing spirit they brought to politics.

> Our judgement would certainly be very different had our information stopped short at 1933 or 1934. At that time, in Germany as well

as in Italy, there were not a few things that appeared plausible and seemed to speak in favour of the regime... And after the stagnation and decay of the post-war years, the refreshing wind that blew through the two countries was a tempting sign of hope.   (Jung, 1946, p. 205)

In fact, even though Jung later repudiated his Nazi associations, he never admitted any kind of culpability for his actions or views during the 1930s, and claimed to be at least bemused by the reputation he had acquired: 'I must confess my total inability to understand why it should be a crime to speak of a "Jewish" psychology' (Diller, 1991, p. 191). Grossman (1979) points out that Jung made no reply to criticisms of his attitude towards Hitler until after the Second World War and never published anything encouraging resistance to the Nazis. There is some evidence of a gradual change in attitude on Jung's part towards the late 1930s. For example, he claimed to have been 'blacklisted' by the Nazis for comments made in 1937 condemning 'the amazing spectacle of states taking over the age-old totalitarian claims of theocracy, which are inevitably accompanied by suppression of free opinion', although Grossman notes that this claim was never substantiated (p. 254). He seems gradually to have shifted his views on the healthiness of the Führer-dominance of the Germans: 'The impressive thing about the German phenomenon is that one man, who is obviously "possessed", has infected a whole nation to such an extent that everything is set in motion and has started rolling on course to perdition' (Jung, 1936, p. 185). Bair (2004) also shows that from 1943 onwards Jung was marginally involved in German plots against Hitler and provided a useful commentary on Nazi psychology to the Americans. However, even in 1945 Jung was unwary enough of the changing political scene to write pretty openly anti-Semitic comments in his personal correspondence. Samuels (1993, p. 304) quotes the following as an example: 'It is however difficult to mention the antichristianism of the Jews after the horrible things that have happened in Germany. But Jews are not so damned innocent after all – the role played by the intellectual Jews in prewar Germany would be an interesting object of investigation.' Samuels (p. 305) also reveals that 'In 1944, a secret appendix was added to the by-laws of the Analytical Psychology Club of Zurich, limiting the proportion of Jews who could be members at any one time. The quota for full members was 10 per cent and for guest members 25 per cent... the quota for Jews was not removed until 1950.'

Thus, even though Jung later claimed that his earlier apparent celebration of Nazism had in fact been a warning about its power, the evidence suggests that this was a post-hoc rationalisation rather than a
justifiable clarification of misunderstood prophecy; at the time he said
little that was critical, reserving this for the period after Nazism was
clearly on the wane. As Samuels notes, criticism of Jung's attitudes does
not depend on historical hindsight. He gives the example of Walter
Benjamin who in 1937 was studying Jungian thought as an aspect of
the politics of 'Aryan' race theory and, according to a letter to Gershom
Scholem, finding it 'the devil's work' (Samuels, 1993, p. 295). Thomas
Mann in 1934 noted that 'Jung's thought and his statements tend to
glorify Nazism and its "neurosis"... He swims with the tide' and by
1942 was commenting that Jung 'was always a half-Nazi' (Hayman,
1999, p. 319). Immediately after the war, too, in energetic evidence to
the Nuremberg tribunal, Maurice Léon (1946) called Jung a 'Pseudo-
scientist Nazi auxiliary', though there is some evidence that Léon held
a lasting personal grudge against Jung for the effects of his analysis of
his wife in the 1930s (Bair, 2004). In 1936, when Jung was invited to
the tercentenary celebrations of Harvard, there was considerable opposition to him because of his suspected Nazi sympathies; he did attend,
but Bair (2004, p. 421) notes that he made a bad impression partly
'because of his remarks about differences in the racial psychology of
Germans and Jews and his earlier unfavourable articles about American
women and American Negroes.'

It is not too hard, in the light of material such as this, to see Jung
as an out-and-out villain, as defenders of psychoanalysis have
been delighted to do. However, away from the axe-grinding disputes
about exactly how anti-Semitic Jung might have been, there are
two sets of issues of considerable importance for any enquiry into
the way in which 'depth psychology' in general functioned when
faced with the immense destructive energy of the Nazi phenomenon. The first of these relates to the engagement of psychotherapy
with the politics of the time; this has been extensively described by
Cocks (1997) and so will be relatively briefly summarised below for
the lessons it teaches about the possible critical role of a psychoanalysis not in thrall to political expedience. The second theme
concerns the intellectual basis for Jungianism's seduction by, or
adherence to, Nazi philosophy. The issues here can be sub-divided
into two related themes: the idea of psychoanalysis as a 'Jewish' psychology to be opposed by a properly 'Aryan' science, and the idea
that the individual, through mobilisation of the 'creative' energy of

the unconscious, might come to be of service to the newly dynamic State.

Politicking with the Nazis

Cocks (1997, pp. 147–8) offers the following summary account of what brought Jung into the public eye in relation to German psychotherapy under the Nazis.

> Jung... did not involve himself unilaterally in the domestic affairs of Nazi Germany. He was in fact sought out by psychotherapists there who felt his association and endorsement would add lustre to their bid for professional autonomy from then dominant nosological psychiatry and dissociate them from Freud in the eyes of the regime. The German Jungians in particular... were of course eager to promote Jung for generally defensive as well as partisan purposes. So though Jung could hardly have been averse to the advancement of his school of thought at the expense of that of Freud, he was involved in a project that he could rightly claim served the survival of psychotherapy in general.

The anxiety felt by the psychotherapy profession in Germany in 1933 was understandably great, and was fuelled by the general popular and political association of them with the 'Jewish' discipline of Freudian psychoanalysis. If the whole profession was tainted with this Jewish stain, it could destroy them all. On the other hand, there were real opportunities: many psychotherapists resented the supposed link with, and domination of, the Freudians and were themselves immersed in a nationalistic strand of the German romantic tradition. For them, the Nazis' declared aim of liberating the creativity of the masses in order to achieve a new flowering of German culture was not necessarily anathema, and the idea that psychotherapy might contribute to this great scheme, for instance by helping people overcome neurotic conflicts, was appealing. This was especially the case in relation to the ongoing jostling with psychiatry for professional superiority; if the psychotherapists could offer something more than just classification and eugenics, they might really find an approved and funded place in the State.

Jung himself seems to have had several, sometimes competing, reasons for accepting the 'call' to make his presence felt in Nazified psychotherapy. As will be discussed more fully below, Nazi philosophy was seductive because it resonated with some ideas that could generically be called 'Jungian' (for instance, the racial stratum of the collective unconscious) and some that were distinctively Jung's (excitement over 'primitive' mystical expressions of irrationality such as those to be found in the Wotan cult). Features of the Nazi scene such as its 'Führer-fixation', its mobilisation of mass energy, its use of myth, its engrossment in spectacle and its rhetoric of striving and national fulfilment were all congruent with Jungian perspectives and made Germany an ideal testing-ground for Jungian theory and practice. Specific antagonism to Freud and Freudianism, mixed in with some pretty blunt anti-Semitism, was another appealing strand in this: this was a spectacularly unmissable opportunity to triumph over Freud. In addition, Jung seems genuinely to have believed that he could indeed act as a saviour for the threatened profession of psychotherapy in Germany, uniting it under his own non-Freudian banner and thus making Jungian psychology the dominant 'depth psychological' force in the Third Reich.

Internationalising German psychotherapy under Jungian leadership could also be a way of protecting it, as well as (to take Jung at his word) offering an umbrella under which threatened individuals might shelter. For the psychotherapists, calling on Jung to take on the mantle of leader of the General Society for Medical Psychotherapy in tandem with Göring (who Jung regarded, in 1933, as 'a very amiable and reasonable man' – Cocks, 1997, p. 133), allowed them to draw on his international prestige and his non-Freudian and non-Jewish credentials in their negotiations with the new German rulers. That Jung allowed himself to be sucked in so far as to deliver approval for Hitlerian leadership, attacks on 'Jewish' psychology, and paeans to the potential Aryan unconscious was an added bonus for the campaign to make psychotherapy an integral part of the state (and state-supported) apparatus. Jung himself claimed that when Kretschmer stood down he would not have agreed to take his place were it not that there had to be a non-German at the helm to give the movement international standing; but in reality, the dual attraction of being wooed by the German psychotherapists and believing that circumstances had arisen under which Jungianism might triumph over psychoanalysis, was too strong for him to refuse. Rationalisation is a powerful defence for psychotherapists as for everyone else; here one might ask whether the argument that psychotherapy had to be 'saved' in Nazi Germany was a convenient rationalisation for people whose desires for conquest and domination were not out of line with the national agenda, however uncomfortable it might have been at the time (and subsequently) to recognise that fact. That is, the psychotherapists appealed to Jung and Jung answered their appeal out of anxiety, for sure, but also out of an ambition to make use of the Nazi phenomenon for their own ends.

As it happened, Jung's influence on the course of psychotherapy in the Third Reich was limited, and much less substantial than that of his co-leader of the General Society for Medical Psychotherapy, M.H. Göring, even though his intellectual impact was significant. Goggin and Goggin (2001, p. 75) state that 'The Göring Institute did not need to develop a separate theory of psychotherapy for Germany. Jung's own theory provided an almost perfect match for National Socialism', but in fact, by the time the Göring Institute came into being, Jung and Jungianism were becoming relatively unimportant. Jung was not directly involved in the Göring Institute, which, as will be seen later, was the dominant force in the integration of the psychotherapies (including psychoanalysis) into the service of the Third Reich, nor was he involved in the German General Society for Medical Psychotherapy. After 1936, his role faded to one of trying to preserve some integrity for the International Society; he eventually failed in this, with the Germans taking over the International Society and Göring becoming sole editor of its journal, the *Zentralblatt für Psychotherapie*. By 1939, Jung was no longer of significance for the Nazis, and he was increasingly distant from them and intent on extricating himself from his position in their psychotherapy movement. As psychotherapy fell in line behind Göring, and with the coming of war, the priorities became those of serving the state in practical terms, rather than through the mystifying pseudo-theology of Jungian thought. Göring proved himself to be sufficiently competent in doing this for the Institute he led to have a very significant position in the Third Reich; what this meant for psychoanalysis is an issue pursued below. What it meant for the Jungians, however, was that while they could continue to claim to be loyal citizens, they were not to be leaders – and Jung himself became something of an irrelevance. 'Aryan' psychology of the Jungian variety turned out to be less in demand than a psychotherapy that might work.

The history of Jung's involvement with the German psychotherapists is an instructive one from the point of view of the sociology of conformism as well as an interesting one in relation to the specific history of psychotherapy in Germany. From the point of view of *psychoanalysis*, however, some of the elements in Jung's pronouncements on 'Jewish' psychology are more important, in that they not only say a good deal about the climate of the times and about Jung's personal attitudes, but also articulate through contrasts what might be of importance in the 'Jewish heritage' of psychoanalysis, and what was experienced at the time as most threatening and subversive. Jung, that is, articulated in his anti-Freudian and anti-Semitic rhetoric some of the most rabid prejudices about psychoanalysis and the Jews, but one effect of this was to make the potential anti-Nazi credentials of psychoanalysis that much clearer.

Jewish and Aryan psychology

Under Jung's editorial guidance, the *Zentralblatt für Psychotherapie* published many articles which promoted anti-Semitism more strongly than might even have been required for the sake of survival, and many of Jung's own pronouncements on the topic have become infamous (though Bair, 2004, claims that some of them have been systematically and misleadingly mistranslated). Thus, in 1934, he wrote in an introductory article to the *Zentralblatt*, 'The differences which actually do exist between Germanic and Jewish psychology, and have long been known to every intelligent person, are no longer to be glossed over' (Jung, 1933, p. 533). Also in 1934, he wrote to a colleague, 'The Aryan people can make the point that with Freud and Adler specifically Jewish viewpoints are preached publicly, and as can be proved similarly, viewpoints that are essentially corrosive in character' (Hayman, 1999, pp. 319–320). His most famous pronouncement, again from the *Zentralblatt* of 1934, runs at length as follows.

> The Jew, who is something of a cultural nomad, has never yet created a cultural form of his own and as far as we can see never will, since all his instincts and talents require a more or less civilised nation to act as host for their development.
>
> The Jewish race as a whole – at least this is my experience – possesses an unconscious which can be compared with the 'Aryan' only with reserve. Creative individuals apart, the average Jew is far too conscious and differentiated to go about pregnant with the tensions of unborn futures. The 'Aryan' unconscious has a higher potential than the Jewish; that is both the advantage and the disadvantage of a youthfulness not yet fully weaned from barbarism. In my opinion it has been a grave error in medical psychology up to now to apply Jewish categories – which are not even binding on all Jews – indiscriminately to German and Slavic Christendom. Because of this the most precious secret of the Germanic peoples – their creative and intuitive depth of soul – has been explained as a mass of

banal infantilism, while my own warning voice has for decades been suspected of anti-Semitism. This suspicion emanated from Freud. He did not understand the Germanic psyche any more than did his Germanic followers. Has the formidable phenomenon of National Socialism, on which the whole world gazes with astonished eyes, taught them better?   (Jung, 1934b, pp. 165–6)

This last quoted passage expresses many aspects of Jung's position in the 1930s both in its apparent celebration of the impact of Nazism and its active denigration of Jews, drawing on both traditional and Nazi anti-Semitic stereotypes, such as that of 'parasitism' ('all [the Jew's] instincts and talents require a more or less civilised nation to act as host for their development'), and incorporating Freud into this anti-Semitic rhetoric. By way both of contrast and context, it is worth taking the promotion of 'Aryan' psychology first. As has already been described, Jung was initially enamoured of the Nazi leadership style, a position he never fully renounced even after he had started to see both Hitler and the German response to him as 'psychotic'. What particularly appealed to him was the idea that the potential of the German people, which up to this point had been both profound and inchoate ('The "Aryan" unconscious has a higher potential than the Jewish; that is both the advantage and the disadvantage of a youthfulness not yet fully weaned from barbarism') might be released by the charismatic power of Hitler, thus allowing its potential truly to flower and express the Germans' 'creative and intuitive depth of soul'. As has been pointed out by many authors, the vision of a therapeutic approach which could free the person from neurotic illness and allow her or his basic creative energy to flourish was an element in Jungian thought linking it with the tradition of German Romanticism and setting it up as a potential servant of the state – and it was very different from Freud's ironic view of the aims of analysis, 'converting hysterical misery into common human unhappiness' (Breuer and Freud, 1895, p. 393). The romanticism in Jungianism was expressed not just in this idea of a pure Aryan unconscious waiting to be released, but more generally in the pursuit of wholeness, of integrity both of the individual personality and of the individual in her or his relationship to the collective. That is, the Jungian perspective shared with the broader German Romantic tradition the idea of an elemental state of Germanic being, present in every single (Aryan) German, seeking its fulfilment and perhaps requiring – or certainly benefiting from – a saviour to bring this state of being into existence. Such a process would be almost bound to involve violence, as the old order of timidity and repression is cast off and a new era – a new Reich – dawns. Thus, as Grossman (1979, p. 234) shows in the following series of quotations, Jung like many Germans saw Hitler as a messianic figure who would lead the Germans into a new land – as, indeed, he temporarily did.

> Many of the references Jung made to Hitler prior to World War II tended to support the latter's claim to messianic leadership. 'If he is not their true Messiah, he is like one of the Old Testament prophets; his mission is to unite his people and lead them to the Promised Land.' In a 1937 interview Jung said of Hitler, 'He is the mouthpiece of the Gods of old... Hitler is the Sybil, the Delphic oracle.'... The Führer had that prime requisite of personality, the ability to listen to his inner voice. 'He himself has referred to his voice. His voice is nothing other than his own unconscious, into which the German people have projected themselves...' Evidently Hitler was a man with a vocation, a man able to tap the resources of the collective unconscious. 'He is the loudspeaker which magnifies the inaudible whispers of the German soul until they can be heard by the German's unconscious ear.' On this basis, 'Hitler', in Jung's opinion, 'had perceived the true balance of political forces at home and in the world; he has so far been infallible. The source of his success lay in the fact that he had exceptional access to his unconscious and that he permitted himself to be moved by it; he listened to his inner voice. The true leader is always led.'

The unconscious is not the Freudian arena of conflict and necessary renunciation, but a driving engine, the irrationality of which, under the right circumstances, can be given direction to fuel great things. For Jung, well in step with much German emotion of the time, Hitler was creating these circumstances; he was the leader arising out of the German unconscious and giving it expression ('The true leader is always led'), infallible so long as he continued to 'tap the resources of the collective unconscious'. This praise of the Führer, couched so nearly in Nazi terms, of course did Jung no harm in the Germany of the time, and his emphasis on the rootedness of Nazism in the German personality, with its holistic assumption of the link between individual and collective, was exactly what was required to endear Jung, the Jungians and their psychotherapeutic fellow-travellers to an astute but ideological new set of political masters.

This same celebration of the irrational, mystical and mythical, the spiritual and the powerful, fuelled Jung's rather exhilarated evocation of the Nordic god Wotan as an Aryan alternative to the alien perspective imposed on the Germans by Christianity and hence, initially, by Judaism. For Jung, the arrival of Nazism was evidence that Wotan had been resurrected, its energy now released and available to the newly awakened Germanic masses. Hitler and Wotan together would set the Germans free. As asserted by the German Faith Movement, the religion for the new Germany was not Christianity, towards which the Nazis were hostile, but this pagan force which was seen as deeply embedded in the Aryan psyche and hence, once realised, as a channel for the German masses' awakening energy. The Nazis were thus credited with releasing something primeval and holy; they were not a mere political party, but a movement with a 'religious' core offering salvation to its people. The irrational is holy under these conditions, because it is the spiritual home of a fundamental mode of true being. In his article on Wotan from 1936, Jung saw the Nazi phenomenon as enlivening of the nation as a whole: 'The Hitler movement literally brought the whole of Germany to its feet, from five-year-olds to veterans, and produced a spectacle of a nation migrating from one place to another. Wotan the wanderer was on the move' (p. 180). The parallels were very direct, as, fascinated by the spectacle of a whole nation overcome with irrationality and seeking to live out a myth, Jung turned to an eschatological reading of history that also happened to be politically highly expedient: 'The maenads were a species of female storm-troopers, and, according to mythical reports, were dangerous enough. Wotan confined himself to the berserkers, who found their vocation as the Blackshirts of mythical kings' (p. 185).

Jung's emphasis on the spirituality of the Nazi phenomenon, or at least its access to spiritual dimensions of the Germanic psyche, was a reflection of his life-long deviation from Freudianism, with its focus on the material, specifically the sexual, as the key causal force underpinning human activity. This was not news: Jung broke with Freud ostensibly over the concept of libido – arguing that it was generally 'energic' rather than specifically sexual – and the priority he gave to myth and symbol as expressions of human striving was always radically dissimilar from the reductive tendency in psychoanalysis. Under the Nazis, however, this aspect of Jungianism became thoroughly imbued with, and expressive of, anti-Semitic stereotypes that fitted the period very well, and give the lie to his claim that all he was doing in differentiating 'Aryan' from 'Jewish' psychology was providing a neutral description of two differing world-views. 'Materialism' was always a code-word for 'sexual', but where it gained potency was that it could trade on images of the materialist Jew whose aim was to corrupt the spirituality of the gentile, as well as drawing in some of the antagonism towards communism and capitalism that Nazi political philosophy embodied, and Jung explicitly shared (Grossman, 1979). This was linked with the Jungian and Nazi emphasis on the rootedness of the Aryan psyche in the earth – its spirituality, that is, grows out of its commitment to, and integration with, the land, and this is what makes the individual and the nation so powerfully at one. The Jew, by contrast, lacking the 'chthonic' relationship to the earth, can have no genuine creativity or national culture; rather, as in the quotation given earlier, the Jew is a 'cultural nomad', trading and stealing, and in the process bringing about the destruction of spiritual values.

The idea of the Jew as either or both a money-grabbing swindler and 'rootless cosmopolitan' has long been a staple of anti-Semitic prejudice, as has a fascination with the supposedly perverse sexuality of the Jew (both male as castrated and female as seductive). Jung managed to combine all these stereotypes in his evocation of the differences between 'Aryan' and 'Jewish' psychology, and in his attacks on psychoanalysis. His ideas on this were not new in the 1930s, but had a long history that might have been dormant during the years of association with Freud, but certainly sprang to consciousness thereafter. The following piece dates from 1918; as Bair (2004, p. 436) explains, it was taken up and enthusiastically if selectively quoted by German psychotherapists in the 1930s 'to justify their tactics of discredit and exclusion of the "Jewish" science propounded by Freud and Adler.'

As a rule, the Jew lives in amicable relationship with the earth, but without feeling the power of the chthonic. His receptivity to this seems to have weakened with time. This may explain the specific need of the Jew to reduce everything to its material beginnings; he needs these beginnings in order to counterbalance the dangerous ascendancy of his two cultures. A little bit of primitivity does not hurt him; on the contrary, I can understand very well that Freud's and Adler's reduction of everything psychic to primitive sexual wishes and power-drives has something about it that is beneficial and satisfying to the Jew, because it is a form of simplification. For this reason, Freud is perhaps right to close his eyes to my objections. But these specifically Jewish doctrines are thoroughly unsatisfying to the Germanic mentality; we still have a genuine barbarian in us who is not to be trifled with, and whose manifestation is no comfort for us and is not a pleasant way of passing time.   (Jung, 1918, pp. 13–14)

The mixture here of linking psychoanalysis' supposed reductionism (everything is reduced to sex) with the rootlessness (lack of the 'chthonic') of the Jew, so that it actually serves the Jew's needs, is consistent with Jung's later statements, as is the implicit celebration of the 'barbarian' aspect of the Germanic people, with whom Jung identifies: '*we* still have a genuine barbarian in *us* who is not to be trifled with'. What is being conveyed here is the familiar anti-Semitic thesis that, free from national identification, the Jew's intelligence is employed to 'simplify' – or, in other versions, to corrupt – the Germanic striving for fulfilment. This striving, with its threat of violence ('the 'barbarian...not to be trifled with'), is 'no comfort', but it is real and true, deriving from the fundamental association with the earth. By the period of the Nazis, it had become clearer that in Jung's thought the psychoanalyst, like the Jew, is someone who revels in the corrosion of Germanic values by the peddling of sex. 'The psychoanalyst's every second word is "nothing but" – just what a dealer would say of an article he wanted to buy on the cheap' (Jung, 1934b, p. 170). The Jew as trader, tricking the relatively slow but true gentile out of something of value, is again a familiar stereotype; here it is used to suggest that psychoanalysis is such a Jewish trading system, cheapening the Aryan unconscious, staining the Germanic soul. This sexual reductionism, asserts Jung, 'will never prove that the symbol or symptom so explained really has that meaning; it merely demonstrates the adolescent smutty-mindedness of the explainer' (ibid.). Thus Freud is confined to the sexual self-abuse of Jewish adolescence.

As well as being sexually subversive, the Jew was also represented in nineteenth century anti-Semitic propaganda as feminised, with circumcision/castration being the fascinating sign of this. Jung again draws on this pre-existent and convenient social discourse (perhaps he would have thought of it as an 'archetype'), to convey the Jewish taint in Freudianism.

Freud and Adler have beheld very clearly the shadow that accompanies us all. The Jews have this peculiarity in common with women: being physically weaker, they have to aim at the chinks in the armour of their adversary, and thanks to this technique which has been forced on them through the centuries, the Jews themselves are best protected where others are most vulnerable.   (Jung, 1934b, p. 165)

Unlike the physically strong Aryan, who draws strength from the relationship with the land, the Jew has developed an intellectualism arising out of the portability of Jewish culture; this intellectualism is reflected in Freud's inability to let himself enjoy, or suffer, the demands of spirituality and romantic identification with the nation and its struggle. In making this claim, Jung is not totally at odds with Freud's own view: as described in Chapter 2, Freud was also convinced that a saving grace for Judaism and the Jewish people was its relinquishment of the concrete and its turn to ideas. However, whereas Freud saw this intellectualism as a cultural advance making Judaism superior to other religions and promoting the longevity of the Jews, Jung saw it as a ducking-out from the demands of manly existence, a way of achieving superiority as women do, that is, by seductiveness and deceit. The image is one of conflict, in which the pure knight is deceived by the wanton seductress; writ large, in the language of Nazi politics, this is also the image of the German state being poisoned by hidden and secret Jewish influence, which must, for the sake of survival, be wiped out. The Jungian triumph over psychoanalysis can therefore be seen as an aspect of the Aryan triumph over the Jews.

As has been noted already, Jung gradually distanced himself from the Nazis and by 1939 was more or less an irrelevance to them. He also defended some individual Jews and did create some organisational structures that might have had the effect of allowing Jewish psychotherapists to retain international links. He never, however, accepted any form of culpability for trading on anti-Semitic stereotypes or for offering support for the Nazi phenomenon; he barely even accepted that he might have been 'mistaken'. After the war, he was inclined to re-write his own pre-war position as one in which he had warned of the potential effects of Nazi power, and also to reinterpret Nazism not as a true expression of the Germanic unconscious, which is how he had seen it previously, but as a distortion produced, like so much else, by the depredations of contemporary industrial society, warping the mind and separating the people from their necessary origin in the soil. This deflection of responsibility did not speak well for Jung's integrity: not only is the historical record against him, with his celebration of Nazi philosophy, his enjoyment of the spectacle of German energy and force rising to power ('To protest is ridiculous – how protest an avalanche? It is better to look out' – Jung, 1934c, p. 538), his political manoeuvring and his tainting of Freudianism with anti-Semitic invective; but his continued focus on 'racial' elements of collective life, and his thrusting towards 'spirituality' based in a romantic notion of wholeness, plus his uncompromising continued denigration of psychoanalysis, speak to a failure to learn from history or from personal experience. Jung gave succour to the Nazis; they did not need it much, but it remains a nasty tale.

In the wider scheme of things, the Jungian adventure reflects something more pervasive about tendencies within German psychotherapy in the 1930s, tendencies that did not leave the psychoanalysts untouched. While Jung's anti-Semitism was undoubtedly fuelled by his antagonism to Freud and his general opportunism; and as Samuels (1993) has shown, while Jungianism's theoretical base always laid it open to racist concepts; it is indicative of a more widespread phenomenon that can also be seen in the writings of Müller-Braunschweig and others. This reflects an admiration for the leadership of Hitler and for the idea of the German nation finding its 'destiny' through Nazism. For Jung and some at least of the 'Aryan' psychoanalysts who sought appeasement of the Nazis, the question was not, or not just, one of sustaining depth psychology in the face of the nightmare, but of finding a place for psychotherapy in a system in which what was promoted was nationalism and authority. Freud theorised an opposition between the individual's desires and society's needs; with the Nazis, individuals disappeared in the mass, their only value being what they could contribute to national revival. Some participants, Jungian and psychoanalytic alike, got very excited about this and sided with the 'Aryan' mass, an act which automatically led them to discard or even (psychologically speaking) assault their Jewish associates. Jung is an easy target, because his anti-Semitism is so transparent, but there was plenty of it around.

Rescued by Göring

While Jung was leader of the International General Medical Society for Psychotherapy, the German Medical Society for Psychotherapy was headed by Matthias Heinrich Göring, who was a psychiatrist and had undergone Adlerian analysis. M.H. Göring was a member of the Nazi Party from 1 May 1933 onwards; Brecht et al (1985, p. 152) comment that, 'Göring's identification with National Socialism remained clear until... April 1945,' and Goggin and Goggin (2001, p. 117) opine, 'In general we believe that M.H. Göring was an enthusiastic Nazi but he showed variation in his ideological concerns.' According to Cocks (1997, p. 36), 'By all accounts, Matthias Heinrich Göring was a shy, gentle man with a stammer', and his association with the Nazis grew out of his old-style patriotism, loyalty to his family, and general belief in the worth of 'the common man', which might be realised under the Nazis' reforming zeal. Göring himself, writing in response to the invitation to take on the leadership of the German psychotherapists, phrased his views as follows (ibid., p. 103).

> In the interests of our society I wish to accept your offer, because I am a National Socialist not in name only but wholeheartedly in the spirit of Adolf Hitler, because moreover I bear the name of the Prussian Minister-President and am related to him. Also in the interests of National Socialism I must not refuse, for I believe that we psychotherapists have a great mission in the new state.... we are called to educate children and adults in the right spirit.

In the same 1933 edition of the *Zentralblatt für Psychotherapie* in which Jung made his distinction between Aryan and Jewish psychology, Göring announced the clear orientation of the new German Medical Society for Psychotherapy:

> The society has the task of uniting all German doctors of medicine in the spirit of the German National Socialist Government, who have adopted the idea that in medical treatment the doctor has to consider the whole person of the patient, that he must not disregard the soul; especially such doctors who are willing to teach and practise psychotherapy on the basis of the National Socialist Weltanschauung. The Society expects all its active members, especially those teaching and publishing, to have thoroughly read Adolf Hitler's fundamental book *Mein Kampf* and acknowledge it as basic. The Society wishes to participate in the undertaking of the Volkskanzler [people's chancellor] to train the German people to adopt a heroic and sacrificing conviction. (Göring, 1933, p. 140; in Thomä, 1969, p. 684).

The terms of this statement of goals – unity, holism, attending to the 'soul', adopting the Nazi 'Weltanschauung', studying *Mein Kampf*, training 'the German people to adopt a heroic and sacrificing conviction' – leave no room for manoeuvre; in the new leader's eyes at least, this professional body for psychotherapy was to be an agency of the Nazi state.

From the very start, therefore, the psychotherapists in the Third Reich pinned their colours to a masthead already painted in the Nazi red and black. Whatever else might have happened later, it is clear that the act of inviting Göring in, just as with the encouragement given to Jung, was not forced on the psychotherapists by the new rulers of the land, but was their pre-emptive attempt to secure their survival and curry favour. It should also be noted, once again, that amongst the psychotherapists there were plenty who shared at least some of the aims of the Nazis, or rather their perception of those aims. Some of this was a simple matter of professional advancement. Cocks (1997, p. 66) notes that 'by 1933 many doctors, especially younger ones whose careers had begun under the adverse economic circumstances following the First World war, supported National Socialism. The Nazis promised to lift doctors out of their economic difficulties and to rid the field of Jews and women.' Clearing the decks of these competitors meant more jobs for the gentile boys. In addition, there were many psychotherapists who sympathised with the idea that therapy should aim to integrate the personality and create unity between the individual and society; the massification of the social order under the Nazis, and their clear injunction that the value of each person lay in her or his capacity to serve the Reich, could be seen to be part of – perhaps even the quintessential expression of – this influential strand of German Romanticism. As Göring put it in his 1934 address to the opening conference of the International General Medical Society for Psychotherapy, 'Like the Führer, we claim that character can be developed and because of that psychotherapy is of the greatest importance. For psychotherapy, as Jung has emphasised over and over, is not just about curing sick people, but about making fit people who lack the correct attitude toward life' (Cocks, 1997, p. 117). Indeed, the 'Master race' philosophy offered an opportunity to the psychotherapists to test their capacity to release the greatness in each German psyche. The psychotherapists were consequently very active in organising themselves to meet the demands and opportunities of the new era. Their first task was to create a clear separation between German psychotherapy and Jewish psychoanalysis, so that the regime would not taint them with the brush of the latter; their further, connected tasks, were to show their loyalty through establishing sympathetic political links with the Nazi rulers (hence the value of Göring) and articulating a vision of psychotherapy in line with Nazi ideals. In all this they had considerable success, aided by the possibly unexpected competence of Göring himself in managing the situation with aplomb.

Psychoanalysis, however, was under deep threat and it was rapidly apparent that its future in the Third Reich would be bound up with the psychotherapists and hence with the person and organisation of Göring rather than with the continuation of the German Psycho-analytic Society, the DPG. Indeed, the psychoanalysts took it upon themselves actively to seek the protection that Göring's name offered. As early as 1934, the new leaders of the DPG, Boehm and Müller-Braunschweig, and some of their non-Jewish colleagues met with the Jungians and with other psychotherapists to discuss joining together under a planned new institute headed by Göring. In February 1936, Boehm was told by the Ministry of Culture that psychoanalysis would be allowed to continue if the Berlin Psychoanalytic Institute would join with other branches of psychotherapy in an organisation under Göring's leadership, with a commitment to developing a 'New German Psychotherapy' (Goggin and Goggin, 2001, p. 104). It seems that in his negotiations with the Nazis, Boehm had been told that while there was no possibility of psychoanalysis being preserved under Jewish domination or with an explicit adherence to Freud, the government was favourable to its continuation on pragmatic grounds. Simply, as Rickels (2002) has shown, the Nazis believed that its effec-tiveness as a mode of treatment for soldiers had been demonstrated during the First World War, and they were keen to exploit this efficacy in any forthcoming conflicts, whatever might be the ideological objec-tions to trading with a 'Jewish science'. The solution would be for the remaining psychoanalysts (the Jews had resigned from the DPG in 1935, as described in the previous chapter) to form together with the psychotherapists, who would thus gain the use of their organisation and building; for the psychoanalysts, this would mean that they could continue to work and have influence over the new state-recognised organisation. Boehm met with Anna Freud to discuss this, apparently gaining support from her, and the German Institute for Psychological Research and Psychotherapy – known, colloquially and lastingly, as the Göring Institute – was set up on May 26th 1936. In July 1936, Göring, Boehm and Müller-Braunschweig met with Jones to gain the approval of the IPA, promising that the independence of psychoanaly-sis would be maintained within the Institute. This promise, however, was not kept: psychoanalytic training came to be combined in most important respects with that of other psychotherapies. The DPG handed its building over to be the base for the Göring Institute, useable by the analysts for only two evenings a week (Eickhoff, 1995, p. 951); the experience of the remaining analysts was thus that their 'home' had become occupied, and they were allowed only shared and partial use of it.

In October 1936, Göring gave his inaugural remarks on the new German psychotherapy, which was to be founded on a non-Freudian, pro-Nazi and antisemitic basis; reading of *Mein Kampf* was made an obligatory part of the training and the remaining Jews were excluded, both as staff and as patients (although neither of these last two moves was fully enforced, and some Jews and half-Jews survived in the Göring Institute until the end of the war, possibly protected by Göring himself (Cocks, 1997, pp. 104, 273). Henceforth, Freud's texts were kept (literally) under lock and key, and either Göring or his wife attended every seminar in order to monitor proceedings (Goggin and Goggin, 2001, p. 43).[1] Freud's eightieth birthday in 1936, bizarrely, was actually celebrated at the Göring Institute, though with all Jews excluded. Otto Fenichel, in his typically scathing way, described Boehm's subsequent attempt to patch things up with Freud. After an occasion at the Göring Institute when 'people had to "fall in", whilst Göring gave a lecture on the Jewish libido conception of Freud and the Aryan one of Jung,' Fenichel states,

> Boehm had such a bad conscience that he went to Vienna to assure Freud of his loyalty and to obtain absolution. He was not given it; Freud said to him: 'Different peoples, with different destinies, have developed a capacity, varying in strength, of holding on to their convictions, even if they have to be abandoned on the outside. Our Jewish people have had the misfortune, or fortune, of accumulating a host of experiences of this kind... Other peoples are less capable of resisting, and when they give in on the outside, they eventually give in on the inside too. It will all depend on what you hold onto inside.' After Boehm had left he said he did not believe that analysis would last in Germany: 'They are a submissive people.'   (Fenichel, *Rundbrief* of 30th November 1936, in Eickhoff, 1995, p. 951).

---

[1] Cocks (1997, p. 104) comments on the uncertainties around Göring's attitudes towards Jews: 'It is difficult to gauge the degree of anti-Semitism in Göring... His words and actions during the Third Reich leave no doubt over his condemnatory public stance then toward Jewish influence in his discipline. But what of his private attitude towards Jews themselves? Ernst Göring has recalled the many Jewish patients his father had and what mutual devotion existed between them and Göring. And yet in 1937 Göring would assert that between 1930 and 1933 only eleven Jews came to him and that he was unable to help any of them because of the "racial" difference.'

Freud's assertion of a mode of Jewish superiority is notable here, in the light of the continuing attempt to appease the Nazis and to accommodate to their own ideology of racial superiority; as described in the previous chapter, there was also an increasingly widespread view amongst the international leadership of the psychoanalysts that Boehm was not only compromised in relation to the Nazis, but weak.

That the psychoanalysts were compliant with the formation of the Göring Institute was clear to everyone: whilst Göring himself ran it, Boehm was its secretary and Müller-Braunschweig its treasurer (Cocks, 1997, p. 177). By the end of 1938, the psychoanalysts had ceased to exist as a separate organisation. At the end of his report on the 'German Psycho-Analytical Society' in the 1939 issue of the *Bulletin of the International Psycho-Analytical Society*, Müller-Braunschweig announced, 'In November 1938 the German Psycho-Analytical Society, transformed into Arbeitsgruppe A of the Deutsche Institut für psychologische Forschung und Psychotherapie, resigned its membership of the International Psycho-Analytical Association' (p. 134) – the second time it had done so, the first resignation having been rescinded in 1936 as 'too hasty' (Müller-Braunschweig, 1938). This formal dissolution of the DPG seems to have come about almost by accident, although it is also likely that Göring was looking for an opportunity to act against the analysts. After the Anschluss between Austria and Germany in March 1938, Göring entrusted Müller-Braunschweig with the task of visiting Vienna and negotiating to bring the psychoanalytic institute there into alliance with the Göring Institute. Whilst there, perhaps through political incompetence or maybe out of feelings of guilt, Müller-Braunschweig wrote a letter of homage to Anna Freud, in which he 'expressed his unconditional loyalty to her father's work and contradicted Göring by expressing the hope that the institute in Vienna could maintain its own separate existence, not only in order to ward off Nazi influence but also to avoid the consequences of the long-standing rivalry between analysts in Berlin and Vienna' (Cocks, 1997, p. 200). This was in a context in which an attempt was being made to 'Aryanise' the Vienna Institute and make it part of the DPG and hence linked with the Göring Institute in Germany – an attempt which resulted in the exclusion or resignation of all but two of the thirty-six analysts left in Vienna. The letter from Müller-Braunschweig to Anna Freud was intercepted by the Gestapo, resulting in the interrogation of both of them; Göring claimed to see it as an act of treachery and used this as a pretext to deny Müller-Braunschweig the right to teach or publish, and Felix Boehm to offer training analyses, though both were allowed to retain their private practices and to continue to participate at a senior level in the running of the Göring Institute. Eventually in Vienna, following the departure of Freud and his immediate family for England, the Psychoanalytic Institute was wound up. In Germany, meanwhile, following Kristallnacht and in the wake of the mistrust between Göring and Müller-Braunschweig, the DPG was closed down (on 19 November 1938) and absorbed into the Göring Institute, although the psychoanalysts retained some identity as 'Workgroup A'.

A non-Jewish psychoanalysis

The Göring Institute had a surprisingly important place in the hierarchy of the Third Reich, apparently invested with the expectation that it could serve the needs of the German people in developing a Nazified psychotherapeutic process serving national ideals. When the second conference of the German General Medical Society for Psychotherapy took place in Düsseldorf in 1938, a telegraph was received from Hitler thanking the Society for its 'vow of fidelity and for the announcement of the establishment of a German Institute for Psychological Research and Psychotherapy' and wishing it 'great success in [its] work' (Brecht et al, 1985, p. 146). Throughout the war, the Göring Institute was involved in psychotherapy and leadership training (particularly with the Luftwaffe), and attracted a substantial budget; it had 128 members in 1937, rising to 240 by 1941 (Cocks, 1997, pp. 335–8; 178). This was partly testimony to the Nazis belief in the effectiveness of psychotherapy – ironically, especially psychoanalytic psychotherapy – in dealing with psychological disturbances produced in soldiers and especially SS men by the experiences of war. Cocks (1997) documents examples of SS men treated as a consequence of their own experiences of killings and other atrocities, which presumably they were responsible for; it is also likely that members of the Nazi leadership were treated for such things as addiction (this may have included Hermann Göring) and possibly homosexuality. A major point here was that the *psychiatrists'* focus on hereditary degeneracy was not much help when it was the state's elite who were suffering; the psychotherapists were therefore on strong political ground in arguing that they should be given a chance to cure sufferers of their (implicitly temporary) neurotic conflicts and return them to active service. This was, too, the rationale behind the Göring Institute's enthusiastic treatment of homosexuality: given the large numbers of homosexuals in the military and the Nazi party itself, it was not possible to be too ruthless about the extermination policy, nor was it ideologically advisable to argue that homosexuality was always an incurable pathology. This does not mean, however, that the Institute operated a liberal regime: its treatment of homosexuals was not only selective, but it also perpetuated the notion (not only limited to Nazi philosophy, it must be admitted), that homosexuality is a disorder in need of treatment or extermination. Cocks (1997, p. 300) lucidly summarises the logic behind the Institute's work in this area.

> The efforts of psychotherapists and psychoanalysts to 'cure' homosexuality represented (1) an attempt to enhance and protect professional status; (2) a desire to 'help' the 'sick'; (3) support for the regime's insistence on a productive populace; (4) an alternative to the policies of punishment, imprisonment, castration and extermination carried out by psychiatrists, the SS, and the military; and (5) a resultant lack of resistance to overall Nazi persecution of homosexuals and thus, as in other matters and in general, degrees of participation in an inhuman system.

While the Göring Institute's practical activities were valued as a contribution to the war effort, it was its efforts towards the development of a Nazified psychotherapy that distinguished it most – as its proponents were the first to acknowledge. In a newspaper interview from May 1939 (Brecht et al, 1985, p. 151), Göring answers the question of, 'how *psychoanalysis*, a very modern branch of medicine, could once have had *so destructive an effect?*' His answer is that, 'since Freud, it has been almost exclusively the domain of *Jewish doctors.*' Freud, as a Jew, could not understand that the unconscious is not a domain of repressed sexual activity, but the 'foundation of life', the source of creativity.

> It is clear that it is precisely in a field of work like that of the mind that Judaism could bring its destructive influence to bear most fruitfully. For the Jews, psychotherapy became a business, and the poisoning of mental life a necessity, so that they could then undertake to cure the poison. *Today a thoroughly German form of psychotherapy has been developed.*

Whilst Jews welcomed neurosis on business grounds, because it provided work for psychotherapists, the 'new German psychotherapy' was idealistic, aiming to 'strengthen belief in the meaning of life and reinforce the link with the higher world of values; it was to convey to the patient the consciousness of being bound and incorporated into the common destiny of the German people' (Brecht et al, 1985, p. 152). As Nazism took control, so there would be greater integration of the individual and the state; the task of a genuinely patriotic psychotherapy was to work in the service of this integration, releasing the patient from neurotic conflicts that might prevent its realisation. In this way, the psychotherapy profession could participate in the spiritual growth of the German people, marching positively forward, leaving incurable antisocials such as the irrevocably mentally ill and the Jews (exterminated) by the wayside. This offered a new and rather rewarding role to psychotherapists:

> The psychotherapist was to be less of an analyst and more of an active agent of the community, leading his or her patients to healthy, productive lives. The partnership between doctor and patient was to involve the joyful exercise of authority on the part of the former and a willing subordination... on the part of the latter (Cocks, 1997, p. 92)

Insight gives way here to mobilisation; psychotherapy, not for the last time, becomes a form of ideological instruction.

It is clear from this that what was being proposed was a psychology without the critical doubt so central to Freud – without, that is, something of what might be thought of as its 'Jewish' heritage. Instead, the objective of psychotherapy was to facilitate in the patient the discovery of an unconscious energy and purpose that could be activated in the service of the German state. That the orientation of the work was towards the collective and not the individual is evidenced both in the expressed aims of the 'new German psychotherapy' and in some of its practices, for example its involvement with so-called 'euthanasia', something leading members of the Institute, including Boehm, came to accept as a solution for the 'untreatable' patient (Goggin and Goggin, 2001, p. 123). This involvement is one of the arguments that the Goggins employ to demonstrate that psychoanalysis could not have survived under the Third Reich: as exterminating supposedly untreatable patients is so obviously contrary to the ethics of psychoanalysis, anyone implicated in it must have thereby ceased to be an analyst. Certainly, there is evidence that senior members of the Göring Institute knew what was going on, for example in declaring numerous children (around 6%) referred to them for treatment as 'hereditarily disordered' and untreatable, thus allowing them to be sent to asylums where murder took place. Herbert Linden, the chief administrative officer of the Institute had daily operational control of the 'euthanasia' programme from 1941, and Göring himself actively refused pressure to criticise the programme. Boehm and Kemper supported extermination for some homosexuals and others, although their post-war defence, and that of others in the Göring Institute, was that by taking on numbers of supposedly untreatable patients they protected them from otherwise certain death. Goggin and Goggin (2001, p. 123) comment,

> While it is clear that the psychoanalysts were not major perpetrators, they were not immune from becoming part of this brutality. By the war's end, Boehm had given up his humane principles and accepted extermination as a way of disposing of 'uncured' homosexuals, while Kemper had participated in establishing the death penalty as a special form of treatment for 'incurable' forms of battle fatigue. Extermination as a means of treatment had become an acceptable method for two of the most distinguished psychoanalysts at the Göring Institute.

More cautiously, Cocks (1997) suggests that the active involvement of psychotherapists from the Göring Institute in the euthanasia programme is not well documented, although their verbal support for it is.

The relevant point here is that despite this apparent displacement of key psychoanalytic assumptions and ethical values in favour of a Nazified psychotherapy, and even after the formal dissolution of the DPG in 1938 and the closing down of all the major prewar psychoanalytic journals (including the *Internationale Zeitschrift für Psychoanalyse*, which moved to Holland in 1939 but ceased publication in 1941 – Thomä, 1969, p. 683), psychoanalytic activity continued within the Göring Institute in an explicit manner. Brecht et al (1985, p. 154) note:

> In fact the training of psychotherapists was to a great extent the responsibility of the 'Berlin psychoanalysts'. After the events of 1938 they did indeed lose some official responsibilities and were partially restricted in their teaching activities. But they were able to keep their influential position and expand it through clever staffing policies. They managed to keep the Polyclinic, the heart of the Institute, as their responsibility.

Thus, the psychoanalysts continued to have an impact in the Göring Institute. Boehm led the programme for homosexual soldiers; Werner Kemper helped work out treatment programmes for soldiers suffering

from war neuroses; Marie Kalau vom Hofe ran an unsuccessful psycho-
analytically-based service for criminals with 'mental illnesses'; and
Müller-Braunschweig remained responsible for lecture organisation and
the teaching programme of the Institute. Gerhard Scheunert, director
of the outpatient clinic, was a psychoanalyst specialising in 'the short-
term application of the "passive-contemplative" approach of psychoanalytic free association' (Cocks, 1997, p. 229). Even the Goggins
acknowledge that the training programme involved training analysis,
supervision and 'conventional-sounding' courses (2001, p. 109) and
that 'between 1938 and 1945 Working Group A [the Freudians] had
trained thirty-four people' (p. 112). Rickels (2002, p. 216) claims that
during the war, Göring's son wanted to be analysed: 'So to get round
Nazi law, Göring argued that his son was already pretrained with a
nonanalytic therapist and therapy: the analysis could proceed under
cover of its being second or secondary place.' Göring's wife Erna was
certainly treated by the analyst Werner Kemper, during which sessions
she allegedly passed on information from her husband regarding
colleagues 'who were in proximate or immediate danger from the
authorities' (Cocks, 1997, p. 277).

   Chrzanowski (1975), in a relatively early interview-based study,
notes that, 'Neither the people inside the Institute nor organised
German psychiatry outside of the Institute believed that psychoanalysis had been extinguished' (p. 496).

> Our research demonstrates that those analysts who remained in
> Germany, under the Nazis, were doing 'regular analytic work'
> during the critical years. Not one person interviewed by us express-
> ed the slightest doubt that he had continued to function as a psy-
> choanalyst throughout the Hitler years. We have no doubt as to
> their sincerity.   (pp. 494–5)

According to the testimonies given to Chrzanowski, the psychoanalysts
and psychotherapists in the Institute worked well together during the
Nazi years, which, while it might have been an example of banding
together against a common threat, also suggests a shared purpose and
enterprise – sometimes relatively liberal, in attempting to maintain
psychotherapeutic standards under extreme circumstances, sometimes
more solidly in alliance with the programme for the 'new German psychotherapy'. Again, however, this relinquishment of the highest psychoanalytic ideals does not allow one to say that psychoanalysis did
not exist. Spiegel (1975, p. 488) describes how 'The aim of Group A was

to maintain rigorously the theory and practice of the Freudian mode of analysis, with the meticulous dedication that put one in mind of the oral tradition for historical accuracy in preliterate societies.' Whilst Göring's scrutiny of the formal seminars may have meant that analytic ideas could not be discussed openly, there were plenty of opportunities for informal meetings 'at which time Freudian terminology was openly and spontaneously used' (ibid.). Chrzanowski does point to the mutual fears of betrayal by analysts and patients as powerful factors interfering with the therapy; however, while this is of considerable importance, it does not in itself imply that the activity being engaged in was not psychoanalysis, and there are no known cases of any such betrayals actually occurring.

Documentation of the extent to which psychoanalysis was actually practised within the Göring Institute is important to Cock's (1997) argument that it participated in the relative growth of psychotherapy as a profession under the Nazis. Cocks shows how the Institute operated particularly through short term therapies along neo-Freudian lines, partly in order to ensure insurance coverage, which was lacking for the kind of long-term analysis that had been more characteristic of the BPI. However, psychoanalytic training activities continued, even though Göring himself exercised personal censorship of Freudian terms and concepts and the members of Workgroup A accordingly had to resort to euphemisms (e.g. 'depth psychotherapy' instead of 'psychoanalysis'). Some cases were handled by depth analysis including free association and the use of the analytic couch. Increasingly, as time passed, the psychoanalysts became more influential within the Göring Institute, largely as a consequence of their greater experience and technical competence. 'Like other therapeutic means in the field,' Cocks comments (p. 276), 'where Freud worked, Freud was used. Ernst Kris, a psychoanalyst who had fled from Austria, observed during the war that the German army and the Ministry of Propaganda incorporated a psychoanalytic perspective in their psychological work, unconcerned that Freud's works had been publicly burned in 1933.' Rickels (2002) notes in this connection that when one looks outside the Göring Institute it is possible to find a great pervasiveness of Freudian thought in the German military-psychological complex: as in England, there was an especially lively interest in its application to groups. Cocks (p. 277) summarises the trend:

> The psychoanalysts, spurred by peril as well as by the opportunity, were particularly visible and active in the running of the outpatient

clinic. And like the other two 'working groups', the Freudians kept up their own regular series of meetings and lectures. Even Göring himself, who had been one of those most bitterly opposed to 'Jewish psychoanalysis', gradually came round to tolerating and even accepting psychoanalysis by virtue of its theoretical and practical contributions to the work of his institute.

As Cocks (2001) notes, none of this means that all the analysts were Nazis or Nazi sympathisers, but it does reveal that during the period of the Göring Institute, non-Jewish analysts carried on with their work as best they could, with varying degrees of collaboration with the aims of the new German psychotherapy, including implication in the euthanasia programme. Few analysts, with the pre-war exception of Edith Jacobson (whose experiences are described in the previous chapter), Käthe Dräger, who distributed anti-fascist materials as a member of the communist underground, and the wartime martyr John Rittmeister, rebelled, although few actually joined the Nazi party (Chrzanowski, 1975, estimated that of the approximately 100 people connected with the Göring Institute a maximum of 5% were members of the Nazi Party, with few if any psychoanalysts amongst them). Over time, whatever their occasional protective actions towards individual patients, the psychoanalysts within the Göring Institute became more, rather than less, implicated in its functioning and in its service to the state. At the very least, this meant that they lent passive support to the activities of the Third Reich; but as has been suggested, there was also a good deal of active collaboration as well, both by reformulating Freudian theory and practice and by political actions in excluding psychoanalysis' Jewish members. As John Rittmeister (1939) famously commented, psychoanalysis was going on 'in a most peculiar way', but going on it certainly was.

The figure of John Rittmeister provides a short coda to this chapter. Rittmeister, an analyst, was Director of the Göring Institute outpatient clinic – quite an extraordinary situation in its own right, given that he was known by Göring to have anti-Nazi views. Rittmeister had actually chosen to return to Germany from Switzerland in 1937 in order to complete his training analysis. He joined the underground resistance movement, focusing mainly on educational activities until becoming involved in 1942 with the more active spy group around Harro Schulze-Boysen. The collapse of this group in 1942 led to the arrest of Rittmeister and his wife, who were charged with treason, and to the eventual execution of Rittmeister in May 1943. For the Göring

Institute, this was a cataclysmic event, spawning sympathy for Rittmeister and anxiety in good measure, but also complicated by the idea that Rittmeister might actually have been treasonous during wartime and hence a genuine threat to the country. Cocks (1997, p. 331) comments, 'The result was that many regarded Rittmeister with a mixture of patriotic indignation, anxious and angry resentment, and some pity.' Göring seems mostly to have been exercised by panic at the thought of what the ramifications might be for the Institute; he certainly moved into overdrive in connecting up with his cousin in order to protect the Institute, and possibly to have action taken against Rittmeister so that no more harm could be done. Subsequently, whilst no measures were taken against the Institute itself, Workgroup A was disbanded, leaving the analysts to meet only in secret, with a disguising title, and marking the formal end of Freudianism in Germany under the Third Reich. Rittmeister was later praised as a psychoanalytic martyr, both in East and West Germany, and there seems to have been quite a scramble to claim links with him, but the evidence suggests that he was abandoned to his fate so as to protect psychotherapy from attack; that is, whether or not it would have made any difference, no one acted on his behalf.

5
The Repressed Returns

Re-branding psychoanalysis

The impact of collaboration between psychoanalysts, psychotherapists and the Nazis continued until well after the demise of the Third Reich. For many years, as noted in Chapter 3, this history was a relatively secret one, as the psychoanalysts set about rebuilding their organisation and their myths, specifically presenting themselves – like many other Germans – as always having been victims and possibly opponents of Nazism. The debate over whether psychoanalysis had survived or not during the Nazi time was relevant to this issue: for those who claimed that it had been suppressed, there was an easier route through to defending its anti-Nazi credentials. Helpfully for this side, Ernest Jones himself asserted that psychoanalysis did not survive in Europe during the war years (Chrzanowski, 1975). For those who accepted that psychoanalysis had survived, the issue became one of establishing that it had managed to maintain some form of resistance to corruption, and hence that there was a certain degree of heroism to be found in those who had kept the psychoanalytic flame burning. Karen Brecht, whose role in clarifying history has been very significant, notes about the situation in the thirty years after the war that, 'Most German publications on the history of psychoanalysis during the Third Reich, originating as they did from contemporary witnesses who presented the analysts as victims, were apologetic and not really informative... The picture of German psychoanalysts presented by oral history was one of secret resistance fighters and inner emigrants' (Brecht, 1995, p. 291). Käthe Dräger, for instance, who trained in Germany during this period, claimed that psychoanalysis had been 'blanketed' by the Nazis rather than killed off; 'In her judgement what actually survived was the conviction of the eternal spirit connected with psychoanalysis and the intactness of its basic ideology' (Chrzanowski,1975, p. 493). However, Dräger, in a paper given at a conference to celebrate the fiftieth anniversary of the founding of the Berlin Psychoanalytic Institute also asked, 'whether it would not have been better for all analysts to emigrate in 1933' (Chasseguet-Smirgel, 1987, p. 436), a similar point to one quoted by Chasseguet-Smirgel (1988, p. 1061) from two other German analysts, H.M. Lohmann and L. Rosenkötter: 'it would be easier to write the chronicle of the years 1933–1945 if today we were able to say: At a certain stage of its development, "Aryan" psychoanalysts simply said "no".'

The rendering of psychoanalytic history as a resistance struggle was aided by the prominence of Alexander Mitscherlich as the leading figure amongst German psychoanalysts in the 1960s and 1970s. Mitscherlich had clear resistance credentials: having been arrested and imprisoned by the Gestapo in the 1930s, he had been an observer at the Nuremberg trials, and in the post-war period he devoted some of his very considerable intellectual talents to a psychoanalytic examination of the German response to the Nazis, culminating in the publication in 1967 of *Inability to Mourn: Principles of Collective Behaviour*, written jointly with his wife. Mitscherlich promoted himself as the founder of psychoanalysis in post-war Germany, and was eagerly accepted in this role as he could clearly be thought to represent a new beginning, or at least a link with a healthier brand of German culture, and his multi-media criticisms of Nazism and the development of post-war Germany greatly aided the presentation of psychoanalysis as a socially radical discipline. Brecht (1995, p. 292) comments that Mitscherlich's 'political notoriety and influence created an atmosphere in the West German institutes which led at least the candidates and younger psychoanalysts... to believe that German psychoanalysts had resisted rather than collaborated with the National Socialists.' Rickels (2002, p. 9) is characteristically more sardonic: 'Mitscherlich got away with claiming to be the sole custodian of a purely victimized Freudian tradition that the Allies brought back.' As Brecht persuasively shows, the truth about Mitscherlich is rather more complex than the legend; as will be seen below, it is certainly not the case that Mitscherlich was the founder of post-war German psychoanalysis, nor was there anything like a clean break with the past. In fact, he did not join the new psychoanalytic association, the Deutsche Psychoanalytische Vereinigung (DPV) until 1956 – several years after it was founded – and did not receive a training analysis until 1958, when he went to London to be analysed by Paula Heimann. His achievements were real: not only did he found and run the highly influential Psychosomatic Clinic in Heidelberg, which did indeed incorporate psychoanalytic ideas into the training programme for doctors, but he also founded the Sigmund Freud Institute in Frankfurt in 1964, and organised a series of high-profile psychoanalytic lectures that 'benefited not only the public reception and the reputation of psychoanalysis but above all the vast need for psychoanalytic learning in the expanding DPV' (Brecht, 1995, p. 302). He established a Professorship of Psychoanalysis at the University of Frankfurt and made a lasting influence on the public reception of psychoanalysis in Germany, and of German psychoanalysis abroad. He was, therefore, easily claimable as the acceptable face of German psychoanalysis at a time when that was what was needed; a consequence was that important parts of the *real* history, which showed rather a lot of continuity with the past, could hide behind him. Mitscherlich was a 'good German' in many important respects, particularly in promoting acknowledgement of the Nazi past; this was something Germany certainly needed, and the psychoanalysts amongst the Germans needed it as much as anyone else. Identifying this function of the Mitscherlich myth, however, Brecht (1995, p. 308) also puts her finger on its profound danger:

> This position of higher morality is the key to understanding Mitscherlich's influence in the sixties and seventies. But this position closely relates to a philosophy which divides people into superior and inferior beings. This polarizing moral attitude does not lead to the idea of, and wish for, reparation. Actually the DPV is still struggling with this misleading position.

Coming to terms with the past requires more than the joyful embracing of a salvational myth.

The process of uncovering the history of psychoanalysis in Germany in the Third Reich had to wait for a considerable time after the Second World War, and required a rude shock to set it going. This shock was the product of a remarkable piece of political incompetence on the part of the German psychoanalysts. In 1977, at the International Psychoanalytic Congress held in Jerusalem, the Germans proposed that the next but one Congress, to be held in 1981, should take place in Berlin. One might have thought that they would realise that raising this issue at a Congress held in the Jewish state would not be a wise move, and perhaps it is an indication of just how much the Germans were out of step with general opinion that they did not realise the furore they would unleash – although it is also worth noting that the Executive Council of the IPA initially supported their request (McLaughlin, 1978). Chasseguet-Smirgel (1987, p. 434) represents the events as follows.

> Those who took part in the Jerusalem Congress in 1977 will no doubt remember that our German colleagues then invited us to Berlin. This aroused an outcry because the majority of the members of many of the world's psychoanalytical associations are Jewish. One after another, well known and respected analysts took the stage, saying: 'It's too soon for Germany' or 'Never in Germany'.... It must be said that our German colleagues – of course, it is not easy to be German today – facilitated matters by not connecting their invitation with the highly symbolic venue of that particular Congress.

In the event, after the issue was opened up to the entire membership of the IPA in the President's Newsletter, the German analysts' request was turned down. This provoked a period of difficult self-examination culminating in the exhibition held at the first post-war Congress that did actually take place in Germany, the Hamburg Congress of 1985, an exhibition which also built on the pioneering critical work of a young German psychoanalyst, Regine Lockot. The results of this and the historical work it spawned have been outlined in the previous two chapters, though it has to be noted here – and will be returned to below – that the Hamburg Congress itself was far from successful in dealing with the relationship between the German psychoanalysts and the Nazis. What has been revealed, however, is clear enough now: that psychoanalysis was compromised by its involvement with the Nazis and with the Göring Institute, and that this process needs to be understood in the light of its own hidden history of Jewish influence and embedded anti-Semitism. However, before considering the final implications of this, it is important to outline in a non-sanitised way one more strand of what happened in Germany: the actual emergence of psychoanalysis from the ashes, that is, its rather sordid path back to international acceptance.

At the International Psycho-Analytical Congress held in Zurich in August 1949, the first after the war, Ernest Jones initiated a debate at the business meeting on whether the Deutsche Psychoanalytische Gesellschaft should be allowed back into the International Psycho-Analytic

Association. His introduction is worth quoting in full, as it lays bare the issues facing the IPA and the DPG, and makes it readily apparent that what was exercising the psychoanalysts was not the question of how to deal with the possible and actual connections between the German psychoanalysts and the Nazis, but rather how to manage a situation in which, because of the enforced amalgamation of psychoanalysis with psychotherapy in the Göring Institute, there were doubts about the purity of German psychoanalysis as a theoretical and practical system. Indeed, in an act of appropriation of history in line with the tendency described already to make the analysts into resistance heroes, Werner Kemper is quoted in the minutes of the meeting as describing,

> some of the difficulties of practising psycho-analysis in Germany when, for instance, to treat a Jewish patient invited being sent to a concentration camp. Their group was formerly stigmatised as Marxist, and more recently as a Bourgeois deviation. But they had not a single Nazi among them, which could be said of no other German Society   (A. Freud, 1949, p. 186).

Kemper was arguing for the readmission of the Germans into the International Association; the leaders of the DPG at this point, and those pressing most strongly for entry, were two well-known names from negotiations with the Nazis, Carl Müller-Braunschweig and Felix Boehm. Müller-Braunschweig was the key figure here, having reformed the DPG as early as October 1945, although the candidates of the DPG were actually being trained in Kemper's Institut für Psychotherapie – a matter of great significance as this Institute was state supported and offered trainees regular or freelance employment at a time when most of the medical establishment was hostile to psychoanalysis (Thomä, 1969). It was important for the psychotherapists that they drew on the name of the DPG as an organisation that had been disbanded under the Nazis, rather than acknowledge any continuity with the Göring Institute, but in fact the persons involved in the new DPG were very much the same as those who had worked and trained together during the war. Even some of the ideology was not yet completely hidden: for example, at a Committee meeting of 7th August 1945, Boehm, in response to a query from Müller-Braunschweig about how the practice in the new organisation might differ from that of the old Berlin Psychoanalytic Institute, is recorded as saying 'what was on his mind, that personally he had always suffered from the preponderance of Jews in the old institute' (Brecht et al, 1985, p. 195). What was particularly problematic, however, was not the perpetuation of anti-Semitic attitudes, but rather that the outstanding figure in the Institute was Harald Schultz-Hencke, who in fact took over its directorship when Kemper went to work in Brazil in the late 1940s. Continuing the 'deviation' from Freudianism that had begun well before the war and had been organisationally embedded in the Göring Institute, Schultz-Hencke and the majority group within the 'new' DPG promoted a form of 'neo-analysis' that very happily chimed with the other psychotherapy groups in Germany, including the Jungians. This, for Müller-Braunschweig and the majority of analysts *outside* Germany, was anathema, a more threatening betrayal than anything that was admitted so far about the links between the pre-war analysts and the Nazis, and Müller-Braunschweig's efforts were thenceforth steadily along the lines of trying to (re-) establish a properly Freudian basis for the DPG. However, within the DPG itself Schultz-Hencke was a very significant figure, and he had benefited during the Nazi period from being allowed to continue teaching and recruiting students, unlike both Boehm and Müller-Braunschweig. In a critical account, Thomä (1969) describes how this special position, alongside his central place in the post-war training Institute for Psychotherapy, meant that 'Psychoanalysis was represented most strongly by Schultz-Hencke, and naturally in the manner understood by him' and that, 'The students around Schultz-Hencke were linked to him emotionally as well as intellectually and thus favourable conditions were created for forming a group' (p. 685). Boehm was largely supportive of Schultz-Hencke, perhaps representing a wish for unity amongst the Germans arising as a defence against being torn apart by recriminations; this meant that the putative director of the DPG, Müller-Braunschweig, was actually in a minority position.

Jones set up the debate at the Congress in his usual direct way, reviewing the history and provocatively giving expression to his doubts. The question was, how pure ('true, real') could the German Society be, given its history of involvement with other psychotherapeutic groups? The previous day, Schultz-Hencke had given a powerful defence of his post-ideological approach and Müller-Braunschweig had responded by criticising him for 'dogmatic conceptual narrowness' in a reply tendentiously entitled 'The neoanalysis of Schultz-Hencke seen from the perspective of psychoanalysis'. This paper included as its opening summary statement the claim that 'Neo-analysis has resulted from drastically eliminating from psychoanalysis all those points which in the course of the development of psychoanalysis aroused resistance' – one of the standard ripostes of traditional Freudians to new departures (Brecht et al, 1985, p. 203). This debate clearly weighed heavily in Jones' scales: in his introduction, he singles out Müller-Braunschweig's contribution for praise and, by implication, damns Schultz-Hencke.

> The German Society was dissolved before the war, just as the Vienna Society was. After the war, Dr Müller-Braunschweig in 1946 notified us of its reconstruction and we naturally welcomed this informa-tion, which was tantamount to a provisional acceptance. Since then, however, information about the state of the German Society has been very mixed... It would appear that steady pressure in the direction of amalgamating different forms of psychotherapy – Jung, Adler, Freud, Neo-Analyse (*sic*) – under one heading must have some effect in ten to twelve years on the members. It would not be human to expect otherwise. The probability is that some analysts have remained true, real, genuine analysts and are clear about its relation to other work. Dr Müller-Braunschweig gave an excellent example of this yesterday. At the other extreme there would appear to be some who we should not consider to be psycho-analysts. In between there is also an indefinite number (we do not know how many or how confused), and so the total picture is undoubtedly somewhat bewildering. Discussion in the Central Executive was therefore to the effect that this large Society which still works under the Institute of German Psychotherapy, so that the training is therefore mixed, is not altogether what we should call a psycho-analytical Society. The question is what steps our colleagues from Germany think they should take to remedy this complicated state of affairs.   (A. Freud, 1949, p. 186)

In response, Müller-Braunschweig expressed his disappointment that there was any difficulty concerning readmission, claiming that the psy-choanalysts 'preserved their own autonomy and independence' and planned to establish their own Institute; but after some debate about how best to manage the situation with Schultz-Hencke, the decision went against him, with acceptance of Heinz Hartmann's motion 'that the Central Executive pursue its investigation further, that provisional acceptance of the German Society be continued, and that the Central Executive report to the next Congress' (ibid., p. 187). This rebuttal seems to have come as a shock to the Germans, who were heavily invested in the idea that they had saved psychoanalysis during the Nazi period and that, as Thomä (1969, p. 687) puts it, 'They had been unable to prevent anything, and everything that was done on their part as a result of the demands of the regime always had Freud's sanction or the approval of the representatives of the International Psycho-Analytical Association.' The public revelation that the DPG was severely split was a narcissistic injury that was particularly hard to deal with, resulting in feelings of betrayal that became increasingly overt. Müller-Braunschweig, as the representative of orthodoxy and the IPA's preferred model of a psycho-analyst, bore the brunt of these hostile feelings.

Subsequent to this meeting, Müller-Braunschweig renewed his efforts to make the DPG more psychoanalytically orthodox; Schultz-Hencke not only opposed this, but refused to leave the DPG himself in order to restore it to psychoanalytic credibility. The degree of acrimony between the protagonists in this dispute became increasingly marked, with Schultze-Hencke claiming that Müller-Braunschweig had delib-erately misrepresented his position in Zurich. After Schultze-Hencke turned down an initial approach by Müller-Braunschweig suggesting a face-to-face private meeting, their correspondence rapidly degenerated into personal abuse. On 10th November 1949, Schultze-Hencke wrote to Müller-Braunschweig that, 'I want to tell you quite frankly that in my opinion you are under a total illusion about the motives for your actions and words, and always have been' and went on to argue that his version of neo-analysis was such that 'I am as completely justified in describing myself as a psychoanalyst as I ever was, at any rate as the Americans in question call themselves Neo-Psychoanalysts' (Brecht et al, 1985, p. 206) – a legitimate point. Three days later, Müller-Braunschweig responded: 'How could you let yourself go as you did in your last letter? It is bristling with slanders, misrepresentations and insults. I was tempted not to reply at all' (ibid., p. 207). The battle lines hardened, with the major-ity group supporting the idea that psychoanalysis could operate within the broader remit of the DPG and the Institute for Psychotherapy, whilst Müller-Braunschweig's group tried to resituate the centre of gravity in what they regarded as a more purely psychoanalytic direction. By January 1950, Müller-Braunschweig was writing to 'all members of the DPG' the following non-conciliatory tract:

> I should like to draw your attention to a question of organisation which has been worrying our Berlin members in particular for a long time. It concerns the relationship of Schultze-Hencke and his friends with our society. A number of our Berlin members see in Schultze-Hencke's membership of the Psychoanalytical Society

a problem urgently demanding a solution. The participation of Schultze-Hencke and his friends in the work of our meetings is seen by a number of our members as scarcely productive and adding nothing to the particular objects and tasks of a psychoanalytical society. The group of members who take this view feel that if the work of the Society is to continue to be undisturbed and fruitful, it is desirable that Herr Schultze-Hencke should give up his membership of the Society.   (Brecht et al, 1985, p. 209)

Perhaps not surprisingly, this did not resolve the situation and Schultze-Hencke refused to leave quietly. Eventually, Müller-Braunschweig gave up his attempt to wrest control of the DPG and took an action that once again provoked the language of betrayal. On 10th June 1950 a new organisation, the Deutsche Psychoanalytische Vereinigung (DPV) was formed by Müller-Braunschweig and a few others; its existence was announced in a circular to the members of the DPG in September. At this time, Müller-Braunschweig was still Chairman of the DPG, and the members of the new organisation did not actually resign from the old one, hoping instead to provoke a split. Matters came to a head at a General Meeting of the DPG of 3rd December 1950 (Brecht et al, 1985, pp. 211–3). Müller-Braunschweig reported on the situation, Schultze-Hencke responded, saying that his theory was 'two-thirds Freud' and implying that Müller-Braunschweig had been plotting (which he had). Boehm, in the first of a series of increasingly vitriolic interventions, commented that 'The outsiders among us must be wondering what sort of a scientific life the DPG has been leading in the last two and a half years. The whole of Müller-Braunschweig's report and the discussion up to now must give the idea that there is no Society, but two men with different viewpoints.' Franz Baumeyer accused Müller-Braunschweig, 'Is it not drastic for a Chairman like you to fail so grossly in his duties? So gross a violation justifies measures of distrust.' Müller-Braunschweig defended his actions, explaining that the DPV group had not resigned from the DPG because they wanted to continue their collaboration and wished to have a 'friendly discussion'; however, 'instead of that I was answered with massive countermeasures which confirmed our fears.' Boehm then gave an extraordinary report on Müller-Braunschweig's five year period as Chairman of the DPG, minuted as a series of nineteen points, which included praise for his work in some areas, but also contained the following criticisms.

5) Müller-Braunschweig as a representative in the public eye: Boehm had constant complaints that Müller-Braunschweig always gave the

impression that he had not prepared his lectures, lost the thread, often repeated himself, etc.

7) Müller-Braunschweig brought dissension into every kind of collaboration.

11) Müller-Braunschweig had staged a public quarrel that was no longer objective. Müller-Braunschweig's appearance before the international public in Zurich was, he said, a typical humiliation of Germans in front of foreigners. Müller-Braunschweig's behaviour had been justly criticised in the press and in letters from foreigners. The IPA's rejection was Müller-Braunschweig's fault.

15) The alienation exists because Müller-Braunschweig is doing everything to eliminate his mortal enemy, Schultze-Hencke.

19) In 1945 Müller-Braunschweig took over a flourishing Society. As a result of his 5 years of activity he leaves a ruined Society, a mere rump.

Given the actual situation in Germany in 1945, this last accusation was especially egregious. After this assault, the proposal 'not to exonerate' Müller-Braunschweig was carried by ten votes to seven (recorded in the minutes as 'Müller-Braunschweig's friends'), with two abstentions; Müller-Braunschweig and seven others then resigned. Thus a split in German psychoanalysis became institutionalised, with the DPG representing neo-analysis and alliance with other psychotherapies, and the DPV representing psychoanalytic orthodoxy. In the years to come, the former was to be portrayed as continuing the tradition of the Göring Institute whilst the latter was credited with restoring psychoanalysis to health; but in fact both organisations were deeply implicated in the past, and the founders of the DPV had actually themselves been members of the Göring Institute, and had exerted influence within it.

At the 1951 International Psycho-Analytic Congress in Amsterdam, the question of the admission of the German psychoanalysts into the IPA came up again for reconsideration. This time, the Congress President was Leo Bartmeier, who summarised the issues as follows (Bibring, 1952, p. 253):

You will remember that during the last Congress we gave only provisional recognition to the German Psycho-Analytical Society (Deutsche Psychoanalytische Gesellschaft) because of problems concerning its composition and the scientific trends in the group. The main question under discussion was the role which Dr Schultz-Hencke's neo-psychoanalysis played. The last Congress felt that this should be clarified and that the German Psycho-Analytical Society should first re-establish its psycho-analytic orientation before a final decision could be made. After unsuccessful attempts to carry out these suggestions, Dr Carl Müller-Braunschweig organized a new group, the German Psycho-Analytical Association (Deutsche Psychoanalytische Vereinigung). The membership has now increased to eleven, and Dr Müller-Braunschweig has applied to the International Psychoanalytical Association for recognition of this new organization. The Executive Council suggests to the Congress acceptance of this application for full recognition.

Müller-Braunschweig then explained the background more fully, stating that he had 'tried to influence analysts of this [DPG] group to leave [the DPG] and form a new group based exclusively on psychoanalytic principles' (ibid.), but the majority of analysts had refused this suggestion, leading to the decision to break away and form the DPV with 'a small group of colleagues'. The resolution to accept the DPV 'under the direction of Dr Müller-Braunschweig' was unanimously accepted. There then followed a debate on what to do about the DPG, which was now under the chairmanship of Boehm. Bartmeier proposed, on behalf of the IPA Executive, that its provisional recognition should be withdrawn. In reply, Kemper gave a historical review of the development of the German Psychotherapeutic Institute, which was, he claimed, 'at the time when the existence of psycho-analysis was threatened in Germany, the only place where the work could be continued' (ibid., p. 254). He proposed continuing with the DPG's provisional recognition, a request Boehm supported, arguing that he had only taken on the chairmanship of the DPG in October 1950 and claiming that it 'would be able to prove its scientific value for psychoanalysis between the present Congress and the next one' (ibid.). He also protested about the view that there were in fact two groups in the DPG – the psychoanalysts and Schultz-Hencke's group – and 'raised the question of the basic meaning of the contemplated rejection of the old German Psycho-Analytical Society. He felt that this implied a rejection of himself, as if his teaching and writing had shown a deviation from the system of psycho-analysis, and he protested against this implication' (ibid.). Anna Freud then intervened to say that it had never been a personal issue; rather, 'It would be a unique occurrence if the International Psycho-Analytical Association were to accept an institute that was not working independently' (ibid.); on this basis, the resolution not to extend the DPG's provisional recognition was passed with only four votes against. The new German psychoanalysis was ready to begin. Later on, faced with the trauma of the 1977 Congress and questioning by young German analysts, controversy over the role of both Müller-Braunschweig and Boehm re-emerged in Germany, and the shame of appointing Gerhardt Scheunert, who had been a Nazi, as the DPV's second President was openly revealed. There was also a process of reconciliation between the DPG and DPV, although it was not until 2001 that the DPG was readmitted to the IPA as a 'provisional society'. For a long period what was dominant was a motivated forgetting of history and instead a focus on how to purify psychoanalysis, not ethically – not, that is, to make up for its involvement with Nazism – but in terms of its disciplinary and professional autonomy.

Even a cautiously psychoanalytic reading of the events of these congresses might suggest the triumph of a defence over something repressed, in line with the argument proposed by many of the younger German analysts and others: rather than deal with what had happened to psychoanalysis under Nazism, including the possibly collaborationist activities of its leaders, the IPA attended to the preservation of the supposed purity of psychoanalytic theory and practice against the depravities of other psychotherapeutic groups. Schultz-Hencke, who probably did have a certain amount to answer for, was made into the necessary bad object; Boehm, who did not distance himself quickly enough from Schultz-Hencke, became contaminated; and Müller-Braunschweig was cleared. 'After a series of organizational manoeuvres, he succeeded in having himself and a small group of colleagues accepted back into the IPA, leaving Schultz-Hencke out in the cold as not only the neo-Freudian – which he was – but also as the displacement object for their common guilt, the designated sole Nazi collaborator – which he was not.' (Antonovsky, 1988, p. 227). The psychoanalytic movement could carry on, apparently reconciled, though as usual the repressed always threatened to return, and eventually did. The immediate effect, however, was to aid German psychoanalysis in its continuing silence about history, through offering instead an alternative set of myths relating to various ways in which psychoanalysis was saved and betrayed. This in turn had some very substantial effects, which were commented on revealingly by Ursula Kreuzer-Haustein (2002), Vice President of the DPG, in a panel discussion on 'Psychoanalysis and Psychoanalysts in Germany after the Shoah' put on by the European Psychoanalytic Federation. Kreuzer-Haustein focuses on the 'unbearable unconscious feelings of guilt and shame among German psychoanalysts of the post-war period, leading to a form of collective defence that lasted for decades' and that was accentuated in the DPG by its isolation from the rest of the psychoanalytic world. In particular, the impact on training analyses was very profound: 'If the training analyses are not just a matter of identifying with the psychoanalytic method, but also of deep processes of identification with the training analyst, then the "hushed-up guilt" over having betrayed Freud and psychoanalysis creates a blind spot in the transference, with serious consequences.' These included an inability to face the destructiveness that was turned against the Jewish elements in psychoanalysis during the Nazi period, covered over by a claim that 'Well, actually we're all descendants of Freud,' seen by Kreuzer-Haustein as a 'blatant (and perhaps also unconscious) example of a justification strategy'. A further defence was to find an alternative object on which to place the blame for the DPG's exclusion; here, the usual suspects could suffice:

> a quite specific myth about the post-war DPG was operative until the early 1970s, in the form of a projective defence. Many non-Jewish psychoanalysts, including Schultz-Hencke, for example, had fought for the survival of psychoanalysis at the Reichsinstitut during the war. However, the IPA had never acknowledged this; the DPG was the victim of foreign (Jewish?) intrigues by being denied readmittance to the IPA. The DPV's founding was also an act of disloyalty... This myth about the post-war DPG bears distinct signs of a justification strategy, in which one's own role as an accomplice, the responsibility for driving the Jewish psychoanalysts out of the DPG, is turned around and becomes a myth of expiatory sacrifice.

Continuation of the accusation that 'the Jews were responsible' is one hidden theme in this material, to be returned to again later. In terms of the organisational situation, the DPG held to the thin thread of its links with psychoanalysis through denying Schultz-Hencke's 'deviation', but also suffered from an ambivalent sense of, on the one hand, how it had been mistreated, and on the other that there might be something true about the claim that it represented a continuation of a Nazified institution. Polemics between the DPG and DPV along the lines of which was genuinely psychoanalytic, which more open and free, which more traditional and which more creative, continued until very recently, being replicated even in a 1996 conference of the two societies on 'The Division of the Psychoanalytic Community in

Germany and its Consequences'. Kreuzer-Haustein comments that this conference was marked by 'intense aggressive conflicts' between individual members and between the two organisations.

> The arguing rituals were clearly used in the service of defending against feelings that were difficult to bear, of shame, guilt, fear of annihilation, hatred, desperation and also mourning. These feelings did not take shape until later, and then, too, were still repeatedly interrupted by unfruitful arguing rituals. Unconscious enactments in the large group dynamics prevented the constitution of a group on the theme of the DPG and DPV's common historical responsibility and a possible common taboo about learning and practising psychoanalysis.

Not much, it seems, had changed.

Reckoning with 'Our Hitler'

The meeting of the International Psycho-Analytic Association in Hamburg in 1985 included in it the exhibition on psychoanalysis in Nazi Germany recorded in Brecht et al (1985), and thus was to some extent set up as a reckoning with the past. The Congress was opened by the Mayor of Hamburg, Klaus von Dohnyani, who gave a remarkably well-informed and direct presentation of the issues and feelings that were involved in holding the Congress on German soil – probably a more direct account than that given by any of the psychoanalysts involved. He began with a reminder (*Opening Ceremony, 34th IPA Congress*, 1986, p. 3):

> More than half a century has passed since the International Psychoanalytical Association last met in Germany. The International Psychoanalytical Congress, then held in Wiesbaden in 1932, hardly appears to have been aware of the imminent threat posed by National Socialism which, only a few months later, set up in Germany the most brutal dictatorship in human memory...

Noting that the fiftieth anniversary of Hitler coming to power and the fortieth anniversary of the end of the Second World War had provoked a new focus on 'those years of German history', von Dohnyani commented that, 'the question: "What really happened then?" has also been engaging the attention of psychoanalytic associations in the

Federal Republic of Germany. In particular, the debate concentrates on the situation, the development and role of psychoanalysis and the German Psychoanalytical Association (*sic*) after 1933' (ibid.). Von Dohnyani then called on the work of the Mitscherlichs, which described, 'how and why we Germans had turned away from the reality of our history, why we were attempting to repress it, and yet would not be able to escape it. Why we remain – as, indeed, we still are – hostages to history for as long as we refuse to confront the truth' (ibid.). And here's the sting:

> It therefore is my opinion that your colleagues who have described the weaknesses of psychoanalysts and their associations in the years leading up to and during National Socialism have helped to free us from historical entanglements by showing us how it really was – with respect to psychoanalysts, too, even Sigmund Freud. For fear of losing everything, bit by bit was sacrificed, every step being rational – and yet at the same time always in the wrong direction. Here a compromise concerning persons, there a compromise of principles, but always in the pretended interest of preserving the whole – which in the end was lost.   (ibid., p. 4)

Von Dohnyani then asked whether psychoanalysis could 'help us not only to understand ourselves better, but also to be and act better' (ibid.); his doubts on this subject were clear for all to see. And finally, looking the issue of owning the past straight in the face:

> It seems we Germans remain a nation in danger, always fearful of being left behind, of being unloved, of not being appreciated sufficiently. It is probably not by accident that the three great innovators Marx, Freud and Einstein all spoke German as their mother tongue. But then, it is also no coincidence that they all were driven out of the country and regarded English as a language of liberation. Whoever says: our Bach and our Beethoven, must also say: our Hitler. This, too, will be one of your topics.   (ibid.)

This powerful speech was not matched by anything of equivalent power from the psychoanalysts. In his response, the President of the IPA, Adam Limentani, acknowledged that there had been a 'prolonged period of debates and thoughtful appraisals' (ibid., p. 5) but focused on the achievements of the DPV since its founding, for instance in becoming the second largest psychoanalytic association in the world. For his part, Dieter Ohlmeier, President of the DPV, did acknowledge the issues faced by Germans struggling to come to terms with the past, but made this an aspect of psychoanalytic history only in so far as the analysts were themselves German: 'German psychoanalysts have increasingly attempted to become conscious of and come to terms with the guilt, the shame, and the mourning which they, as Germans, have to bear' (ibid., p. 6). Psychoanalysis itself, however, was seen as amongst the victims: 'Psychoanalysis shared the fate of all scientific disciplines for which freedom of thought and absolute truthfulness are of supreme importance, and which endeavour to guide mankind on a path which will enable people to understand each other and treat each other in a humane way: it was suppressed, outlawed and destroyed in National Socialist Germany' (ibid.). As has already been argued, this is too easy and exonerating a claim, whatever caveats hedge it about.

In his comments on the Congress, Weinshel (1986, p. 89) remarked that, 'Although that portion of the Congress programme dealing with the "Nazi Phenomenon" occupied less than 25 per cent of the actual meeting, the emotional impact of that phenomenon preoccupied a much more significant part of our time in Hamburg.' He noted that many of the visitors to Germany were surprised at the strength of their feelings, that they kept expressing their concerns and asking questions about the Germans, and repeating 'It's so moving.' By the end of the Congress, Weinshel claimed, 'most of these questions and concerns appeared to be put to rest. Our German colleagues were not only colleagues but very often friends' (ibid.). However, it is clear from the accounts of others present that not everyone agreed, but rather thought that, in what might perhaps be seen as a common defensive move, the past was invoked at the Congress precisely in order that it should not be fully faced. Rafael Moses and Rena Hrushovski-Moses (1986) spoke on behalf of many Jewish analysts when they expressed their unease and disappointment at the way in which the impact of Nazism had been so contained in a seminar on 'identification and its vicissitudes in relation to the Nazi phenomenon' as almost to disappear: that is, the IPA's reluctance to deal with anything but *clinical* issues surrounding Nazism can be seen as a way in which they could claim to be dealing 'scientifically' with the past without dealing *emotionally* with it at all. Moses and Hrushovski-Moses begin their paper commenting, 'We left Hamburg before the official farewell party. We were feeling vaguely depressed. The general atmosphere was that something had been missed. The central issue of this Congress – that it was the first one to be held in Germany since the Second World War and since the Holocaust – had been very much in the air but had not been adequately dealt with' (p. 175). They note that a similar 'papering-over' had occurred in the 1969 Congress in Vienna, which had been opened by Anna Freud, whose 'opening speech did not tackle in a very direct or forthright way the problem of her relations with her country of birth and with the city in which she had been born and raised. Wounds that were not yet healed were covered over and hidden rather than given acknowledgement and care. The feeling with which many people – many analysts – were left was then, too, one of something missed, of a courageous stand not taken, of politeness and lip service, of things left unsaid' (ibid.). The parallel here with what actually happened in Germany – a 'courageous stand not taken' – are striking enough.

Moses and Hrushovski-Moses go on to describe a sequence of events during the Congress in which both German and non-German (including Jewish) analysts stepped back from actually enunciating and confronting the feelings swirling below the surface of the Congress, as if they did not want to risk blowing something fragile apart. The theme on 'identification and its vicissitudes in relation to the Nazi phenomenon', they note, was part of a series on identification and various pathologies, thus diluting its specificity; in any case, 'to call the events of the Nazi era, to name what was done by human beings to human beings, a phenomenon, is to elevate brutal events into the realm of more intellectualised abstractions… It is a watering down of something we are looking in the face' (p. 176). This watering down process could also be seen in the tendency to equate the Nazi Holocaust with other 'holocausts' in different parts of the world, or even in individual patients' family histories, referring to the way their parents' treated them: in the specific context of the Hamburg Congress, these were ways of avoiding dealing with what everyone could feel. Even where 'reality aspects' of the situation did surface – in the discussion groups, for example, when people did speak about their responses to being on German soil – they were dodged: 'they could be sensed, but they were not talked about' (p. 177). Moses and Hrushovski-Moses suggest that behind all this there was a complex of dynamic forces, including particularly a fear on the part of German analysts that they were going to be attacked, so that they and the organisers of the Congress worked hard to avoid confrontations, and a complementary sense amongst non-German analysts that they wanted to move on, 'that the Germans of today could not and should not be held responsible for what their parent generation had done; that peace must be made and the past put aside' (p. 179). The concern then became that the Congress should 'go well' rather than deal with the issues, the kind of thing that often happens both in individual psychoanalytic sessions and in organisations and meetings of all kinds. 'The main emotional subject was placed in the middle of the Congress, padded on all sides' (ibid.); nothing could be grasped hold of, with the consequence that no resolution could be achieved, but the cancerous mistrust and disturbance of unacknowledged yet deeply felt emotions continued to fester. Kijak (1989, p. 218) adds to this the suggestion that, 'there was another important factor which I believe was not discussed: the obligation of coming face to face, not only within the Congress, with the colleagues who are children of the generation that perpetrated the Holocaust, but also outside the Congress with the very Nazi assassins who actually carried out the genocide and who are now enjoying a happy and prosperous life, many of them remembering proudly how they served their fatherland, with no conflict in a society which, in part unconsciously and sometimes consciously, approves and legitimizes their history.' *They should be disturbed*, one might think, in need even of psychoanalysis; but instead they are happy and it is the victims who continue to suffer. Silence over this issue too, Kijak implies, hung densely over the Congress participants.

It has to be said that there was some recognition of these problems at the Congress itself. For example, Ostow (1986), responding to the papers on 'identification and the Nazi phenomenon', prefaced his remarks with the following justification for the focus on clinical work.

> It is no secret that this Congress assembles with a certain degree of tension that reflects the unresolved residue of mutual reserve between those of us who were actual or potential victims, and those of us who failed to distinguish ourselves sufficiently clearly from the persecutors during the Nazi apocalypse. It is also obvious that all of us hope this meeting will go far toward overcoming this reserve, by virtue of collaborative work on professional problems, and open and co-operative discussion of the kinds of issues that have come between us. It would seem to me that our panel this morning is designed as just that kind of reconstructive endeavour. (p. 277)

Treating the Nazi period as a kind of aberration, Ostow went on immediately to 'infer' that 'those Germans who have associated themselves with the Nazi movement, and who have returned to the historically normal way of thinking since its collapse, face a... need to account for the discontinuity in their mental life, and to make some sense of the bizarre, unnatural, and in fact delusional views that they espoused and promulgated – or at least tolerated – during this episode' (ibid.). By the end of his subtle paper on the clinical issues, Ostow was arguing that preventing 'another apocalypse and [defusing] prejudicial tensions' could be psychoanalysis' 'contribution to *tikkun olam*' – that is, the healing or perfection of the world (p. 284). The clearly deeply felt movement here, from acknowledgement of the tension in the Congress, through clinical work, to the idea that psychoanalysis could through these mechanisms of professional understanding of 'delusion' be a major force for good, is representative of a certain kind of slippage in the thinking of the psychoanalytic movement as a whole. The tension, which was real enough, gives way to the distancing of the phenomenon either through focusing on explanations of Nazism itself or on discussions of how Nazism affected *patients*; the point at issue – the implication of *psychoanalysis* in Nazism – consequently is covered over or lost. Psychoanalysis might indeed be a force for moral good, for *tikkun olam* (the reparative intention here is perhaps emphasised by being expressed in Hebrew), in many of its aspects, but it also has a darker side, just like the unconscious itself.

A startling and provocative account of all this is given in a compelling paper by Janine Chasseguet-Smirgel, published in the *International Review of Psycho-Analysis* in 1987. She comments that even though it was agreed that the Congress would focus on an 'essentially clinical exercise' and that several German analysts had written to the President of the IPA demanding that Germany's past should not be concealed at the Congress, 'Nevertheless, when the day devoted to the Nazi phenomenon was announced, I received a telephone call from Germany accusing me of wanting to put the Germans in a concentration camp' (Chasseguet-Smirgel, 1987, p. 435). Some Germans told her that they were staying away from the Congress 'because they feared hurtful attacks by colleagues, which they were already experiencing daily' (ibid.). A storm brewed: it became obvious at the Congress both that psychoanalysis had not been 'liquidated' in the Nazi period, but rather had found ways of participating in the Third Reich, and also that the degree of passion and vituperation surrounding this hidden history was not conducive to dealing with it. In fact, as Chasseguet-Smirgel points out in her summary comment (p. 437), both denial and split-off blame can serve the interests of repression.

We must regretfully conclude that our analytical identity is fragile and that courage and independence of mind are rare. If the German psychoanalysts lost their souls during the twelve years of the Nazi regime, the new generation of analysts will not gain them by failing to show sorrow or pity. On the contrary, the hatred expressed in some documents – for example, the collection of letters on this matter published by the DPV, couched on both sides in outrageously violent terms and exchanged hell-for leather like as many blows – shows that those involved are principally concerned with getting rid of their guilt by projecting rather than confronting it. As it happens, the word 'guilt' hardly ever features in these documents. The word that recurs insistently is 'shame'. This is to say that it is not a matter of assuming responsibility – by identification with the parents, and possibly with the analytical parents – for what happened in Germany. When opening the Congress, Klaus von Dohnanyi exclaimed: 'If we say "our Beethoven, our Bach", we must also say "Our Hitler".' Thomas Mann entitled one of his articles 'Bruder Hitler'. After all, the problem is one of identification.... *What is one to do with a Nazi father?* Apparently, the only solution is to reject him. If you speak of the need to integrate your identification with that father, you are immediately treated as a Nazi yourself... In order to become a human being in the full sense of the term, we have to be able to discover, confront and own, the *Hitler in uns*, otherwise the repressed will return and the disavowed will come back in various guises.

This complex argument is worth examining closely. The DPV set itself up as some kind of clean break with the past, leaving the old DPG to carry the blame of association with the Göring Institute and through that with the Nazis – despite the fact that those involved with the DPV, including its President, were deeply implicated in the Göring Institute. Discovering this past, and more generally realising that the institutions of psychoanalysis could not be idealised as bastions of resistance to the Third Reich, led to bitter acrimony and the rejection of their predecessors by a new and searching generation of German analysts. Chasseguet-Smirgel's argument is that the terms of this were such as again to replicate the splitting between 'good' and 'bad', rather than to create ownership of what had happened and the possibility of working it through, accepting guilt and promoting reparation. In a parallel paper (Chasseguet-Smirgel, 1988), she heightens the pressure on contemporary German analysts by arguing that this 'substitution of "shame" for "guilt"' is an indication of a failure of responsibility, because it represents an identification with parents rather than a recognition that 'the son of a Nazi will only be able to exorcise Nazism by facing up to, recognising, and sublimating his identifications with the Nazis'; without going through this process, 'the repressed will always return; whatever has been denied will reappear in persecutory form and render *all sublimation impossible*' (p. 1062). In particular, what is not acknowledged is 'the *Hitler in uns*', both at the ordinary level of the question, 'how would we have behaved?' and at the unconscious level of identifying the temptation towards hatred in everyone.

Specifically, for the non-Jewish analysts, this means identifying and owning anti-Semitic hatred. In her reflections on the impact of the Shoah on German psychoanalysis, Kreuzer-Haustein (2002) argues that deep ambivalence towards the 'Jewishness' of psychoanalysis, and towards Jews, continues on the German scene, in large part as a consequence of guilt at having betrayed psychoanalysis during the Nazi period. Psychoanalysis might have been a German-language creation and therefore something to take pride in; nevertheless, Kreuzer-Haustein suggests, the post-war psychoanalysts 'still had to reckon with their own hostile associations with psychoanalysis as a "Jewish science" that had been developed by Freud, a Jew, and was persecuted under National Socialism.' She further identifies a series of troublesome emotions that materialise in the various settings in which German and Jewish psychoanalysts come together (especially the Nazareth conferences on relationships between German and Israeli psychoanalysts) and that require facing up to if progress is to be made. These include:

a tormented feeling of guilt and shame;
a collectively operative paranoid fear of annihilation that is hard to bear, the fear of reprisal by the Jews. One German member phantasized that the hotel in Nazareth was a concentration camp where the Jews had locked us up in order to kill us all;
destructive phantasies and affects: the hatred for the Nazi fathers and their real or phantasized crimes and the hatred for the Jews, combined with murderous phantasies...This hatred was also disguised in idealizations of the Jews and what is Jewish. I understand this hatred as the expression of an anti-Semitism that we have to reckon with in ourselves today, but also as an 'anti-Semitism after the Shoah' that has something to do with hating the Jews because they are always reminding us of our guilt.

This last mode of hatred identified by Kreuzer-Haustein feeds into another tendency, that of finding ways to blame Freud and his Jewish circle for anti-Semitism within the psychoanalytic movement. Reviewing a book edited by J-L Evard on 'Psychoanalysis Under the Third Reich', Chasseguet-Smirgel (1988) discusses a comment from the editor that Freud 'never showed a will to face up to events... Despite the fact that he is endowed with all the necessary moral authority, he lets the institution that he has created become enmeshed in abjection and allows it to endorse the pogrom that was required of "Aryan" analysts by the Hitlerian regime... "Yes to psychoanalysis with the Nazis" say the psychoanalysts of Germany, faced with the abstentionism (tinged with cynicism) of Freud' (p. 1063). Chasseguet-Smirgel takes issue with these 'reproaches' on a variety of practical grounds, such as Freud's age and the complexity and intensity of the Nazi phenomenon. But her more spirited critique arises from teasing out the anti-Semitic aspects of the attack on Freud, aspects that have resonance in relation to wider (and wilder) accusations that the Jews were in some way responsible for the Holocaust.

> But most suspicious of all is that Germans (although they are not alone in this) reproach Freud for the fate of Jewish analysts and for Germany's agreement to become *Judenrein*. What a convenient solution to the whole problem! And how reminiscent – after the War, was it not rumoured that Hitler was a Jew? Could there be a better way of washing one's hands of the genocide than to reduce it to a Judeo-Jewish affair? Six or seven million Jews were exterminated by a Jew. This proves that Jews are indeed diabolical... (p. 1065)

The point is a general one: without acknowledging quite how pervasive anti-Semitism might have been in the psychoanalytic movement, and the various forms it might have taken, it is hard to see how anti-Semitism, or the Nazi past, can ever be securely put to rest.

How, then, can one move on from here? Chasseguet-Smirgel (1988, p. 1059) comments that, 'When the history of psychoanalysis under Nazi rule in Germany is concerned, it is almost as if one had quite literally obeyed the order: "Your are requested to close the eyes" appearing in one of Freud's dreams. *One must not see.*' If one refuses to look away, however, there are still numerous ways of understanding the somewhat sorry tale of psychoanalysis in Germany in the Nazi period. At the simplest level (which is not to say that it does not have its own complexities), it is a story of individuals faced with circumstances hostile to the continuation of their professional work, who were also caught up more or less strongly in a phenomenon of stupendous power, with its threat and its excitement. At the very least, these individuals went along with the dictates of the Nazi machine, retaining what dignity they could (less as time went on), plying their trade and preserving their profession as much as possible. This may have been ignoble, but perhaps not more so than those who did exactly the same in other walks of life. Psychoanalysts were certainly no more malevolent than many others who should and might have done better, being representatives of a class or professional group which was built upon self-reflection or accurate analysis of personal and political situations, or which had around it a clear ethical framework: lawyers, doctors, academics. Whilst there were heroes of resistance in all these fields, as a group they did not cover themselves with glory; psychoanalysis may not have had many heroes, but it also had relatively few perpetrators of Nazi abuses, and at least most of its Jewish representatives escaped.

However, there is something else to be explored here. Psychoanalysis had some kind of special status not (or not *just*) because it is premised on an idea of awareness of personal motives, but more (or also) because of its position as a paradigmatic 'Jewish science'. As noted, this was a term of Nazi abuse and carried with it all the racist connotations that are instantly recognisable: something corrupting, parasitic, demeaning and impure, which should be wiped out. However, psychoanalysis was also seen by many of its *practitioners*, including Freud himself, as having a special connection with Jewish culture, history and identity, a connection that had made psychoanalysis 'Jewish' well before the Nazis made this an index of abuse. Not only were the vast majority of European psychoanalysts secular Jews, but it was also the case that analysts and others alike could see that Jewish assumptions and ways of thinking were key elements of the psychoanalytic approach, however much it hungered for the apparent objective universalism of 'science'. Chasseguet-Smirgel (1987, p. 433) comments on the reasons why all analysts should be interested in 'the Jewish problem': 'they are all in effect of Jewish stock, through their identifications with Freud and the pioneers of psychoanalysis, and should therefore perhaps think about the links between Judaism and psychoanalysis – and hence themselves.' Under such circumstances, it might have been possible to hope that German psychoanalysis, with its outstanding history of political engagement, would provide a source of political and cultural resistance to Nazism; in the name of its own values and origins it might have resisted appeasement even if that meant exile, as happened in France, Holland, Norway and even Austria (Roudinesco, 1986). In fact, as soon as it was tested, the opposite was the case.

There is little doubt about the anti-Semitism of some of the players in this game: Jung, Göring, Müller-Braunschweig, probably Boehm. More profoundly, however, there was an antisemitic *movement* at work, which fed off and into Nazism and represented a serious attempt to rewrite the future of psychoanalysis. Jung thought he could bid for it and become the dominant force in an 'Aryanised' depth psychology; the Göring Institute was the institutional centre for the more formal attempt to put it into practice as a 'new German psychotherapy'. But what may be dimly perceived in all the scheming, the appeasement and collaboration, the rapid process whereby the Jewish analysts were turned against by their 'psychoanalytic brothers and sisters – with whom they shared classes, seminars and analysts' (Goggin and Goggin, 2001, p. 101), the forced resignations and (at least in the case of Wilhelm Reich) secret expulsions, is the enactment (albeit probably guilt-ridden, as Müller-Braunschweig revealed in Vienna) of a wish to eradicate the Jewishness from psychoanalysis. This *consciously* involved opposition to Freud and the centrality of sexuality, it also meant *consciously* replacing the Freudian critical stance and the theory of the opposition between individual desire and social order with an approach that gave primacy to the interests of the latter – recast as the 'Aryan nation' – and asserted that individuals could be psychologically enriched by falling in with these interests. It also meant constructing a theory of leadership congruent with the Nazi 'Führer-fixation', and converting a theory of necessary psychic conflict into one in which wholeness and integrity, in the service of the state, is possible. All this was *conscious* and can be read out from the writings of the representatives of psychoanalysis in the Third Reich.

The *unconscious*, however, was also at work, as it always is. What could have been the meaning, for gentile psychoanalysts, of finding themselves caught in the web of a 'Jewish science', subservient to its demands and, through their own transferences and the trust they had put in mainly Jewish training analysts (not to mention their institutional idolising of Freud), personally implicated in this Jewish cultural product, at a time and in a place in which things Jewish had become the defining mark of corruption, antisocial activity, parasitism and defilement? If Jewish analysts felt at home with psychoanalysis because of its compatibility with their culture, however much they had repudiated the beliefs of Judaism as a *religion*, then non-Jewish analysts were always likely to have a sense of marginality within their chosen profession, have the tables turned, as it were, be the uncomfortable outsiders who have to learn the rules to 'pass' – the reverse of the usual social situation. Once the Nazi hegemony was established, as it was in Germany extraordinarily quickly, these same non-Jewish analysts found themselves in a bind: hold out heroically as representatives of a Jewish culture to which they would always be outsiders, but to which they had given themselves through their training and professional affiliation, or join the new path and become central, insiders again. Part of the unconscious attraction of this latter course might well have been relief at the prospect of freeing themselves and psychoanalysis from the yoke of being 'a Jewish national affair'; that is, there is plenty of evidence that many analysts were, to the say the least, uncomfortable with being within a movement defined by insiders and outsiders alike as 'Jewish'. One has to recall that anti-Semitism was no historical aberration, but rather was the primary unifying political and religious force in Christian Europe throughout several centuries. Political and 'racial' anti-Semitism built on this and was at one of its peaks in the 1930s; thus, finding oneself using the language and thinking the (conscious and unconscious) thoughts of anti-Semitism may have gone against the official psychoanalytic line, but it would not necessarily have felt completely odd or morally repugnant. Given powerful circumstances in which engaging in practices detrimental to the Jews could be rationalised as protective of psychoanalysis itself, as was the case in Nazi Germany, the anti-Semitic elements that were never completely expunged from most non-Jews' identities could, and did, easily swim to the surface. That these should have been so difficult to face in the post-war period, resulting in the institutional histories of defence and deception described in this chapter, should also come as little surprise.

The summary situation before the war may therefore have been something like the following. Coupled with the general uncertainty about whether appeasement was an appropriate political policy, and added to the genuine dangers of speaking out, of resistance; and mixed in with some no-doubt unconscious fratricidal urges towards their Jewish analytic peers; and perhaps enraged by the loss of so many senior Jewish analysts, whose disappearance might have been experienced unconsciously as abandonment at a time of need; it perhaps did not require more than an average dose of moral turpitude and self-serving ambition to side with the apparent historical victors. Psychoanalysts of the Third Reich kept going throughout the Nazi period, quietly most of the time, doing good sometimes, but collaborating, losing their way, corrupting the psychoanalytic movement. They did so not only for all the compelling reasons that make it so hard to resist totalitarianism, but also because it was a form of revenge against the Jews. Afterwards, the shame attached to this was so profound that the past became hidden, repressed, only to keep bouncing back into view – not least as an unacknowledged but often pervasive seam of anti-Semitism.

Part III
Anti-Semitism and the Other

6
Psychoanalysis of Anti-Semitism I: A Christian Disease?

It is clear from the history rehearsed in the previous chapters that the Jewish connection with psychoanalysis is more than just a historical accident. The conditions under which psychoanalysis arose were strongly marked by shifts in modern identity generally, and Jewish identity specifically, occurring at the end of the nineteenth century in Europe. As well as determining the make-up of the early psychoanalytic movement, the marginalised and ambiguous status of Jewish identity lent psychoanalysis acuity of perception, a sharp, ironic and iconoclastic interpretive facility. Whilst this proved to be an immensely creative legacy, the price of this Jewish heritage was also great. It meant that anti-Semitism was programmed into the new discipline: psychoanalysis always embodied the mixed pride and prejudice of being a 'Jewish science', provoking erratic emotions amongst its adherents and opponents, Jewish and non-Jewish alike. This 'virus', carried by psychoanalysis throughout its early history, burst into activity in Germany when the Nazis came to power, with effects that have been visible ever since.

If psychoanalysts in certain circumstances *enacted* anti-Semitism, one might also ask of them that they should be capable of *understanding* it. After all, anti-Semitism has many of the attributes of the excessive, self-damaging, irrational and yet persistent psychopathological complexes that are the meat and drink of psychoanalysis' clinical and theoretical activity. Few other social phenomena are better set up for psychoanalytic exploration, because the intensity of anti-Semitism, its perseverance over generations, its continued operations even in the absence of Jews, and its characteristic failure to be in tune with reality, all have the hallmarks of a phenomenon saturated with unconscious emotion. Add to this the particular relevance of anti-Semitism for understanding psychoanalysis itself, and this seems a research seam of such potential richness that it could not be missed. As will be seen, however, whilst there have been creative attempts to theorise anti-Semitism from a psychoanalytic perspective, the work overall has been disappointingly limited, leading one to ask whether there is something in psychoanalysis itself that creates a systematic blind spot in this area.

It is curious to note, given how explicit Freud was about anti-Semitism and how powerfully Nazism impacted upon the psychoanalytic movement, that very little has been written about anti-Semitism from a psychoanalytic perspective, and that whilst there was some notable work by European Jewish émigrés after the war, by the 1960s psychoanalytic explorations of anti-Semitism had dried up (Bergman, 1988). Ostow (1996a, p. 4) comments on this,

> Aside from Freud's many references to antisemitism in a number of papers, psychoanalytic literature was relatively silent about the matter until the Nazi period. When European psychoanalysts reached safety, a few of them undertook an essay, or in a few cases even a book, on the subject. For the most part, these offered explanations based upon the common defense mechanisms of displacement and projection, yielding the scapegoat theory and Oedipal determination. Some spoke of the influence of Christian mythology, especially the charge of deicide and the symbolism of the mass. Others attempted an approach via group psychology.

However, at least until the stirring events of the 1985 Hamburg conference let various cats out of the bag, this work on anti-Semitism was desultory at best and, as will be argued below, failed in particular to develop a set of concepts attuned to the pervasiveness of anti-Semitic phenomena. Indeed, Freud's own work in this area – as in many other areas, one might suggest – remained well ahead of that of his followers, despite advances in historical and cultural theory that meant they had much better explanatory resources upon which to draw. Ostow is actually of the opinion that the early analysts' avoidance of contestation of anti-Semitism alongside their active repudiation of religion represented more than just a statement about scientific priorities.

> With respect to the early generations of analysts, if we consider their general derogation of the Jewish religion and its practitioners; their failure to express an interest in Jewish affairs and Jewish destiny until the confrontation with Nazism made these issues unavoidable;

their reductionist and simplistic efforts to 'analyze' Jewish religious
ritual and liturgy with which they were barely familiar, while simultaneously taking no psychoanalytic interest in antisemitism with
which they were very familiar, we are forced to infer the existence of
a degree of Jewish shame and self-hatred.   (ibid., p. 24)

Such a psychological reading of the early analysts' behaviour is supported by consideration of their cultural context, which provoked
them to try to distance themselves from the East European stereotypes
of the Jew as part of their own assimilationist strategy for coping with
anti-Semitism. As has been seen, even Freud was not immune from this
dynamic; and the psychoanalysts' appeasement policy towards the
Nazis during the 1930s might be seen as the extension of an attitude
that anti-Semitism would cease if the Jews would only hide. Non-
Jewish analysts also bought into this attitude, with Ernest Jones exem-
plifying the ambivalence surrounding their involvement with the
'Jewish science'. As late as 1951, in his paper, 'On the Psychology of
the Jewish Question', Jones could locate a source of anti-Semitism in
Jewish separatism and their 'superiority complex', as well as, following
Freud, to circumcision and castration anxiety. The most likely solution
to anti-Semitism, according to Jones, was assimilation into the surrounding community.

Freud's account of anti-Semitism, as we have seen, is rather more
thorough, focusing on how the Jew represents elements in the anti-
Semite's psychic constitution that are uncomfortable or threatening,
and are consequently repudiated, yet are also objects of fascination.
Because of the history of Christian anti-Semitism, which laid the
important mythological groundwork for the pervasiveness of anti-
Semitic beliefs in Western culture, the Jew is the chosen carrier of these
unwanted yet seductive projections. In addition, there are real attributes of Jews and Judaism (such as circumcision, monotheism, and the
idea of the 'chosen people') that fuel this set of compelling myths. In
the limited bibliography of psychoanalytic studies of anti-Semitism,
this generally Freudian account has continued to hold sway. Knafo's
(1999, p. 36) list of themes included in 'the more salient early attempts
to explain' anti-Semitism remain true of later attempts too, and can
mainly be traced back to Freud: 'displacement, projection, scapegoat-
ing, castration anxiety (as linked to circumcision), latent homosexuality, sibling rivalry, intolerance of small differences, rejection of dark
pigmentation because of its association with feces, Jewish disavowal of
the murder of the father, Jewish masochism, psychopathy, paranoia,

and envy of the Chosen People.' These 'themes' have helped to fill out the possible dynamics of the anti-Semitic state of mind, but also reveal something of the limits of psychoanalysis when faced with such a complex, emotive, psychosocial phenomenon.

Anti-Semites on the couch

One might have thought that the catastrophic events of the Nazi period would be a spur to detailed psychoanalytic investigations of the motivation for, and capacity to engage virulently in, anti-Semitism, yet this was the case to only a small extent. The relative silence of psychoanalysis on the topic is especially audible in reports on clinical work with anti-Semitic patients, where there are very few studies and where those that have been carried out have been concerned mostly not with cases of strong anti-Semitic belief or activity, but with patients (several of them Jewish) who have expressed some anti-Semitic sentiments in the course of the work. Loewenstein (1952) presents a clinically-oriented account of anti-Semitism that begins with an acknowledgement of the fact that, 'The cases which are best known to us and which furnish particularly good opportunities for studying the problem, are those in which the patient exhibits only a latent or moderate degree of anti-Semitism when he comes for treatment' (p. 37). Over the course of therapy, however, such patients tend 'suddenly' to reveal 'strong anti-Semitic prejudice', leading Loewenstein to believe that the dynamics involved are those present in anti-Semites generally. In fact, Loewenstein implies that there is no real need to make these kinds of distinctions, at least amongst non-Jews, because the power of anti-Semitic stereotypes of the Jews is so great: 'At some point in the course of analysis almost all non-Jewish patients will manifest varying degrees of anti-Semitism' (p. 38). Almost always, the Jew is regarded as a figure of 'fear and hate', and in the transference these feelings become directed towards the analyst, *especially* (though not only) if she or he is Jewish. Presumably, the ethnicity of the analyst is not a crucial factor here because psychoanalysis itself is so strongly perceived as 'Jewish'; that is, *all* analysts are Jewish in the minds of their necessarily anti-Semitic patients. This link, however, has an additional psychodynamic meaning that gives it sharpness and poignancy: for Loewenstein, in line with much psychoanalytic thinking on anti-Semitism, what is revealed from the clinical material is the association of the hated Jew with the hated and feared father. For most 'classical' psychoanalysts, the analyst, representing authority, necessarily takes on the attributes of the father, but what is added here is the idea that there is a psychic equivalence between the Jew as represented in social discourse – in particular, as will be seen, in Christian-influenced ideology – and the father, so that the working-out of Oedipal conflicts in the transference brings anti-Semitic impulses to the fore. Additionally, as castration fears emerge so the 'superstitious horror' (p. 40) produced by the Jew's circumcised state becomes manifest; more generally, anti-Semitic patients experience their own 'inadmissible instinctual drives' (p. 39) as placed inside them by the analyst, whose own 'dirty Jewish imagination' is responsible for corrupting their minds. Finally, some anti-Semitic patients show very clearly how sadistic impulses towards the Jews arise:

> Neurotics who suffer from an intense sense of guilt and who live in anticipation of punishment protect themselves by projecting their faults onto the Jewish analyst or onto Jews in general. They would like to see the Jews tortured and punished in order not to feel guilty themselves. To avoid punishment they would like to assume the punitive role themselves.   (p. 40)

This is the 'classic' anti-Semitic dynamic linking the transitory manifestations of anti-Semitism that occur during all analyses with the characteristic state of mind of those who are truly and stably anti-Semites.

A more recent study by Ostow (1996a,b) presents a lengthy account of the work of a large group of analysts plus a couple of academic specialists (including Yerushalmi), which met over an extended period to explore the psychodynamics of anti-Semitism. Ostow comments, 'The first thing we learned was that there were very few antisemites in analysis with members of our group. That was just as true for the patients of the non-Jewish analysts as for the patients of the Jewish analysts... Mostly we dealt with antisemitic comments or sentiments offered by patients who could not be designated as antisemites by any reasonable definition' (Ostow, 1996b, pp. 15–16). In fact, Ostow and his colleagues spent nine years in regular seminars, yet dealt only with ten case histories 'in some depth' and four cases 'less intensively' plus five others who were 'mentioned briefly' (Ostow, 1996a, p. 43). The thinness of their clinical material is thus remarkable given the effort they expended. What they did note was that when anti-Semitic comments occurred, analysts were very reluctant to take them up. Other widely referenced and important studies, such as those deriving from the work of the Institute of Social Research in the 1940s (e.g. Ackerman and Jahoda, 1948; Adorno et al, 1950) similarly used relatively 'mild' instances of anti-Semitism or studied people who were rarely expressive of very strong anti-Semitic sentiments. Even the useful and relatively recent paper by Knafo (1999), set up to redress the silence about anti-Semitism in the clinical setting, is based on only three cases, one of them Jewish and one half-Jewish, and perhaps not surprisingly therefore concludes that the anti-Semitic sentiments brought up during therapy usually turn out, on analysis, to be subsidiary to deeper unconscious concerns. That is, she argues that anti-Semitism in these patients is mainly the form taken by more pervasive conflicts, and should be interpreted as such – not backed away from, for sure, but nevertheless not seen as a powerful psychosocial phenomenon. Whether this claim would hold for genuinely anti-Semitic patients, or in strongly anti-Semitic cultural settings, is a moot point; under such conditions, it might be expected that the specific characteristics and attractions of anti-Semitic ideas could come more strongly into view.

Knafo notes the reluctance of most analysts to engage with anti-Semitism and attributes this to a discomfort that has countertransference roots: 'Our personal oversensitivity and defensiveness with regard to this issue, I believe, frequently results in silence or avoidance, which too often is rationalized as analytic neutrality' (pp. 37–8). This is especially true for Jewish analysts, in her view. But if the failure to engage fully with anti-Semitism arises in part or whole from unresolved traumatic responses on the part of analysts, the effect of this failure is rather strongly to parallel the effect of the German psychoanalysts' failure to deal adequately with the history of their involvement with Nazism: it becomes an invitation to blame the victim, to see the sources of historical and continuing anti-Semitism as lying in the provocations of the victims themselves, the Jews. That is, failure adequately to theorise what might be the dynamic origins and phenomenology of anti-Semitic beliefs and actions does precisely what psychoanalysis has been accused of elsewhere: it directs the light of interrogation towards places where it does not belong; it states, 'if we can say nothing of the perpetrators, then we are left only with the psychology of the victims.' Chasseguet-Smirgel (1987), as described in the previous chapter, pointed out how this phenomenon could operate in relation to the psychoanalysts' culpability under Nazism: Freud himself got blamed. Here, in a parallel argument, is a bitter outburst from Kijak (1989, p. 217).

> Over the twenty years during which I have participated in the psychoanalytic world, I have frequently read and heard variations on the theme of the participation of the victims in their own destruc-

tion. The causes of this participation may be found, according to these psychoanalysts, in the predominance of Thanatos, in the masochism of the Jews, in unconscious guilt, in submission to castrating parents, in the fact of generating the hatred of their neighbours through their behaviour and habits, in the use of pathological defences to impede the perception of danger, and many other like explanations. All these opinions express a common ignorance of the historical context in which the events occurred and also express the desire to apply theories taken from individual psychopathology to phenomena of such complexity as the Holocaust.

Kijak goes on to argue that, 'We can infer that forcing such complex situations into the Procrustean bed of previous opinions and theories is a result of the inability to face the painful facts, to recognize such a high degree of perfected aggressiveness as mankind had never before reached' (p. 218), a suggestion that carefully avoids attributing responsibility to any sustained anti-Semitism amongst analysts themselves. Rather, what is suggested is that the sheer magnitude of Nazi brutality during the Shoah has still not been processed – or had not been at the time Kijak was writing, more than forty years after the event – and that instead analysts engaged in defensive manoeuvres to reduce what was felt to be unknowable (or at least unbelievable or unprocessable) into what was more familiar, the already-known. Where an honest attempt to articulate the murderous form of anti-Semitism embodied in Nazism failed, recourse to blaming the victim followed.

There are a number of strands of thought here, which need to be disentangled. Psychologising explanations of systematically social phenomena such as anti-Semitism need to be placed within a context in which, at the very least, there is acknowledgement of the power of the social; the 'blaming the victim' school of (avoidance of) thought fails to do this, but many psychoanalysts have been scrupulous in setting their attempts to theorise anti-Semitism in its broader context. Simmel (1946a, p. xx), for example, introducing the volume of essays that arose out of a symposium on anti-Semitism commissioned by the San Francisco Psychoanalytic Society, asserts that 'It is only through psychoanalysis that we can hope to shed some light on [the anti-Semite's] obscure entanglement of irrational hatred and neurotic misery,' but then goes on immediately to make this subordinate to social forces.

However, anti-Semitism cannot be understood merely through an understanding of the anti-Semitic individual. It is his problem, to be sure, but beyond this it is a social problem involving political groups, classes and nations.

The general agreement amongst psychoanalytic investigators is that anti-Semitism is the expression of a more generic type of pathological prejudice, taking the specific form it does because of the way in which anti-Jewish stereotypes and beliefs are endemic in western society. Psychoanalysis, because it is a method of investigating the minds of *individuals* is appropriately limited in its contribution to what Fenichel (1946, p. 11), writing in the same volume as Simmel, calls 'the psycho-analysis of the anti-Semite, not of anti-Semitism'. As he phrases it, 'The question is what can the comparison of psychoanalyses of many anti-Semites contribute to an understanding of the social phenomenon of anti-Semitism?' Fenichel has a clear account of what it *cannot* do: 'After a study of the influences determining the structure of the anti-Semitic personality and of how this structure functions, the questions of the genesis of these influences and of the social function of the anti-Semitic reaction still remain unanswered' (p. 12). In essence, the restricted claim of these politically highly sophisticated analysts is that psychoanalysis can offer accounts of the internal dynamics of the anti-Semitic individual – a crucial component of any complete theory – but that anti-Semitism itself, as a social phenomenon, requires explanation at a different level. For Fenichel, drawing on his background in Marxist theory, this is a primarily economic level of explanation: given a situation of social disorder, the misery experienced by people is matched by a lack of clarity as to the causes of this misery, 'partly because the underlying causes are too complicated, and partly because the existing ruling class does everything in its power to obscure the true causes' (p. 15). Under these circumstances, the victim of this social disorder seeks 'someone in the environment' who can feasibly be seen as the cause of the misery. 'For centuries,' writes Fenichel (ibid.), 'it has been the Jew, in his role as money lender and as tradesman, who has appeared to those confronted with financial need as the representative of money, regardless of how much Jewish poverty there prevailed at the same time.'

Ackerman and Jahoda (1948, pp. 243–4) express a similar idea about the relationship between individual pathology and social hatred as follows.

The common denominator underlying an anti-Semitic reaction in our cases is, thus, not a similarity of psychiatric symptoms, or total character structure, but rather the common presence of certain specific emotional dispositions. These trends are not in themselves specific for the production of anti-Semitism. They may as well be the dynamic basis for other irrational group hostilities. Undoubtedly, they can exist without anti-Semitism. But in the culture in which our patients live, anti-Semitism does not develop without these character trends. They represent, therefore, an emotional predisposition, a necessary though not sufficient cause of anti-Semitism. In a different culture these character traits may be released in some other hostility reaction.

Thus, the 'emotional predisposition' for irrational group hostilities is laid down through particular developmental experiences and becomes part of the character structure of the individual; their expression as anti-Semitism is due to the 'culture'; a different culture would produce different types of 'hostility reaction'. Ostow's (1996b, p. 15) view is similar, albeit couched in a more extended historical analysis; he too places weight on the social ('stereotypical myths') as overriding what he terms 'individual dynamics'.

After the definitive secession of early Jewish and Gentile Christ followers from the Jewish community at the end of the first century Common Era, the Jews were stigmatised and demonised by them and by the early Church fathers and labelled as a principle of evil, along with Satan, that was to blame for all Christian misfortune. The many antisemitic myths that evolved throughout the history of the Christian West all concurred in this theme. Apocalyptic thinking required such a principle as the source of the death phase, so that the elimination of Jews became the condition for the rebirth phase. In the presence of a sense of disorganisation and chaos, societies congeal into fundamentalist groups that require a mythic enemy. These groups tend to cultivate apocalyptic paranoia. Under those circumstances, anti-Jewish sentiment and discrimination become active persecution.

What is particularly interesting about this analysis is that anti-Semitism is viewed as the product of many centuries of Christian myth-making, interpreted according to psychodynamic principles. Ostow holds that Christianity needed an enemy in order to create its own mythology of death-and-rebirth, and the Jews were selected as such because of the fact that Christianity had begun as a 'secession' from Judaism and thus benefited from heaping abuse on its progenitor. The explanatory structure here reads cultures much as it reads individuals: just as the psychic equilibrium of a person might be maintained by the 'myth-making' propensity to project hostile urges into an outside other, so Christian culture as a whole maintained its own organisation by the construction of Jews as the despised other. When external pressures are particularly hard, individuals project more strongly and with more extreme content to their projections; the same is true of cultures: 'In the presence of a sense of disorganisation and chaos, societies congeal into fundamentalist groups that require a mythic enemy' and persecution follows.

Despite the emotional power of this kind of historical conjecture, one has to ask whether it really solves the problem of welding together social and psychoanalytic perceptions. It seems rather to reduce the social to the individual, treating an entire (and very complex) culture as if it has the kinds of feelings and disturbances that can be observed in analytic patients. Nevertheless, Ostow's account is socially interesting in its implication that the 'stereotypical myths' promoted by the culture may be best viewed not as empty vessels into which individual psychopathology is channelled (the disturbed person becomes anti-Semitic because culture makes available that route for expression of the disturbance), but rather as forces that construct forms of consciousness, that is, that make subjects in their image. Put more simply, the social inheritance of anti-Semitism is so powerful that it serves as one of the building blocks upon which western subjectivity is built. This is the case despite Christianity's relative loss of power in the past two hundred years: as many scholars have shown (e.g. Gilman, 1991), the Christian heritage of anti-Semitism has been passed down very firmly through biological, racial and social theories to retain considerable hold amongst those in the west, even if the traditional imagery of what Ostow terms the 'principle of evil' is no longer as widespread as it was. This kind of heritage is not just a channel for expression of emotional disturbance, though it can be useful as such; it is, rather, a way in which the unconscious dynamics of each person's psyche are marked. Jews and non-Jews of all kinds have a connection to anti-Semitism, are 'positioned' in relation to it, and its expression in an individual therefore needs to be understood as a manifestation of a social force. There is no magic here, nor does it require an appeal to a Jungian 'collective unconscious'; rather, anti-Semitism is so embedded in the culture that it can be understood as one of the taken-for-granted kernels of meaning out of which each western subject is constructed. Žižek (1997,

p. 76) comments, 'The (anti-Semitic figure of the) "Jew" is not the positive cause of social imbalance and antagonisms: social antagonism comes first, and the "Jew" merely gives body to this obstacle.' Culture's investment in this figure of the 'Jew' produces it as an element in the unconscious, and with it arises the widespreadness of anti-Semitism itself.

A Christian disease

Freud's analysis of anti-Semitism as arising out of Christianity's sibling rivalry and displaced guilt for parricide is a theme taken up strongly in the post-Freudian literature. For some earlier writers, there is a direct relationship between the emotional ambiguities of Christianity itself and the construction of an anti-Semitic vessel to 'hold' these antagonisms in place. Simmel (1946b), for instance, proposes that deicidal wishes are provoked and expressed by the Christian ceremony of eating the holy wafer (devouring the Lamb of God), but such wishes are untenable, and hence are projected outwards. The projection finds as its historically-constructed target the Jew, to whom this murderous inclination becomes attributed. Thus, anti-Semitism arises from the guilt feelings of Christians due to their own ambivalence. Simmel sees a direct link between this dynamic of Christian anti-Semitism and the fantasies held and played on by the Nazis.

> The Hitler blood accusations against the Jew – that he wants to defile Aryan blood by penetration – is nothing but the well-known projection of denying one's own devouring tendencies by accusing the Jews. In a different form, it is a repetition of the accusation of the desecration of the holy wafer: the Jew causes the bleeding of the wafer which, to the anti-Semite, signifies the actual body of Christ.   (p. 63)

Rappaport (1975) presented a more 'environmental' account of how the individual might suffer from Christian influences experienced during childhood, suggesting that the 'anguish' of the anti-Semite is 'caused by his futile resistance against a sick, irrational behavior pattern which he introjected in the early years of his childhood when he was exposed without protection to the unmitigated influence of his environment, parents and educators' (p. i). The crucifix, with its celebration of death, is impressed on the consciousness of the child, producing unmanageable anxiety about death; as a way of defending against this anxiety, the child develops compulsions, delusions and doubts and an unconscious disbelief in the divinity of Jesus. This disbelief is projected onto the Jews as the people defined by their lack of belief; accompanying the projection is all the intense angst of the death-disturbed individual. Under the right social conditions, in which uncertainty and threat are dominant, these individual histories can become the dynamic fuelling an entire social movement.

Loewenstein's (1952, p. 44) exploration of what can be learnt from expressions of anti-Semitic prejudice during analysis also offers a kind of 'developmental' account of the impact of Christianity on the child, linking it in a familiar way with Oedipal conflicts.

> The Jews, who are described in the gospels as unbelievers and executioners of Christ, become in the imagination of the child so taught the symbols of these bad instincts, the incarnation of every wickedness the child has repressed in himself. On the other hand, since the Christian child identifies with the Son of God, God the Father whom the Jews recognize becomes associated in his mind with the Jews. The Jews are pictured in his mind as the 'elders', the older generation – in other words, they become the transformed image of his own father. Thus, the ancient conflict between Christ and the Jews which took place nineteen hundred years ago reflects the child's own past conflicts with his father, and becomes the unconscious symbol of his Oedipus complex.

In addition to this schematic account of how the Jew and the father might become associated in the child's mind, Loewenstein also argues a more general historical point that for the Christian the association of the Jews with the crucifixion means that the Jews were necessary for the founding of their own religion. That is, the Jews were (in Christian mythology) actually responsible for the act making Christianity possible; psychologically, they enacted the aggressive wishes embedded in each child's Oedipal struggle. 'The Jew,' writes Loewenstein (pp. 44–5), 'is held responsible for the crime from which the Christian reaps moral and psychological benefit in redemption from sin. Thus, the Christian child learns not only that the Jews were essential to Christianity in the past; he learns that they can serve even now as the scapegoat for the personal sins of every Christian.' Mixing together theological and psychological stories, the child imbibes the notion that the Jews are both essential and despised, that she or he is connected to them, even dependent upon them, but that they are also the carriers of hate. In this theory, an irrational set of socio-historical beliefs and claims about the Jews fits neatly with the irrationality of unconscious, Oedipal conflicts to provide a satisfying outlet for the child's – and later the adult's – imperfectly formulated yet continuously troubling aggressive impulses.

Grunberger (1964, 1989), whose account of the narcissistic compo-nent of anti-Semitism (discussed in the next chapter) represents one of the most compelling psychoanalytic conceptualisations of the phe-nomenon, also roots his understanding of its systematic nature in the history of Christianity. A key element in the argument derives from Freud's formulation of monotheistic Judaism as an advance on Christianity, or rather the latter as a regression away from the greater abstraction and father-centredness of the former – a formulation that, as Boyarin (1997) has shown, can itself be understood in part as a response to the anti-Semitic association of Jews and Judaism with 'sensual' femininity. Grunberger similarly characterises Judaism as an Oedipal religion, whereas Christianity is more narcissistic (1989, p. 85).

> Monotheism in cathecting the father as an object has obscured reli-gion and cooled it down. In taking away the maternal figure, as Freud has shown, religion has favoured spirituality, but also removed that source of warmth and love, the mother. Christianity later repaired this frustration by deifying the maternal figure, but on a plane already transformed by the collective superego. This led to an exacerbation of the conflict in the Judaeo-Christian unconscious. *The Christian, the son, is in effect reunited with the mother, the father having been deported to heaven*, an oedipal realisation, one which has increased the Christian's guilt in respect to the Jews who have kept their fidelity to the father.   (Grunberger, 1964, p. 383; italics in original)

In Grunberger's account, Christianity appeared at a point in history when, because of the Roman oppression, the unflinching judgemental-ism of Oedipal Judaism, with its emphasis on law, morality and facing reality, gave insufficient succour to a needy people. Christianity then arose as a messianic movement structured around a narcissistic return, a search for the mother who can enfold the believer in her arms, who can, in effect, make reality go away. '*The superego position becomes untenable*, and an idealised form of a return to the narcissistic illusion begins... all the dominant and characteristic features of the religion of Christ... *derive their affective charge from primary narcissism, and represent a challenge to reality and to the order of the father.* The Father is, at least in theological terms, still present, but *this massive narcissistic cathexis* takes as its object the Son, and then the Mother. It is also important to note, finally, that the economy of human sacrifice reasserts itself, and becomes central (the sacrifice of Christ is re-enacted in the Mass)' (Grunberger, 1989, p. 86). Anti-Semitism thus arises as an outcrop of the hostility of the narcissistic maternal religion for the Oedipal judgements of the internalised super-ego; the Jew instantiates the continuation of guilt at the murder/abandonment of the father, thus attracting the hostility of the Christian, which itself is born out of ambivalence. As with the other quoted theories, this one makes the Christian's own guilty hostility the source of anti-Semitic prejudice; the Jew becomes the object of hate because his or her very existence is a reminder that an act of violent repudiation – here, of the father – has occurred.

An obvious rejoinder to these approaches casting the sources of anti-Semitism in Christian hostility towards Judaism, is that Christianity (despite its strength in the USA) no longer has much hold over the beliefs and imagination of the West. Indeed, the most profound anti-Semitic movement of the twentieth century, Nazism, was antagonistic towards Christianity even as it was murderous towards Jews, and *religious* opposition to Judaism was not the main feature of its ideology. The declining power of Christianity was in fact very well established by Freud's time, so there is a sense in which even his theorising on the Christian underpinning of anti-Semitism was anachronistic. 'Racial' and cultural anti-Semitism had long been dominant over religious anti-Semitism, and secularism was as pervasive amongst non-Jews as it was amongst Western Jews like Freud. This suggests that what these psychoanalytic theories are explaining is a dimension of Christian anti-Semitism which may have very limited applicability to modern anti-Semitic phenomena, including the Nazi Holocaust – an ironic situation given that it was precisely that enormous event that motivated most post-Freudian explanations.

The response to this criticism is that whilst Christianity itself may have declined in significance, its heritage lives on in the categories of thought available within Western society. Cultures develop and change, of course, but they do so whilst also perpetuating the basic assumptions concerning experience and perception that have founded them. This can be seen in the stereotyping and mythologising that people engage in when trying to make sense of their lives, perhaps particularly when searching for explanations of troubling phenomena, or indeed – more psychodynamically – when trying to find ways of alleviating their distress and confusion. If people usually proceed through life by creating 'reasonable' narratives of existence, giving accounts of their experiences that make sense and that portray them in a fairly benign light, then it has to be recognised that there are situations and times in which such narratives are very hard to construct, and individuals and social groups who – perhaps because of the nature of their past experiences – are particularly prone to struggle to create such narratives. These 'breaches' in narrative coherence demand repairing, and the way in which this happens is usually to have recourse to some powerful cultural story, a 'myth', that can be bought into and make for a persuasive narrative account. As a result of its two thousand year history, the Christian story about the Jews is one such cultural myth; even without its theological components, the stereotypes and assumptions that it has consistently promoted are so powerfully engrained in Western culture that they surface whenever an enemy is needed, wherever a plot has to be invented to deal with failure or confusion.

Ostow (1996a, pp. 135–6) follows this general line of argument in defining the 'essence of anti-Semitism':

> In each case some person or persons are blamed for current distress, whether or not there is a real reason for that blame. In each case the Jew or the Jewish community is selected for the role and a myth is created that explains how the Jew brings about Christian suffering. That, I would suggest, is the essence of antisemitism, the readiness to select the Jew as the responsible agent. I would attribute that readiness to the continuing influence of Christian authority, both ecclesiastic and lay, preachers and parents, in so stigmatising the Jews since the composition of the Christian Scriptures. Even the Nazis who had no great respect for Christianity, had each absorbed in childhood the message of Jewish culpability. In every case, the Jew is the principle of evil.

'Early Christian teachings,' comments Ostow (p. 176), 'to the effect that the principle of evil is the Jew, have been passed on through the ages and have remained active even among "post-Christian" anti-semites.' The mechanism for this seems to be in childhood experiences, with an assumption that each individual anti-Semite has been exposed to 'the message of Jewish culpability'; one might see this as a direct parental message, but it could also be, simply, that there is an unconscious way in which the culture speaks anti-Semitism, in which it makes anti-Semitic sentiment available automatically as an explanation for everything that goes wrong.

Ostow's own account of the mythological component of anti-Semitism is focused on this idea of the Jews as a constructed 'principle of evil'. From their small number of cases and analyses of literary and mythological material, Ostow and his colleagues concluded that while every instance showed a 'psychologic origin' to anti-Semitism rooted in the need to deal with personal unhappiness, the standardised, stereotypical elements in anti-Semitic rhetoric dominated: 'In every instance, individual differences and idiosyncrasies were overridden by these stereotypical myths' (Ostow, 1996b, p. 16). This was even though the variety of accusations against Jews was very great: linking them was the 'the proposition that the Jew is dangerous because of his hostile designs and because he is alien' (ibid., p. 21). For Ostow, in a move that echoes Freud's own belief in the superiority of Judaism over its rivals, this anti-Semitic impulse represents a kind of return to polytheism by those who cannot face the stringent logic of true monotheism. The monotheistic position is one in which there is no 'principle of evil', but rather a complex deity in which suffering and goodness are united; anti-Semitism, by contrast, is built on the idea that destructiveness must be separated from goodness, so that there is something outside the deity that represents the negative. In this case, it is the Jew who carries the responsibility for evil:

> Other religions have offered religious dualism and polytheism as explanations for evil. The monotheistic religions had to find room for evil within their own domain. The explanation offered by Christianity was that the flow of God's benevolence was obstructed by the Jews. Because what was proposed did not square with what could be seen of the Jews, considering their poverty, lack of power and usually unexceptionable behaviour, it was proposed that Jewish power and malevolence operated secretly. Jews conspired to destroy Christendom, which was therefore justified in persecuting Jews even in the absence of visible evidence of malevolence.   (Ostow 1996a, p. 176; 1996b, p. 28)

In particular, those who are of an 'apocalyptic frame of mind' are attracted to this belief that Jews block the flow of God's goodness to Christians; they are of such a frame of mind because of their own personal experience or perhaps because of 'community misfortune'. 'Apocalypse combines the illusion of Jewish fault with the need to attack and destroy, and yields the illusion of rebirth' (Ostow, 1996a, p. 176). Thus, while anti-Semitism is not correlated with any specific type of psychopathology and is expressed in various ways, its core belief is that Jews are the source of suffering; this paranoid idea derives from the long history of Christian mythologising about Jews, which itself is motivated sometimes by 'realistic' aspects of the relationship with Jews (for example, economic rivalry), but more profoundly by the inability to countenance suffering. The Jew is not so much a scapegoat here, in the sense of bearing the non-Jew's own hateful feelings, but rather offers a narrative framework through which emotional confusion and distress can be managed. Why the Jew? As before, because Christianity has constructed Jews as recalcitrant non-believers, and hence as evil, and the permeation of this presentation throughout Christian culture has continued, in its derivations as racial and cultural anti-Semitism (the Jew as poisoner of the *Volk*, for example), into modern times. The imperviousness of anti-Semitic stereotypes to reason, the existence of anti-Semitism even in the absence of Jews, suggests that these myths serve significant psychic as well as social functions, and that these functions parallel one another. At both social and individual levels, they offer a framework through which suffering can be separated into the 'other', which can then be the object of assault, so allowing personal and social integrity to be maintained. This notion, that the function of the Jew for the anti-Semite is to secure the inner world against doubt or dissolution by constructing a mythological external enemy, is common to many psychoanalytic accounts of anti-Semitism; in Ostow's (1996b, p. 22) version, 'Even when the Christian is attacked by a third party, he believes that he has two enemies, the real enemy and the Jew who caused the misfortune to come about. In fact, he reverses their significance: he considers the mythical enemy real and the real enemy accidental.'

It can be seen that the account of anti-Semitism as deriving from Christian mythologising culminates in a view of the individual anti-Semite as 'suffering' from an inability to integrate painful with benign aspects of the personality – that is, there is a failure to tolerate ambivalence. In Ostow's account, the Jew becomes blamed for everything damaging; anti-Semitic ideation is a kind of lazy way of producing a narrative of good and evil, building easily on time-worn stereotypes. Other psychoanalytic theories are a little different, seeing the Jew as holding aspects of the anti-Semite's own personality; whatever its rather concrete formulation, Simmel's (1946b) notion that the Christian's ambivalence towards Christianity is projected into the

Jew has an intriguing psychological complexity about it. Still other theories, less concerned with the links between anti-Semitism and Christianity, have been more inclined to see anti-Semitism as reflecting a variety of modes of psychic disorganisation; in particular, some of these have claimed that anti-Semitism is connected to borderline or psychotic ways of thinking, and that the Jew as hate figure is therefore needed to keep the disturbed psyche intact. These ideas are considered in the next chapter.

7
Psychoanalysis of Anti-Semitism II: Splitting and Narcissism

The enemy outside

The idea that the Jews as a separate and historically denigrated 'out-group' serve as suitable cultural recipients for the split-off, unacceptable elements of the anti-Semite's psyche is a pervasive one in psychoanalytic theorising on the subject. The general notion is that psychic life is made up of contradictory unconscious impulses or ideas sufficiently defended against so that they can be organised into reasonably integrated patterns. Under some circumstances, such as personal or social trauma, those impulses that are most disturbing to the individual are experienced as powerful enough to threaten the person's stability, leading to impending fragmentation and breakdown. Preserving the psyche becomes urgent, a matter of life and death, and extreme measures are often taken to accomplish it, including ejecting the unwanted impulses into some form of outside carrier. This process of ejection, known in psychoanalysis as *projection*, constructs a useful enemy out of what is available in the outside world; in the case of anti-Semitism, the Jew is thus made into the carrier of what is hated and threatening to the integrity of the anti-Semite's psychic life.

The general model here is best described in the language of Melanie Klein (1946), who roots in it normal development. In her view, the very young infant is threatened by the intensity of her or his own destructive emotions and projects them outwards into the mother's breast; this has the relieving effect of reducing the conflict in the psyche, the threat from within, but it also creates paranoid sensations, a threat from without. The loved and depended-upon breast becomes also the potential source of attack, as it carries the infant's own projected destructiveness; writ large, this links with the combination of fascination, fear and hatred characteristically shown by people – including racists – for their denigrated 'other'. For Klein, things only improve when the infant experiences the outside world – the giving breast – as primarily benevolent, allowing destructiveness to be over-shadowed by love, producing gratitude and making integration of envious and positive feelings possible. This allows for gradual integra-tion of the psyche without denial of negativity; that is, it makes toler-ance of ambivalence possible, with an accompanying capacity to feel more deeply, for example to experience guilt and loss and form inti-mate relationships. If, however, developmental circumstances are such that the infant never feels secure in the basic loving capacity of the depended-upon other, the paranoid state will be exacerbated and inte-gration will be impossible. The 'paranoid-schizoid position' is then pre-served as the dominant way of experiencing the world, giving rise to continued projection and persecutory feelings, powerful hatred with concomitant anxiety, recourse to splitting, and at the extreme, 'border-line' or psychotic states of mind.

Although explicit deployment of the Kleinian model is not very widespread in psychoanalytic investigations of anti-Semitism, there is much use of the general idea that splitting is engaged in to protect the psyche against its own destructive urges and that these urges are then projected into the hated figure of the Jew. This in turn is held in many accounts to lead to the anti-Semite's characteristic combination of fas-cination with, and derogation of, the Jew – a combination familiar in other instances of racism (Frosh, 1997). Anti-Semitism is thus seen as a mechanism offered by Western culture for maintaining the psychic equilibrium of the disturbed individual, but like all symptom-forma-tions this occurs at the price of damaging the psyche even though its function is to protect it. At the cultural level, Simmel (1946b) draws a familiar parallel here:

> Applying our method of psychoanalytic-dialectic thinking, we must infer not that anti-Semitism annihilates the achievements of civ-ilization, but that the process of civilization itself *produces* anti-Semitism as a pathological symptom-formation, which in turn tends to destroy the soil from which it has grown. Anti-Semitism is a malignant growth on the body of civilization.   (p. 34)

For Simmel, thinking back on the Nazi phenomenon, anti-Semitism is a mass psychosis, a 'social disease', despite the individuals concerned not being psychotic; or rather, it is the existence of this mass psychosis that protects anti-Semites from becoming psychotic themselves. The argument here is that anti-Semitism cannot be thought of as a mass *neurosis*, as some analysts construed it, because neurotics do not form together in the kind of groups that distinguish anti-Semitic mass movements. Rather, although it is the case that there may be various neurotic processes at work within individual anti-Semites (Simmel proposes 'the latent homosexual complex, that complex which produces hate as a defense against the dangers of homosexual love' – p. 35), the individual anti-Semite is 'normal'. However, when this person joins a group the crowd dynamic takes over, distinguished particularly by 'unrestricted aggressive destructiveness under the spell of a delusion' (p. 39) – exactly the characteristics of psychosis. This is also the epitome of the splitting process:

> The anti-Semitic crowd man, for the first time in his life, succeeds in finding a temporary solution of his latent ambivalence conflict with the parent. Through participation in the collective ego of the crowd, he can split in two the re-externalized parental power: into the leader whom he loves and into the Jew whom he hates.   (p. 50)

Culture thus makes available a mechanism through which the personal disturbances of its most vulnerable members can be contained; just as generally a group is given greater coherence if it can find another group to hate, so individuals are made more psychically coherent if they can direct their hatred outwards. Membership of the group in fact protects the individual anti-Semite from individual regression and psychosis (Bergman, 1988). All this further clarifies the comfortable way in which the anti-Semite can live with irrational beliefs: 'The anti-Semite believes in his false accusations against the Jews not in spite of, but *because* of their irrationality. For the ideational content of these accusations is a product of the primary process in his own unconscious and is conveyed to his conscious mind through the mediation of the mass-leader's suggestions' (Simmel, 1946b, pp. 51–2).

What, however, might be the exact contents of these destructive urges and the mechanisms for managing them through anti-Semitism? The notion that the Jew might represent the anti-Semite's own anti-Christian feelings has been described earlier, but those theorists specialising in projection have not limited themselves to considering religious doubts and antagonisms. For some writers, taking their lead from Freud, the key issue is the threat posed by castration, the sense that what is most precious is also most at risk. Glenn (1960), for instance, arising from a study of two patients (the generation of grand theories from small numbers being a characteristic of psychoanalysis), argues that 'the anti-Semite may harbour contradictory attitudes towards Jews. Because the Jew is circumcised, he is held to be castrated and effeminate. For the same reason, he is feared and envied as being virile, aggressive and castrative' (p. 398). Building on some proposals from Fenichel (1946, p. 27), who suggests that circumcision gives the anti-Semite the idea that the Jews might seek sexual retaliation against non-Jews, Glenn argues that the male Jew is seen as both feminine and deficient, but that this also arouses the idea that the Jew is threatening and seeking revenge, making him potentially aggressive and virile, and thus a source of envy. This fantasy is a projection of the anti-Semite's own ambivalence about passivity and activity, femininity and masculinity: 'Making the scapegoat both virile and emasculated facilitates bisexual or homosexual projection. The scapegoat can be hated as father or mother, or as representing the aggressor's own bisexuality' (ibid). Thus it is sexual anxiety in the form of an inability to tolerate homosexual impulses that is at the core of the anti-Semite's discomfort; and the Jew, because of circumcision/castration, is the vessel into which this anxiety is poured.

Fenichel (1946), in one of the last papers he wrote, offers a powerful account of both the social and personal dynamic of anti-Semitic feeling. As noted earlier, he takes the common psychoanalytic position that anti-Semitism arises in periods of socially-induced misery: the anti-Semite, immersed in confusion and led astray by ideological forces, 'sees in the Jew everything which brings him misery – not only his social oppressor but also his own unconscious instincts, which have gained a bloody, dirty, dreadful character from their socially induced repression' (p. 29). Jews are the ideal object for projection of these unconscious urges 'because of the actual peculiarities of Jewish life, the strangeness of their mental culture, their bodily (black) and religious (God of the oppressed peoples) peculiarities, and their old customs' (ibid.), which remind the anti-Semite of 'old primeval powers' which non-Jews have given up (p. 18). Jews have a sense of the uncanny about them because of these peculiarities, which adds to the sense of threat and disgust they provoke. However, the most significant element leading to the intensity of anti-Semitic hate is the way the Jew is the recipient of the anti-Semite's own destructive feelings and also of the fantasised retaliation against them, induced by the individual's own super-ego. That is, both the repressed impulses and the punitive internal response to these urges are projected outwards, onto the Jew.

Anti-Semitism is indeed a condensation of the most contradictory tendencies: instinctual rebellion directed against the authorities and the cruel suppression and punishment of this instinctual rebellion, directed against oneself. Unconsciously for the anti-Semite, the Jew is simultaneously the one against whom he would like to rebel, and the rebellious tendencies within himself.   (p. 20)

Why the Jew? Because 'with his unintelligible language and incomprehensible God' the Jew appears 'uncanny' to the non-Jew, yet recognisable in continuing to hold to 'archaic' customs that were once part of the non-Jew's repertoire: 'rejected instincts and rejected ancient times are revived for them in these incomprehensible people who live as strangers in their midst' (p. 22). Linked to this is a more profound identification between the Jew as foreign and uncanny, and the site of foreignness within: 'It can be expressed in one sentence: one's own unconscious is also foreign. Foreignness is the quality which the Jews and one's own instincts have in common' (p. 20). The Jew as foreigner and preserver of archaic customs can be the object of projection of what is feared and hated within oneself, the 'foreign' unconscious; they thus carry the sense of destruction and desire, of 'what is murderous, dirty and debauched' (p. 19), and racist hate is magnified by the anti-Semite's terror of these inner urges. The idea that racist thought runs together the Jew, the 'other' or foreigner/stranger, and the unconscious as a site of foreignness within one, will be returned to later; the key notion here is that the disturbing awareness of the existence of something strange inside one's own self is made tolerable by projecting that strangeness into the outsider, the desired and despised other.

For Ostow (1996a), the intolerable element in the anti-Semite's psyche is not so much sex as aggression:

We found that those patients who exhibited the most militant or active antisemitism, were people who had difficulty in controlling their anger in general. They seemed to fall into such diagnostic categories as borderline personality disorder or adult attention deficit disorder... We inferred that a problem in the disposition of aggressiveness might conduce to militant antisemitism.   (p. 44)

Noting a 'phasic' alternation between anti-Semitism and philosemitism, Ostow and his colleagues describe a 'family romance' in which the supposed family consciousness of Jews was made into an idealised version of what the person wished for in her or his own family – a way, that is, of resolving ambivalence towards the parents through identifying with an idealised family set-up. However, faced with some real or imagined disappointment in Jews, the opposite pole of this idealisation is invoked and the individual swings round to anti-Semitism, bolstered once again by the available categories for this within the culture at large.

> Antisemitism is generated when there is a real, current, though relatively minor reason for hostility toward Jews and when, at the same time, an antisemitic myth is invoked from the myths that circulate, masked or unmasked, in the surrounding society. The relative importance of these two components varies from occasion to occasion and infrequently, one alone may suffice.   (ibid., p. 61)

What is hypothesised here is that the aggression felt towards the anti-Semite's own disappointing or rejecting family is dealt with initially by imagining a warm home in the Jewish world; however, faced with the inevitable disappointment of these idealised hopes (idealisations themselves being the product of splitting, in which what is fantasised as 'good' is kept absolutely and impossibly separate from any impurities, any 'badness'), revenge is sought, the Jew becomes all-bad, and mental equilibrium is maintained through taking refuge in the available anti-Semitic myths and projecting all evil into them. The mechanism here is a paranoid-schizoid one; hence its associated psychopathology is not neurotic, but 'borderline' or psychotic in type.

Knafo (1999) confirms this idea in her small study of anti-Semitic patients, although she is insistent that anti-Semitic material is not special in kind, but rather is produced just as other material is in the context of the therapeutic transference, and hence is expressive of 'underlying' conflicts 'such as anger, trust, competition, envy, ambivalence and self-esteem [which] are at times conveyed in terms of religious, racial or ethnic stereotypes' (p. 40). Asserting that anti-Semitism in patients is multi-determined and needs to be understood in the context of each individual's psychological situation, Knafo nevertheless allows herself some generalisations. These emphasise the non-neurotic nature of anti-Semitic ideation and also the ways in which it is mistaken to see such ideas as solely negative.

> It is necessary to relinquish the notion that anti-Semitism in patients expresses only hatred or evil. ... transference reactions to therapists who are perceived as Jewish are complex and frequently involve a combination of philo-Semitic, idealized transfer-

ence reactions and anti-Semitic negative transference reactions. Anti-Semitism can therefore serve as a ubiquitous carrier of important messages that are revealed in the analysis of each patient's personality dynamics. Most important, each case reveals how split-off parts of the self can be clothed in anti-Semitic ideology and expressions. Anti-Semitism thus may serve diverse defensive purposes, involving a variety of compromise formations and restitutive functions.   (pp. 58–9)

The difficulties raised for Knafo's formulation by her reliance on a tiny number of patients who could be described only very loosely as 'anti-Semitic' have already been mentioned, but her account is nevertheless characteristic of an approach to anti-Semitism that treats it as a psychological survival technique. Again the emphasis is on splitting and projection, with idealisation and denigration of Jews appearing as aspects of the same dynamic process. Hence the characterisation of the defences in such cases as not neurotic, but rather borderline in kind, relying on the repudiation through projection of unwanted impulses, instead of simply managing the psychic economy through repression. 'Since splitting, in severe cases, is related to dissociation,' writes Knafo (p. 59), 'it is bound to incorporate issues of identity as well. Thus, during anti-Semitic episodes, patients are in what Melanie Klein called the paranoid-schizoid position.' Defences are extreme and rigid, organised around keeping 'goodness' in and 'badness' out; Jews can become the carriers of this badness, but the implication is that this link is in some ways accidental, and that the troubled psyche, if it could not find anti-Semitism as its saving grace, would find something else. What is gained here is an understanding of how anti-Semitism might be heavily invested in by individuals who need to maintain such beliefs because without them they would disintegrate; what is lost is all but the most anodyne appreciation of the specific nature and force of anti-Semitic ideology itself.

A more systematic account of the splitting processes endemic to anti-Semitism is provided in a powerful and now classic paper by Wangh (1964), focused on the Holocaust. This paper is unusual in both describing a set of psychodynamic processes through which anti-Semitism might take hold, and linking this with some historical material – or at least speculations – founded in this case on the history of Germany during and after the First World War. The general psychodynamic account centres on the idea that 'differentiation of self from non-self' is a key achievement in the early developmental period, and that this occurs initially in the context of the boundaries of the mother-child couple, presumably in such experiences as slight frustrations or awareness of absence (p. 387). Later on, further distinctions are made, preoedipally as well as Oedipally, in connection with 'the stranger' outside the mother-infant relationship. Given what Wangh terms a 'defective individuation experience, and a consequently disturbed object relationship', the aggressive impulses which might usually be contained within the bond with the mother become displaced or projected onto the stranger and 'will result in fear of him, which in turn will strengthen the need to seek refuge with the prime object. Ethnocentrism and xenophobia, the polar points of prejudice, have their basic roots in these infantile patterns' (ibid.). As the boundaries of self and not-self are manifestly insecure in these circumstances, the individual's sense of identity remains unstable and threatened by internal aggression; the prejudicial projection of this aggression into the other helps to solidify these boundaries, though at the price of harming the integration of the self.

> Projection and the concomitant intensified clinging to the prime-object are undertaken to aid impulse control, to preserve the love-object, and to preserve the integrity of the self. However, these defensive manoeuvres may have an adverse effect. The more projections take place, the more debilitated become both the sense of reality and the sense of identity. An ever-widening repudiation of that which belongs to the self brings about an ever-increasing need to define the limits of the self in terms of that which is not self through a detailed delineation of the characteristics of the out group. In consequence, the ego knows less and less of its own feelings, and supposedly, more and more of those of the alien group. In this connexion, attention may be drawn to the vast bulk of Nazi publications dealing with the Jews.   (ibid.)

Projection of this kind is a desperate measure, creating an external enemy in order to preserve the self, but at the same time investing that enemy with such dire attributes that it becomes deeply threatening in its own right. This makes the enemy impressive and alluring as well as disgusting, contradictory feelings which can be observed at work in most anti-Semitic and indeed generally racist ideation ('the Negro is as sly and diabolical as he is credulous and naïve; the Jew is at one and the same time ugly and seductive, hoards secret wealth and is given to ostentatious display' – ibid.). More psychoanalytically, Wangh proposes a sexual accompaniment to this ambivalence, fuelling the sense that what is most hated is also in significant ways desired. The *obsession* the anti-Semite has with the Jew takes some explaining, and suggests that there is some way in which the desire of the anti-Semite is mixed up with the object of hatred. This is hypothesised as connected with the threat of object-loss and castration that is part of the deep anxiety about dissolution of boundaries: 'It involves a displacement of hostile object-cathexes and a simultaneous glorification of the object. It constitutes a submissiveness which gives rise to strong passive and passive-homosexual unconscious fantasies' (ibid.). The link between anti-Semitism and an inability to tolerate homosexual desires has been made before; here it is seen as unconsciously confirming to the anti-Semite that there is a threat of castration, an emasculatory process, which itself is often defended against by strong reaction-formation: the anti-Semite exaggerates the femininity of the Jew (supported by classical anti-Semitic ideology) and asserts his own integrity through 'a strenuous exhibition of masculine attributes' (ibid.). The Jew is thus once again feared and despised, seen as weak yet a threat, because what the Jew carries is the anti-Semite's own identity crisis: fear of dissolution accompanied by the rageful attempt to stay alive.

Wangh proposes that the degree of anti-Semitism expressed by an individual will depend both on her or his own characteristics and on aspects of the social situation, such as the possibility of sharing these ideas with others and the power of external political circumstances. In the case of the followers of Nazism, he suggests that they 'were young men affected by the [historical] events of their childhood and early adolescence in such a way as to promote a fixation on sado-masochistic fantasies and on specific defences directed against them; and that under the renewed external crisis regression to this fixation level occurred' (p. 391). These young men saw their fathers go to war and come back defeated, and then saw these same fathers as unable to protect them against the ravages of the economic depression of the early nineteen-twenties, with the concomitant impact on mothers who would be in a state of long-term heightened anxiety. Under such conditions, the psychodynamic complex described above comes into play: the mother's anxiety and the father's weakness produces an internal state of boundary loss and fragile identity, which is kept at bay only by increasingly strong defensive operations, specifically splitting and projection. It also made these youngsters (specifically young *men*, it would appear from the article), prone to regression and sado-masochism, so when the renewed troubles of the nineteen-thirties arose, and with it the Nazi promise of safety and revenge in the mass, the response was immediate and powerful.

> The external calamity of the thirties rekindled the anxiety of the war and post-war years and at the same time reawakened the magic, illogical, sadistic defensive methods of childhood. The former wartime enemy, while denounced, was, in fact, for the time being unassailable. Instead, the stranger within, the Jew, was substituted for him and all aggressive methods against fear could be applied to him with impunity.   (p. 394)

The notion of the 'stranger within' has particular resonance here, acting on both the social and the psychological level. The Jew is the culturally given 'stranger' within European society and hence readily available as the recipient of projections and sadistic impulses; the Jew also represents the unconscious, the 'strangeness' within the psyche, with its femininity and fluidity that is such a threat to the insecure fascist, the one who cannot face the breakdown of boundaries that such fluidity entails.

The gender-insensitive account given by Wangh and many other psychoanalysts can be made to cohere with the kind of material to be found in some other, more flamboyant but also feminist-influenced, explorations of the psychodynamics of Nazism. Theweleit's (1977) influential analysis of the writings of the fascist Freikorps of Weimar Germany is particularly resonant. First, he identifies the deadness of the language of these men and their fetishising of the Fatherland and of the all-male soldier world, and of violence; it is a language with emotion drained from it. Then there is their rejection of womanhood in its sexual forms, shown not only in the conventional splitting of women into good and bad, mothers (and idealised sisters) and whores, but also in a desperate and vicious fantasy of total annihilation of the 'red woman'. This woman is partly phallic, armed and violent, but she is also part of the 'red flood', the tumult that breaks down the barriers protecting both the nation and the self. This flood produces ambivalent feelings: excitement at the sweeping away of frozen and dead things, but terror at the dissolution of identity that this brings in its wake. Against such 'flow', fascism sets up its bulwarks; it is not just ambivalence that is feared, but anything threatening the fantasy of purity, anything, that is, with the stamp of complex reality upon it.

> The monumentalism of fascism would seem to be a safety mechanism against the bewildering multiplicity of the living. The more

lifeless, regimented and monumental reality appears to be, the more secure the men feel. The danger is being-alive itself. (Theweleit, 1977, p. 218)

Later, dealing with the energy displayed in the mass rallies of fascism and Nazism, Theweleit comments,

> Men themselves were now split into a (female) interior and a (male) exterior – the body-armour... What we see being portrayed in the rituals are the armour's separation from, and superiority over, the interior: the interior was allowed to flow, but only within the masculine boundaries of the mass formations. (Theweleit, 1977, p. 434)

Femininity here is something unsettling, disruptive of identity precisely because it is fantasised as 'flow', playing into the masculine anxiety that boundaries will be lost. This too may be a link with the emblem of the Jew, always feminised in the Western imagination, through circumcision/castration and the general notion of hysteria and physical weakness. The Jew and the woman, both of them creatures of the night, both of them somehow alluring yet also castrated and castrating; what better groups into which to pour one's anxiety about dissolution, and with it one's rage over one's incapacity to hold onto a self? Whilst few psychoanalytic explorations of anti-Semitism have really grappled with gender issues, the material deriving from studies such as those of Gilman (1991) and Boyarin (1997) make the link with men's fear of the feminine seem very strong; on the symbolic plane at least, this seems to be a fear that fuels the choice of the Jew as the 'bad object' wherein projected destructiveness finds its home.

The notion of the rigidity of the 'character-armour' of the anti-Semite finds further expression in the classic study of authoritarianism by Adorno et al (1950). This book, *The Authoritarian Personality*, was published as part of a set of works called *Studies in Prejudice* edited by Max Horkheimer and Samuel Flowerman, and sponsored by the American Jewish Committee (Wiggershaus, 1986). *Studies in Prejudice* was an outcome of work by the Institute of Social Research, which had originally been located in the University of Frankfurt and had moved (via Geneva) to New York in 1935 and then California in 1941. Known generically as the 'Frankfurt School', and conceptually as adherents of 'critical theory', this was one of the most influential groups of sociologists and social theorists of the twentieth century. In its American manifestation, it was dominated by Max Horkheimer,

Theodor Adorno, Herbert Marcuse and to a lesser extent Erich Fromm, and deeply embedded in the work of Walter Benjamin, who had died in Nazi Europe. Psychoanalysis was one of the conceptual systems drawn on by the members of the Frankfurt School, and its influence can be seen very profoundly in *The Authoritarian Personality*; but it should be noted that psychoanalytic and psychological concerns were always secondary to social and economic analysis, in the case of anti-Semitism as in other aspects of the Institute's work. In the 1930s, this skew to Marxist and sociological theory was especially marked. For example, Horkheimer's (1938) essay 'The Jews in Europe' 'basically interprets anti-Semitism in terms of its usefulness for monopoly capitalism... considering it as a mere ideological façade for the elimination of an entire sphere of circulation, defined by small banks and the vestiges of a market' (Bronner and Kellner, 1989, p. 7). Even in this article, however, Horkheimer manages to convey the energy and intensity of Nazi anti-Semitism as having its origins in the political and economic sphere, 'intimidat[ing] the populace by showing that the system will stop at nothing,' but also serving psychic needs.

> People can secretly appreciate the cruelty by which they are so outraged. In continents from whose produce all of humanity could live, every beggar fears that the Jewish émigré might deprive him of his living. Reserve armies of the unemployed and the petty bourgeoisie love Hitler all over the world for his anti-Semitism, and the core of the ruling class agrees with that love. By increasing cruelty to the level of absurdity, its horror is mollified... Pity is really the last sin.　(Horkheimer, 1938, p. 92)

At this time, Horkheimer was generally scathing about the uses of psychological theories applied to social phenomena, but his analysis here is already pointing to the emotional hold that terroristic forms of anti-Semitism might have, even over those who ostensibly oppose them.

In the 1940s, the Institute for Social Research became heavily involved in work on anti-Semitism, sponsored from 1943 onwards by the American Jewish Committee. Some of the most influential aspects of this work took the form of a set of psychoanalytically inflected empirical social psychological investigations, with questionnaires such as the famous 'F-Scale' developed by Nevitt Sanford and Daniel Levinson being an important component of the general work and of *The Authoritarian Personality* in particular. For Adorno and Horkheimer, however, the stakes were greater, as studies of anti-Semitism came to be central to their broader theoretical project. Wiggerhaus (1986, p. 275) describes how by 1940 Adorno was seeing the Jews as 'the proletariat of the world-historical process of enlightenment, deprived of every vestige of power', so that analysis of the Jewish situation and of anti-Semitism would cut to the heart of the issues of domination and oppression. Adorno himself developed a vision of the Jews as representing 'nature' (in the form of an attachment to 'nomadism') against the depredations of 'civilised', alienated class society. This results in a form of envy amongst non-Jews, with the Jew representing a happier, less constrained humanity, in which the forces of rationality and alienated labour are kept at bay.

> The image of the Jews is one of a condition of humanity in which work is unknown, and all of the later attacks on the parasitic, miserly character of the Jews are mere rationalizations. The Jews are the ones who have not allowed themselves to be 'civilized' and subjected to the priority of work. This has not been forgiven them, and that is why they are a bone of contention in class society.   (Adorno, letter to Horkheimer, 1940, in Wiggerhaus, 1986, p. 276)

This seems an unlikely portrait of Jews, who throughout the twentieth century were consistently imagined as urban and whose distance from 'nature' was so often used in the rhetoric directed against them. However, it successfully captures a sense of the Jew as standing outside the social order – the Jew as other – that is powerfully engrained in much anti-Semitic thinking and that links with the psychoanalytic focus on how the Jew carries the projected elements of the anti-Semite's psyche. Building on this in their magisterial book, *Dialectic of Enlightenment* (1947), Adorno and Horkheimer make a clear link between Jews and women, understanding the hatred towards them both as similarly deriving from their status as outsiders to the coercive power of domination.

> Women and Jews can be seen not to have ruled for thousands of years. They live, although they could be exterminated; and their fear and weakness, the greater affinity to nature which perennial oppression produces in them, is the very element which gives them life. This enrages the strong, who must pay for their strength with an intense alienation from nature, and must always suppress their fear.   (p. 112)

Where Jews differ from other minorities, however, is in the unusual combination of this association with nature and 'weakness', and the striving of the Jew for something non-material or spiritual – an argument very much akin to Freud's (1939) idea that the key characteristic of Judaism is the belief in an abstract God. Wiggerhaus (1986, p. 341) explains, 'The general image of the Jews which Horkheimer and Adorno presented was one of subjects in whom unconformed nature, and unconformed mind or spirit (*Geist*) were conjoined. In this way they represented, as no other minority did, the opposite of the failed civilization: a relation between mind and nature in which the mind was genuinely the opposite of nature and nature genuinely the opposite of mind.' The impact of this, somewhat as in Freud's theorising, is to bring out the envy in those who are subject to the 'failed civilisation'.

Although the Institute for Social research's work on anti-Semitism had a number of components, in terms of a contribution to psychoanalytic thinking, it is *The Authoritarian Personality* (Adorno et al, 1950) that has overwhelming importance. This book emphasises that the 'responsibility' for anti-Semitism lies with the anti-Semite, and that there is nothing in the 'specific nature' of the Jew that is the source of anti-Semitic feeling: 'anti-Semitism is not so much dependent on the nature of the object as upon the subject's own psychological wants and needs' (p. 301). However, the figure of the Jew has usefully been the subject of cultural and historical abuse and so constitutes a ready-made container for the destructive urges of the anti-Semite. Adorno et al hold to a view that individuals are systematically misled by ideology into misreading their own sense of frustration as having a specific external cause, rather than as embedded in the social order; faced with psychological pressure leading to breakdown, their balance is maintained if they can find somewhere for their aggression to go.

> We start with the general assumption that the – largely unconscious – hostility resulting from frustration and repression and socially diverted from its true object, *needs* a substitute object through which it may obtain a realistic aspect and thus dodge, as it were, more radical manifestations of a blocking of a subject's relationship to reality, e.g. psychosis.   (pp. 299–300)

Jews are suitable 'substitute objects' because of the work that has been done on them historically in the culture, producing a fantasy that is compelling, rigid, and exhaustive.

> The 'object' of unconscious destructiveness, far from being a superficial 'scapegoat', must have certain characteristics in order to

fulfil its role. It must be tangible enough; and yet not *too* tangible, lest it be exploded by its own realism. It must have a sufficient historical backing and appear as an indisputable element of tradition. It must be defined in rigid and well-known stereotypes. Finally, the object must possess features, or at least be capable of being perceived and interpreted in terms of features, which harmonize with the destructive tendencies of the prejudiced subject... There can be hardly any doubt that all these requirements are fulfilled by the phenomenon of the Jew.   (ibid.)

The Jew is the ideal, prepared-for hated other for the disturbed individual, who latches onto this escape route in order to preserve her or his psychic integrity when faced with internal destructiveness and an oppressive social order. Added to this is the systematic confusion of the prejudiced person, the sense of being alienated from society, of not understanding how it works or what are the sources of its actual impact. Politically unsophisticated, the anti-Semite seeks respite from a mystifying reality in the reassuring story of the single enemy, a rigid narrative of existence strong enough, and widely-shared enough, to seem to make sense. The Jew's own 'alienness' serves as shorthand for the alien nature of society itself, but the materiality of the Jew makes her or him accessible as an object of hate in the way that society in general is not. 'Charging the Jews with all existing evils seems to penetrate the darkness of reality like a searchlight and to allow for quick and all-comprising orientation. The less anti-Jewish imagery is related to actual experience and the more it is kept "pure", as it were, from contamination with reality, the less it seems to be exposed to disturbance by the dialectics of experience, which it keeps away through its own rigidity' (p. 310).

The search for purity, both pure goodness within and pure evil without, is another key element in the anti-Semite's consciousness; it forms the basis of what Adorno et al refer to as 'psychological totalitarianism', the impulse to keep everything completely in its place, under the sway of one powerful, paranoid organising principle. The cost of this is great: the anti-Semite lives in terror of the persecutory universe she or he has created, but the benefit is that at least this universe makes sense, and nominates one single, identifiable source of danger – the Jew.

It is as if the anti-Semite could not sleep quietly until he has transformed the whole world into the very same paranoid system by which he is beset: the Nazis went far beyond their official anti-Semitic programme. This mechanism makes for the complete disproportion between 'guilt' and punishment. The extreme anti-Semite cannot stop... Hatred is reproduced and enhanced in an almost autonomized, compulsive manner which is both utterly detached from the reality of the object and completely alien to the ego.... The extreme anti-Semite silences the remnant of his own conscience by the extremeness of his attitude. He seems to terrorize himself while he terrorizes others.   (pp. 324–5)

This compellingly captures both the extremity of the anti-Semitic state of mind and its perversity: it is a kind of addiction demanding more and more intense satisfaction if it is not to leave the subject gasping for air. Any 'difference' becomes a threat and has to be wiped out, yet the more tightly the boundaries around what is acceptable and 'same' are drawn, the more likely it is that difference of one form or another will be encountered. So it is that the capacity of the self to tolerate anything 'outside' is continuously reduced, and the intensity of hatred of all that is other is exponentially increased. The Jew becomes a figure chosen initially for its cultural congruence as a hate object, but then excessively invested in as a carrier of all this otherness; in a kind of parody of the famous Lenny Bruce routine, everything becomes 'Jewish', conspiracy is to be found everywhere. This produces a spiralling of paranoia and hatred, as the Jew serves both to contain and to exaggerate the projected impulses of the anti-Semite. Psychosis is in the air, kept at bay only by endlessly increasing rigidity – what Theweleit (1977) references as the 'monumentalism' of fascism – and escalating anti-Semitic hate. The Jew is a safety valve for destructive impulses, but this use of the Jew has a profound personal and social cost.

The narcissistic universe

The emphasis on splitting and projection in the material described in the previous section has linked anti-Semitism with psychosis or at least borderline phenomena – the 'borderline' here referring to a kind of half-world in which the self is shadowy and somehow incomplete, requiring for its survival manipulation and externalisation to a degree that verges on the psychotic. The Jew is selected as the object for projection because of the specific cultural history of anti-Semitism; the Jew's function in this is to hold onto these projections and act as the collecting point for paranoid fantasies. The closest one can get to a formal psychoanalytic theory here is to suggest that paranoid-schizoid mechanisms are at work, and that the specific failure of the anti-Semite's consciousness is the failure to come to grips with ambivalence and consequently to be able to integrate the psyche, including its destructive elements.

This work has some persuasiveness, in particular in its attempt to link individual psychic disturbance with the figure of the Jew as made available culturally. The long history of Christian anti-Semitism, in particular, lays the foundations for this continued use of the Jew in a post-Christian era: the 'mythological', stereotyped status of the Jew continues unabated, even though the belief structure that once underpinned it is on the wane. This account also offers an explanation for the ambivalence that the Jew provokes – the mixture of fascination and hate, sometimes of idealisation ('philosemitism') shifting suddenly into derogation. However, there is another element that can be introduced to sharpen the account and to link some of the material on Christian anti-Semitism with a description of the mental mechanisms through which anti-Semitism in general operates. Once again, this builds on an argument of Freud's, here that what Judaism represents in the world is an affiliation to the father. As noted earlier, one suggestion from various authors is that Christianity is characterised by repudiation of the father, a return to a more 'maternal' mode of comforting and service. Anti-Semitism, therefore, is driven in part by repugnance at Judaism's constant reminder that the father has been Oedipally displaced, with the attendant guilt that act promotes. With the gradual development of powerful theories of narcissism in post-Freudian psychoanalysis (Frosh, 1991), this hostility towards the father has considerable resonance: it suggests that there might be a link between the narcissistic rage produced by the presence of a flat, insecure self, and the broader structures of wish and impulse that can be seen at work in the anti-Semitic consciousness. That is, anti-Semitism is seen by some authors as a reflection of hatred for the father, represented by the Jew, and a regressive urge to disavow Oedipal reality with its injunction to deal with difference (for instance, to accept the prohibition placed on incestuous desires by the father and the social 'law') and instead take refuge in a state of primordial oneness with the mother, in which no outside otherness needs to be faced.

Psychoanalytic work along these lines has appeared at various points since the Second World War, even prior to the popularisation of theories of narcissism as preoedipal regression. Loeblowitz-Lennard (1947), for example, pointed out the various phallic representations of the Jew: 'Some of the peculiar features ascribed to the Jew – and their unconscious elaborations – are horns, tails, tremendous growths of hair and beard, enormous noses, extreme age. The tail as phallic symbol needs no elaboration' (p. 34). The pervasiveness of these representations is seen as bolstering the argument that the Jew serves to symbolise the restrictive, castrating father in Western society, an argument perhaps at odds with the emphasis on the 'femininity' of the Jew to be found elsewhere. 'In the life of the individual, inhibiting, depriving forces are associated with one's father. The Jew, a universal father symbol, came to represent inhibiting, depriving forces in society... The fear of the Jew, symbolised by the anti-Semitic myths, is the fear of the "father", the Jew representing the punitive aspects of parental and societal authority' (p. 36). The roots of anti-Semitism, consequently, 'lie in fear which springs from an unresolved Oedipus in which case the father has not been adequately internalised in the form of a superego' (p. 37).

The beginnings of an account of anti-Semitism as a product of narcissism can perhaps be seen in the work of Ackerman and Jahoda (1948, 1950), which was one of the five studies published as part of the Institute of Social Research's *Studies in Prejudice* project. As with many of the psychoanalytic studies, this work was based largely on the secondary analysis of a relatively small number of analytic cases, albeit more than in other instances (twenty-seven in the 1948 paper, forty in the 1950 book, including eight Jews). Ackerman and Jahoda (1948) note an important characteristic of the patients who they considered: 'None of our patients suffered from a genuine, deep depression... In a few instances, the attack on the Jew seems to serve the dynamic purpose of offsetting a depressive tendency... The existence of an anti-Semitic reaction presupposes a tendency to blame the outside world rather than one's self, and dynamically, such a tendency is in contradiction to the overtly self-destructive trend of a genuine depression' (p. 243). The significance of this observation lies partly in its links to another insight of Melanie Klein's (1946), that being 'depressed' depends on a capacity to feel deeply and to internalise or 'own' one's emotions, specifically those relating to destructiveness. Depression is founded in loss, responsibility and guilt, especially as a consequence of the sense that one has damaged objects one also loves; paranoid-schizoid splitting and projection of such emotions, by contrast, means that there is no such ownership of feeling, and hence no real 'thickness' or depth to the personality. So whilst genuine depression is indeed 'self-destructive', as Ackerman and Jahoda state, it is also indicative of a potential for integration of the personality that is denied those who rely solely on projective defences. Conversely, the inability to feel depression is akin to the inability to mourn; it implies a thinness to the personality that also suggests that the self is fragile, needing constant bolstering by its external objects. In this light, it is not surprising to find Ackerman and Jahoda (1948, p. 244) commenting that, 'All the patients suffered from anxiety...Because of their inner weakness and negligible insight, the outside world seemed hostile, bad, menacing, inexplicably hard... The general impression is one of weakness of personality organisation, disordered self-image and, with this, an exaggerated sense of vulnerability to social injury.' The sufferer from such a flat self struggles with passivity and particularly with intimacy; such people are always likely to show the narcissistic pattern of self-aggrandisement coupled with deep, unconscious self-doubt, and thus to fluctuate between grand schemes and a sense of impotence. They are also likely to seek support in conformity with others, which by its very nature means that they are hostile to difference – one of the factors which Ackerman and Jahoda speculate may be related to anti-Semitism, as the sustained difference of Jews is hard for conformists to bear.

Narcissists of this kind have a 'drab', shallow psychic life, with colourless affect and weak conscience, and an inability to manage feelings of guilt. The source of all this lies strongly in experiences of rejection by the parents, whose coldness and hostility towards one another and towards the child are replicated in the child's own psychic structure; that is, the failure to find a loving and supportive parental context means that the child has little experience of a benevolent world and therefore never develops the ego-strength to resolve internal conflicts arising from ambivalence. Instead, an unbearable hostility breaks forth, paralleling the parents' relational stance; however, the absence of a secure self means that this hostility cannot be managed but instead is projected outwards onto the despised bad object.

> In many cases, one sees a clear, dynamic parallel between the patient's attitude to a parent and the specific meaning of the anti-Semitism. The hatred for 'the Jew' is often identical in content with the hatred for one of the parents, or identical with the hatred of one parent for the other. In the unconscious, Jewishness is sometimes equated with the image of an aggressive, domineering mother. In other cases, it may be symbolised in the father.   (1948, p. 258)

'In this syndrome of anxiety, weakness, confusion, inner doubt, disordered self-image, and instability,' write Ackerman and Jahoda (1948,

p. 248), 'anti-Semitism seems to play a functionally well-defined role.' As with the theories described earlier, the idea is that the anti-Semite deals with inner turmoil through projecting it outwards, finding a convenient receptacle for it in the Jew. Seeking to preserve the self, the anti-Semite uses this external object as a lightning rod for the rage that actually arises from her or his own experience of rejection, whilst also finding safety in the sense of sameness that comes from rejecting all difference. The thinness of the personality is actually maintained in this way, as intense feeling is projected outwards and a protective shell is internalised, so that the anti-Semite comes to feel increasingly less real and consequently more and more envious of anything of value in others. The Jew is once again particularly provocative here: of value as a culturally embedded symbol of rejection, the Jew nevertheless can be idealised as being comfortable in difference. This confusing pattern is made even more complex by the consequences of ambivalence, as some of the attributes despised in the Jew turn out also to be those that are present yet denied in the anti-Semite's own unconscious. The appalling truth is that the anti-Semite sees him or herself in the Jew, because that is indeed where the intolerable elements of the self have been placed, and so becomes ever more strongly tied to the object of hate. The disturbance within the anti-Semite has thus been dealt with by projecting out those feelings that are experienced as too painful to bear, yet this produces not the sought-after sense of relief, but an aggravation built out of identification: 'Thus, the Jew, at one and the same time, stands for the weakness or the strength of the self; for conscience, which reproaches the self for its deficiencies and badness, and also for those primitive, forbidden appetites and aggressions which must be denied as the price of social acceptance' (p. 254).

The account of anti-Semitism given by Ackerman and Jahoda focuses on the devastating consequences of parental rejection and links with what in other places might be termed a 'false self' (Winnicott, 1965) – a search for something conformist and acceptable that will gain approval and hence produce emotional warmth. This, however, involves jettisoning the more deeply felt elements in psychological life, in particular the rage that is a consequence of the experienced rejection. A vicious cycle then is set in motion, in which the projection of rage leaves the self increasingly depleted and hence more fragile and lifeless, resulting in more desperate projection to stave off collapse. Into this maelstrom the figure of the Jew steps, ambiguous and contradictory enough to offer a suitable container for negativity. The use of such a culturally salient category of hate also gives the anti-Semite a sense of being linked with others and thus a false but comforting sense of 'identity'. The Jew is the castrated other to be despised, yet secretly identified with by the anti-Semite who feels castrated by the hostility of the parents; the Jew is also the castrat*ing* other (amongst other things, he circumcises his sons) who is the source of distress and must consequently be wiped out. This is where Oedipal antagonism occurs and is preserved: the Jew is constantly fought against as a consequence of the anti-Semite's passivity and sense of woundedness. The Jew represents both what is most despised in the anti-Semite's own psychic life – the 'castrated', unformed and unwanted self – and also the potent antagonist, the aggressive other. It is from here that the anti-Semite's flat, narcissistic self and the relationship with the father begin to feature.

Narcissism, repudiation of the father and anti-Semitism are drawn together most powerfully in the work of Béla Grunberger, especially in his 1964 article, 'The Anti-Semite and the Oedipal Conflict'. Grunberger's account is based on two linked propositions: first, that anti-Semitism is characterised by regression to preoedipal levels of functioning, and hence is associated with a wish for a narcissistic solution to the problems of reality, in which everything will be 'at one' with the self and no challenging differences will exist; and secondly, that the Jew represents the father and is therefore attacked as part of this repudiation of the Oedipal. As proposed by some of the other theories considered above, the psyche of the anti-Semite is held by Grunberger to be unintegrated, made up of separable components living in an uneasy truce with one another with peace maintained mainly by projection. The area of the personality from which this projection arises is seen by Grunberger as being of great centrality to the individual concerned: 'It is a section of the ego which is more or less radically isolated from the rest of the personality, but attracts to itself a considerable portion of the libido, thereby warping the remainder of the personality' (p. 380). Because of the ego's 'immaturity' it is constantly threatened with disintegration, which is managed through rejection of reality ('He lives in his fantasy, and any reference to reality tends only to irritate him and is rejected' – ibid.) and the rigidity of formulaic but unintegrated moralism amounting to no more than a 'respect for force'. Oral and anal – that is, regressive and preoedipal – components dominate the mind and are revealed vividly in the accusations that the anti-Semite produces against the Jews. Thus, for example, oral aggression is witnessed in the accusation of the blood libel, effectively the claim that Jews drink the blood of Christians; Grunberger also notes, 'the time-worn accusation which turns up in different guises, but always has the same significance: "The Jews have poisoned the wells"' (p. 381). Anal fantasies are most evident in the association of the Jew with the devil.

> The Jew is diabolical, the very incarnation of evil. As we know, the devil represents anal components which are endowed with guilt and whose home is the lower regions of the body. The devil with his colour, his odours, and his manners represents the excremental world. As for hell, region of darkness, place of eternal combustion where a torrent of sulphur burns away the very rocks while pursuing the destruction of the sinner (the bad object), it would seem to be the very projection of the digestive organs, mainspring of the last phase of the anal-object relationship...The anti-Semite prides himself on his ability to smell a Jew a hundred miles away.   (ibid.)

Not only are concerns about dirt and pollution projected onto the Jew – particularly as fantasies about money, the quintessential anal substance – but all forms of aggression of the treacherous kind are included: 'The anal components of sexuality are also projected upon the Jews – lewd monsters who rape innocent German girls in order to pollute the race' (ibid.). As in Kleinian theory (which is not, it should be noted, the point of origin of Grunberger's account), the preoedipal psyche is characterised by extreme projection; what this does, as revealed in these anal and oral examples, is to put into the Jew all the fantasies of dirt, disgust, poison and weakness with which the anti-Semite is afflicted. This in turn ensures that the narcissistic ego is protected from the damage that could be caused it by having to acknowledge and resolve internal contradictions, especially 'unacceptable' desires.

> The anti-Semite's profound satisfaction flows from the fact that his ego is in perfect harmony with his ego-ideal. Having made his projection onto the Jew, he has found his Manichaean paradise: all that is bad is thereafter on one side – the side of the Jew – and all that is good on the other side where he himself is.   (p. 382)

Once again, the Jew is the principle of evil in this split psychic world, the Jew is to blame for all the badness the anti-Semite feels welling up inside.

As described earlier, Grunberger follows Freud in proposing that Jewish monotheism was a move away from the more sensual and material 'mothering' kind of religion towards a more austere, distanced and rule-bound set of beliefs and practices that were not only *about* the father, but also represented the Oedipal mode of functioning: restrictive, prohibitive, moral. *'If paganism gives a very great place to the maternal elements,'* he writes (pp. 382–3), *'Judaism presents itself as above all a worship of the Father,* a severe, omnipresent, omniscient father, an implacable judge; in a word, the superego.' The superego is that structural element in the psyche that forms predominantly as an effect of the Oedipus complex: it is the internalisation of paternal aggression experienced as a prohibitive, limiting function and hence is a product of the reality-demands of the external world. Christianity is a partial rebellion against the harshness of this situation, a return to a more mother-centred religious structure, albeit with some element of distance as the aspect of the mother as virgin shows. For the narcissist, however, the Judaic reminder that the father exists, that there are prohibitions and restrictions laid upon the extent to which one can have what one wants, is an irritant or even, at the extreme, an unbearable assault.

> In a word, the Jew by introducing monotheism has not only banished man from his intimacy with the mother (even with the Christian, the mother has remained the inaccessible virgin) and from his narcissistic universe, but has installed within him a judge to persecute and punish him for his oedipal desires. *The Jew has therefore done exactly the same as the father. He has imposed the rule of the father, which explains why he particularly has been chosen by the anti-Semite for the abreaction of the Oedipus complex.* (p. 383; italics in the original)

This is not to say that the anti-Semite/narcissist rejects the father completely; rather, it is the father in his aspect of law-giver that is renounced. Here the Jew is of especial use, acting as the recipient of hatred and split-off projections that attack the restrictive, Oedipal character of the father and yet allow the anti-Semite to maintain a loyalty to a loved father who is coded into various kinds of idealised absolutes: 'God, ideals, country and fatherland, etc' (p. 384). However, behind this idealised father in the anti-Semite's unconscious lurks the hated father; that is, there remains an identification with the projected hatred of the father that belies the anti-Semite's attempt to keep the inner world pure. The dynamic that consequently arises is one in which the Jew has to be perpetually attacked both as the reminder of the father's reality as an Oedipal figure, and as the container of the anti-Semite's own aggressive impulses. Grunberger notes that the Jew is especially well chosen for this role, culturally speaking, because in addition to representing the father 'he' is perceived as a castrated being, not just because of circumcision, but because the Jew is systematically 'cut off from the collectivity and therefore an "outsider"' (p. 384). For the narcissist, belonging to a social collective is an absolute necessity, and the conformist aspects of the anti-Semite's behaviour have this as their goal; the Jew's status as outsider creates a figure of disgust and a potential victim who the anti-Semite can despise. Even more attractively, the Jew also inhabits the position in which the narcissist would like to see the father: 'lonely wandered, castrated and miserable' (ibid.). This is the way to get rid of a rival, a law-giver who restricts the pleasure to be gained from narcissistic oneness with the mother: throw him out.

Grunberger's argument is that anti-Semitism is a characteristic expression of narcissism in a certain kind of social world, which happens to be the social world of the West over thousands of years. Narcissists cannot tolerate difference and otherness, yet this is precisely what constitutes reality, which asserts the impossibility of the wish for oneness with the mother, of a place in which there will be no contradiction and no restriction on pleasure, in which no-one will say 'no'. Because the narcissistic wish for omnipotence is so strong, scapegoats are needed to hold the projected otherness, to be to blame for the inevitable entry of contradiction into the system. 'And,' writes Grunberger (1989, p. 87), 'because it was the Father, with his laws, prohibitions and reminders about reality, who drove them out of the paradise in which they merged with the Mother, *they attack the first herald of that strict authority, namely the Jew*. No matter who committed the offence, it is the Jew who is held responsible.' This is the legacy of thousands of years of hostility: 'The same accusations are constantly being made, as the Jew has become a symbol implanted in the unconscious of the narcissist; resorting to it is almost a reflex action' (ibid.). What is hated is the paternal order itself; all narcissists, whether non-Jewish or Jewish, hate this, and for all of them the Jew is the cultural category that is available to carry the hate – hence the phenomenon of Jewish anti-Semitism, to which Grunberger, in common with many psychoanalysts, pays perhaps undue attention. Thus, according to Grunberger, anti-Semitism is a social phenomenon only in the sense that it is the social expression of a pervasive psychological structure: an inability to deal with reality accompanied by a wish to 'return' to the fantasised state in which nothing disruptive or restrictive impinged on the mind.

A final variant of this theory is offered by Chasseguet-Smirgel (1990), in an article concerned with the psychodynamic sources of Nazism. As in Grunberger's account, the emphasis is on regressive narcissism as a source of the repudiation of difference and of separation, which is seen as embodied culturally in the Jew. The Nazis epitomised that mode of racist ideology in which the integral link between the people and 'Mother Nature' (the 'soil' or land) is contrasted precisely with the 'rootlessness' of the Jews; unity is what is sought, with the loss of individuality in the comfort of the mass being a reassuring prop to narcissism, an abolition of the paternal barrier. 'All obstacles which, after birth, make access to the mother's body impossible to achieve have to be removed. These obstacles are identified with reality and are presented by the father and the father's derivatives: his penis, children... Ridding oneself of paternal obstacles by emptying the maternal body, fighting against reality and thought, form a single, identical wish: that of returning to a world without organisation, to primeval chaos, to a universe marked by homogeneity and the continuum present before birth' (p. 168). Extreme ideologies such as Nazism promise to remove contradiction and to offer a state of bliss to their adherents; the loss of individuality entailed might seem to be a significant price to pay to achieve this, but in fact it is actively sought after, because it involves absorption of the self in the mass, a state of complete narcissistic oneness with the environment, a return to the time when infant and mother were (fantasised) as blissfully united. The process involved, as Nazism testifies, is a brutal one: obliterating the paternal order is not achieved without violence. Extremist ideologies possess the capacity 'to incite individuals and groups into sweeping away all obstacles they may meet on the road to the Heavenly Jerusalem. They are, therefore, potentially bloodthirsty' (p. 173). In their way stand, in particular, the Jews, who represent separation, division from the earth, intellectualism, a God who abhors sensuality, a set of paternal restrictions on what can be achieved. Here, therefore, what is being described is not necessarily a pathological class of narcissists, but a narcissistic tendency that can be mobilised by ideologies, and that in the process will find the Jew employable as, once again, the culturally constructed representative of denigrated otherness.

Conclusion

The last two chapters have trawled through numerous psychoanalytic accounts of anti-Semitism, finding some consistencies and some provocative material, but also a difficult uncertainty concerning levels of explanation – psychological, psychosocial, cultural. Most of the theories follow Freud in arguing that the roots of Western anti-Semitism lie at least in part in Christianity, and that this has at its source hatred of the restrictive nature of monotheism, which is identified with the father. Rebelling against the father's constraints, Christianity was marked by repudiation of guilt and revulsion towards the Jews, who were experienced psychically as carrying the message of the father forwards, when what was wished for was to escape his wrath. Building on this, Judaism and the Jews became Christianity's scapegoat, and a powerful cultural category was constructed that continues into the (mainly) post-Christian world as a useful repository for hatred, narcissistic rage, and unmanageable negativity. There is general agreement amongst these theorists that anti-Semitism is not a specific psychopathology, but rather the culturally amenable expression of various troubled psychological states, with projective mechanisms characteristic of preoedipal functioning being the dominant defences. Psychotic and borderline type functioning is proposed, and some of the most powerful work rests on the idea that anti-Semitism can be understood as a socially valorised expression of regressive narcissism, with the Jew standing in both for the father and for difference or otherness in general. Hatred of the Jew is hatred of otherness, of anything that threatens to disrupt the hard-fought-for unity of the psyche; the other, the stranger, the outsider all introduce difference and potential conflict, all remind the anti-Semite of uncontrollable elements in the unconscious, and all, therefore, are to be opposed.

Much of what has been described here seems phenomenologically correct, in that it portrays a set of experiences and attitudes that are recognisable in anti-Semites, and psychodynamically interesting in postulating possible unconscious mechanisms. It is also mostly respectful of the social component of anti-Semitism, in that it allows that anti-Semitism is historically produced by a specific culture that has just happened to be dominant, and as such is a *contingent* phenomenon. That is, anti-Semitism is not 'hard-wired' into the psyche, but rather is the culturally available vehicle for the expression of certain psychic conflicts that are themselves more likely to occur under some social circumstances (such as those which prevailed in Germany after the First World War) than others. This largely protects psychoanalysis from the criticism of psychological reductionism (i.e. that social phenomena are being dealt with as if they were purely psychological), although it is still the case that, as one would expect, the psychoanalytic emphasis is on the psychodynamics of anti-Semitism at the individual level rather than in relation to its social causes. This is in important respects simply a statement of what psychoanalysis does: it is an approach to psychology, not sociology (despite its historical application to social phenomena), so it legitimately asks questions about what anti-Semitism 'means' at the psychological level, and how it takes hold of individuals.

That said, however, there is another way of looking at things. An assumption running through the theories dealt with here is that the machinations of the individual psyche produce certain problems (for example, an inability to manage ambivalence, narcissistic regressive fantasies) that are 'solved' through the use of categories (the 'Jew') that are available from within the culture. However, perhaps this is not strong enough in terms of its theorisation of the social. For one thing, it reflects a set of ambiguities to be found within psychoanalysis itself, centring especially on a lack of clarity about the gendered elements in anti-Semitic thinking. For the majority of psychoanalytic theorists, the Jew represents the father and is hated by the anti-Semite because of this, either as a residue of unresolved Oedipal conflicts or as an expression of revulsion against the Oedipal order in total. Yet in most anti-Semitic ideology, the Jew is seen not as masculine but as *feminine*, and this is an aspect of the representation of the Jew that, it is plausibly argued, had a powerful impact on the construction of psychoanalysis itself. It may in fact be the case, as Boyarin (1997) hypothesises, that Freud's representation of Judaism in *Moses and Monotheism* as a religion of the father – and hence superior to Christianity because more abstract and intellectual and therefore more culturally 'advanced' – was not just a way of theorising anti-Semitism, but was also a reflection of his own *internalised* anti-Semitism. That is, in distancing himself from the 'feminine' components of Judaism and Jewish culture – for example, its representation of ideal masculinity as scholarly and meek (like Freud's actual father) rather than soldierly and physically strong (like Hannibal) – Freud might himself have been embracing the anti-Semitic discourse that disparages such 'effeminacy'. The psychoanalytic theorists following in Freud's wake have not redressed the balance here with a more sophisticated understanding of the gender complexities of Jewish culture, which has indeed both 'paternal/ masculine' and 'maternal/feminine' components. Instead, with their own rather unquestioning acceptance of the idea that Judaism is a quintessentially paternal religion, they can be seen to have reproduced a certain kind of anti-Semitic and misogynistic ideology: the feminine (traditionally associated with Jews) is bad; the masculine, good; therefore, to reclaim the Jews from the place in which Western culture has placed them, only the 'masculine' elements of Judaism will be stressed. The transparent gender stereotyping of several post-Freudian theories, in which 'regressive' narcissism is associated with the mother and opposed to the Oedipal/paternal capacity to face reality, shows even more explicitly how the failure of psychoanalysis to explore its own ideological and political investments can result in theories that obscure as much as they explain.

The widespread psychoanalytic assumption that the primary function of the social world is to offer beliefs and practices that can serve as carriers or containers for split-off individual projections is also problematic, notwithstanding the care with which some theorists have argued for the significance of anti-Semitism as a social phenomenon. An alternative framework of at least equal viability is one in which, rather than running parallel to the individual, culture is understood to *construct* subjectivity: that is, one might argue that anti-Semitism, and racism in general, is a key category in the making of the Western citizen. Everyone, whether Jew or non-Jew, has to deal with anti-Semitism if they are to deal with society at all, and in so doing they take up 'positions' in relation to anti-Semitism that enfold psychic processes within them. Put more strongly, one might suggest that the contradictions in society are not simply accompaniments of, or accidental parallels to, the contradictions of the unconscious; they actively *produce* them, through all the micro- and macrosocial processes (parental interactions and anxieties; socialisation practices; familial beliefs; gendered and 'racialised' institutional practices, etc) out of which each person is made. In all this, the figure of the Jew is a particularly powerful instance of the figure of the 'other' in general. Through its historically-derived cultural pervasiveness it is perpetuated as a representation of that which is needed yet despised, that which holds in place the otherwise potentially intolerable destructiveness of a social system founded on inequality and alienation. Such systems *create* their own psychic structures and psychological disturbances; thus, given the organisation of Western society, anti-Semitism is as much an element in the unconscious of every subject as is any other psychosocial state – love, loneliness or loss, for example. The Jew, and more generally the figure of the 'other', is a constitutive feature of Western consciousness, an element out of which subjectivity is made. With this framework in mind, one is left still asking, after considering all the psychoanalytic theories of anti-Semitism, what is the relation of socially-induced otherness to the way in which subjectivity is constructed, and in what ways do anti-Semitism and racism feature as fundamental aspects of psychic life?

8
The Other

It was suggested at the end of the previous chapter that psychoanalytic theories of anti-Semitism consistently founder on the issue of 'otherness', which is often seen as a convenient category into which to project unwanted aspects of the self, but is not fully explored as a fundamental principle of social – and hence psychological – organisation. The argument here is that otherness, embodied in a person or people called 'the other', is a primary source of subjectivity; that is, it is in relation to 'the other' that subjecthood is formed, that the individual comes to experience her or himself as having a self and a psychic life. This is how society works: it defines numerous axes around which personhood is structured (class, 'race', sexuality and gender being the classic ones) and requires every subject to find a 'location' with respect to these axes, becoming inserted along the way in a web of contrasts between different kinds of 'sameness' and otherness'. Socially, this produces various kinds of fractions embodied in the different contrasts (for instance, working class or bourgeoisie, to use the traditional Marxist model, or heterosexual and homosexual to use the categories of contemporary queer theory); psychologically, it produces patterns of identification and repudiation out of which identities emerge. Various kinds of cultural myths arise in the course of history to define certain kinds of others as particularly significant, especially in carrying the unwanted projections of the majority culture. In particular, as described in the previous chapter, the Jew has come to be a kind of 'universal stranger' for Western society (Bauman, 1989; Clarke, 2003), although in the contemporary post '9/11' world there is also considerable use of the image of Islam as radically other; and there is of course continued, virulent, anti-Black 'colour' racism with its history in colonialism. Disputing which of these 'othernesses' is most significant is perhaps one of the effects of living in a society structured around divisions and identifications of this kind. The recent advent of 'post-colonial' theory, for example, has revealed just how pervasive the psychic effects of colonialism have been in their continued hold over Western subjectivity, in some ways displacing the image of the Jew from the centre of opprobrium, though the shadow of the Holocaust looms large and there is plenty of evidence for a rumbling background of Jew-hatred whenever any form of racism raises its head.

The multiple sources of racist hate barely need rehearsing: colonialism, economic exploitation and privation, disenfranchisement and political oppression, the injustices of history, the legacies of domination. Writing the full story of intolerance would take something truly multidimensional and much more than simply 'multidisciplinary' in the academic sense. It would have to imagine not just the economic, political, and social roots of the passions of nations, ethnic and religious groups, social classes, and individuals; but also the specific histories of each conflict, the exact fantasies that each group provokes in the others with which it has contact and dispute, and the interconnected web of deceit and influence that envelops the whole. It would have to be expert at the social and political level, understand economics, know its theology and mythology, above all know its history. Yet all this would not be enough, partly because the situation never stands still, however much it recurs; partly because as well as the various 'rational' factors feeding each conflict – historical and material disputes, interests and investments of various observable kinds – the 'causeless hatred' of racism and bigotry is never quite encompassed by rationality, but always seems to figure something else. That is, at its heart (and 'heart of darkness' is now an inescapable image of the colonial relationship at least, precisely because of its racist connotations), there seems to be something excessive in racist hate, irreducible to its apparent objective causes, something too much and over the top, something full of what Žižek (1991) calls, with bitter irony, 'enjoyment'. This should not be misconstrued: the point Žižek is making is that the emotional investment in hatred of the other is often so intense that it can only be understood as enacting some desire without which the psyche would feel depleted. At times, for instance when mass racist movements occur, this translates into genuine enjoyment of a blatant kind. For example, commenting on Daniel Goldhagen's (1997) *Hitler's Willing Executioners*, Žižek (1997, p. 57) notes,

A close reading of the testimonials from his own book ... demonstrates how the executioners *experienced their deeds as a kind of* '*transgressive*' *activity*, as a kind of pseudo-Bakhtinian 'carnivalesque' activity in which the constraints of 'normal' everyday life were momentarily suspended – it was precisely this 'transgressive' character (transgressive with regard to the publicly acknowledged ethical norms of Nazi society itself) which accounted for the 'surplus-enjoyment' one got from excessively torturing the victims. The feeling of shame thus, again, in no way proves that the executioners were 'not wholly corrupted', that 'a minimum of decency persisted in them': on the contrary, this shame was the unmistakable sign of the excess of *enjoyment* they got from their acts.

On the other side (taking the side of the other, one might say), Levinas (1991, p. 98), writing about the Shoah, refers to the 'useless suffering' caused by murderous racism: 'Pain in its undiluted malignity, suffering for nothing'. Tragically but inescapably, it seems, the two things – enjoyment and useless suffering – often go together.

Psychoanalysis has had its own problems with racist and anti-Semitic thinking, and with compromises with corrupt regimes, as the examples in this book have shown. It possesses in particular a considerable heritage of colonial assumptions with which to grapple. For instance, Brickman (2003) has made a very extensive study of the use of the notion of the 'primitive' in Freud and others, showing how it is 'suspended in a web of social and cultural meanings that have played a prominent role in the discourse of European colonialism' (p. 16). One great discovery of Freud's, which forms a basis for the arguments in this chapter, was that the apparently other, including the 'primitive', could not be separated off absolutely from the 'civilised' self, but rather could be found inside each and every one of 'us' in the form of unconscious impulses and longings. This realisation has considerable significance in undermining any simple differentiation of self and other based on 'good' versus 'bad' and 'superior' versus 'inferior': the attributes of otherness that are at times most disavowed are also elements of our deepest psychic life. However, the parallel between 'basic', 'crude' psychological impulses and the idea of the 'primitive' has also led in psychoanalysis to a long association between the psychologically 'primitive' in the sense of early and undeveloped, and the so-called 'primitive peoples' of classical anthropology, otherwise known as 'savages'. Commenting on Freud's (1914) anthropological speculation in his book, *Totem and Taboo*, Brickman notes,

> by correlating the progression of narcissism, the oedipal stage, and maturity with animism (savagery), religion (barbarianism), and

science (civilisation), *Totem and Taboo* transposed the racial assumptions of the cultural evolutionary scale onto the modern psyche…
The psychoanalytically conceived norm of mature subjectivity was,
by virtue of the correlation of libidinal development with the cultural evolutionary scale, a rationalism whose unstated colour was
white, just as its unstated gender was male.   (p. 72)

The terminology and the conceptual baggage of the 'savage' and the
'barbarian' remained with psychoanalysis for some time and is still
lying only-just-dormant in those references to 'primitive feelings' that
are often the stock-in-trade of clinical psychoanalytic discussions.
Brickman shows convincingly that the slippage here is not totally
accidental, and that it continues to have effects: it is as if the nine-
teenth-century fantasy of the 'dark continent' (a formulation famously
employed by Freud to refer to femininity) is inscribed in the basic
assumptions of psychoanalysis and has never been fully revoked. She
writes (p. 114), 'In the same way that femininity is fundamental to
masculine subjectivity as an excluded yet constitutive other, primitivity is fundamental to civilized subjectivity as *its* excluded yet constitutive other.' The linkage of otherness with 'race' is clear here, and
permeates both the auto-critique of psychoanalysis and the use of
psychoanalysis as a way of studying racism itself.

Despite these caveats, psychoanalysis seems the obvious discipline
to look to for an exploration of the 'excess', the ambivalent kind of
'enjoyment' that seems to invest so much urgency and passion in the
figure of the other. This is because psychoanalysis deals specifically
with the excessive, with what is desired *over and above what is possible*,
that is, with what is unconscious, wished for but usually too dangerous to give expression to. Psychoanalysis' expertise lies in taking
examples of actions that seem 'overdetermined', too heavily invested
in to be easily explained by simple conscious motives, and exploring
what other resonance they may have for the person or group concerned. In the case of anti-Semitism, as described earlier, the psychoanalytic interest is not in how it may sometimes arise out of rivalry for
economic resources, but rather in the way the Jew embodies the split-
off unappeasable self-hatred of the anti-Semite; this is one explanation
of the intensity and ambivalence of anti-Semitic feeling. Applied to
racism and bigotry more generally, there is a history of psychoanalytic
theorising that tends to emphasise processes of projection in which
the denigrated other is made to carry unwanted aspects of the self;
in its more sophisticated version, this has been linked to social and

historical formations of oppression and discrimination (e.g. Fanon 1952; Kovel 1984, 1995; Rustin 1991; Frosh 1989, 1997). This work has proved very fertile in linking established psychoanalytic views of the intersubjective defences of the mind (putting hated and feared elements of the self into the other, for example by use of the mechanism of 'projective identification') with the political structures supporting racism. In so doing, it has compellingly demonstrated how certain groups become repositories for the paranoid, destructive and sexually exciting fantasies of others. Rustin (1991), for instance, shows how the process of racist thought is one in which unwanted or feared aspects of the self are experienced as having the power to disturb the personality in so damaging a way that they have to be repudiated and evacuated or projected into the racialised other, chosen for this purpose both because of pre-existing social prejudices and because, as a category of fantasy, racial 'otherness' can be employed to mean virtually anything. Once the projective impulse takes hold, it feeds on itself, creating a lie at the centre of the personality, something destructive and damaged that must be endlessly defended against, that poisons the world around. Rustin comments (p. 69), 'The "lie" in this system of personality organisation becomes positively valued, as carrying for the self an important aspect of its defence against weakness, loss, or negative judgment.' The more strongly it is held, the more it is needed; the subject falls in love with the lie and fearful of anything that challenges it, and the investment in racism becomes profound.

Kovel's (1995) analysis parallels this account in many respects, but makes an additional contribution by linking the historical trends leading to Western racism, particularly as seen in its American forms, with the psychoanalytic exploration of the workings of the racist psyche. Specifically, he contends that a set of economically motivated social circumstances, with slavery and capitalist accumulation at their centre, produced in the West a psychological imperative to disown multiplicity and sensuality and to project it into the black other. The power of this psychosocial organisation is so great that it can 'enter into the evolution of the psyche' (p. 212), closing down the possibility of responding to any new experience that is not in the interests of accumulation. Instead, the repressed sensuousness of the white subject, preserved unconsciously because otherwise the psyche dries up completely and is 'deadened', is experienced as threatening and subversive, as well as exciting. It is bestial, animal, fit for projection onto those human subjects designated by the complex social drive of capitalist imperialism as nonhuman – in the American context, the slaves.

> A persistent shadow had dogged puritanism, the dominant cultural type of the early capitalist order – a spectre of renunciation and rationalisation, of the loss of sensuousness and the deadening of existence. In this context the animality projected onto the black by virtue of his or her role in slavery became suitable to represent the vitality split away from the world in Puritan capitalist asceticism. Sensuousness that had been filtered out of the universe in capitalist exchange was to reappear in those who had been denied human status by the emergent capitalist order. Blacks, who had been treated as animals when enslaved, became animals in their essence, while the darkness of their skin became suitable to represent the dark side of the body, embodying the excremental vision that has played so central a role in the development of western consciousness. In this way blacks were seen as beneath whites in reasoning power and above whites in sexuality and the capacity for violence. (p. 217)

The racist needs the hated other as a repository of all that she or he has lost and fears losing further; 'Without the spectacle of lost nature to hate and be fascinated by, it is doubtful whether the reduction of the psyche to a homogeneous personality could be sustained' (p. 218). Kovel's account here is similar to, perhaps based on, that arising from the exposition of a politically attuned psychoanalysis to be found in the school of 'critical theory' associated with Adorno and Horkheimer and their associates. Clarke (2003, p. 83) summarises their general view on the relationship between the 'other' and the 'primitive feelings' of the self as follows:

> Firstly, the 'other' reminds us of the peace and happiness that we cannot have, persecuted minorities form a receptacle for the betrayed of modern society. We cannot have it so we will destroy it, an envious attack. Secondly, the 'other' stands as a direct reminder, either real or imaginary, of our repressed longings to return to a pre-social state of nature, to satisfy socially banished instinctual needs; we accuse outgroups of behaving like animals because we long to behave like animals.

The 'us' of Western society needs the 'them' to contain personally and historically split-off aspects of psychic life. Bringing this idea back to the figure of the Jew, Žižek (1993, p. 206) emphasises not just the 'need' of self for other, but also the inseparable link between the two: the other *expresses* those aspects of the self that are most hidden, yet also by virtue of that very fact, most emotionally intense.

> Is capitalism's hatred of the Jew not the hatred of its own inner-most, essential feature? For this reason, it is not sufficient to point out how the racist's Other presents a threat to our own identity. We should rather inverse this proposition: the fascinating image of the Other gives a body to our own innermost split, to what is 'in us more than ourselves' and thus prevents us achieving full identity with ourselves.

These and other adventures in extending psychoanalysis to encompass a theory of racism have been very productive and have done a consider-able amount to remedy the historical silence of psychoanalysis on issues of social hatred. However, one characteristic they share is a limited account of what constitutes the 'other' on the psychological level. For Rustin, it is by nature an empty category, available to be used as the repository of the racist's dark impulses. For Kovel, it is a historically constructed symbolic category made to carry the burden of that which is repudiated from the white psyche. More generally, these theories suggest a relatively clear differentiation between self and other, between what the subject experiences and what the other represents. Yet when one surveys the virulence of bigotry, hatred, and fear of the other as manifested in the intersubjective, interpersonal, and social spheres – when one sees its prevalence and the ease with which what is other becomes what is foreign or alien, and the degree to which this rep-resents a *threat* – then one has to ask, what exactly might be the char-acteristics of, or at least ascribed to, otherness in general, and why does it so strain the tolerance of the self? Kleinians in particular are wont to make it a kind of bad object, into which unwanted unconscious impulses are projected, and many accounts of anti-Semitism are based on this general idea. But this is not specific or detailed enough; the con-nections are so profound, so distressed, that the other must mean some-thing more, something from which each one of us cannot escape.

Primacy of the other

If the figure of the Jew is one quintessential 'other' for Western culture, there still remains a considerable amount of work to do to understand how such a figure becomes constitutive of the individual's unconscious functioning. That is, if the link between the outside other and the 'otherness' embedded in each of us in the form of the unconscious is more than just an analogy, then its nature and the processes through which it arises need to be elaborated. In much psychoanalytic and social theory, there is reliance on what might seem to be an obvious truth that the burdensome otherness of disturbing unconscious ideas becomes projected into the 'real' other outside; yet the connection between these two types of 'other' is not actually that obvious. What, to put it crudely, is the 'Jew inside' that becomes the anti-Semitic figure of the Jew outside; or conversely and more potently, what is it about the outside other, the outside 'Jew', that has such a hold over the unconscious?

Reversing the conventional psychoanalytic wisdom is important here. Instead of seeing the social other as a carrier for the internal turmoil of the suffering subject, the pervasiveness of anti-Semitism and racism makes it at least as likely that the structures of the external world produce the 'inside'. That is, reversing the lens one can argue that the socially constructed anti-Semitic and racialised figure of the other is not created in order to contain the naturally-occurring split-off destructiveness of the individual, but instead it *makes* this inner split occur. From this perspective, the outside other is primary, built into the structures of a society premised on difference and division; and it is in relation to this primary otherness that each individual subject emerges. The figure of the Jew in Western culture is one of those constitutive representations of otherness; it continues to be highly charged and to create psyches in its image, alongside other racialised representations of the black, the 'primitive' and the alien. Psychoanalytically, this raises a question of how it is that what is ostensibly 'outside' gets to be so centrally 'inside', a question which has conventionally been answered through accounts based on notions of internalisation or identification, these being seen as 'taking in' processes in which the attributes of others are incorporated into the self. However, even this explanatory approach seems less than comprehensive, because it implies an already-existing self that can carry out these incorporative acts, as if it is taking in something that is distinct from it. The pervasiveness and intensity of racist fantasy suggests that the external other is more than that, but is implicated in the very production of the self in the first place.

There are now a number of converging theoretical approaches that give primacy to this notion of the other as formative of the self. For some, such as Levinas (1991), this is an *ethical* position, an irreducible feature of the human condition: if we cannot place the other first, we are not human subjects at all. For others, it is a psychological fact that otherness is primary, with whatever social, ethical, and political consequences that may follow. The French psychoanalyst Jean Laplanche is a key source here. Consistently over decades, Laplanche has argued that the great contribution of Freudian psychoanalysis to Western thought resides in its 'Copernican revolution', through which an act of psychological decentring occurs that parallels the earlier realisation that the earth is not the centre of the universe. What this means, as Freud himself claimed, is that psychoanalysis shows that the experiencing 'I', the ego ('das Ich' in the original German) is not the master of mental life, but rather has to struggle against various internal forces threatening to topple it. This is a process of *decentring* because it removes the ego from the centre of personal psychology and replaces it with the unconscious (and, in Freud's 'structural' theory, the Id or 'It'), which reveals with great intensity the alien core inside each one of us. In Laplanche's words,

> The sharpness of [Freud's] vision is testified to by terms like 'internal foreign body' or 'reminiscence'. They define the unconscious as an alien inside me and even put inside me by an alien. At his most prophetic, Freud does not hesitate over formulations which go back to the idea of *possession*.   (1997, p. 658)

The notion that what psychoanalysis reveals is the presence of otherness within is fairly widely shared among contemporary psychoanalytic critics, and its explicitly cultivated use of the imagery of foreignness is another link back to Freud's roots in 'alien' Jewish culture. Political and psychological imagery constantly overlap with one another, as the trope of the other is made to serve as a vision of the unconscious, but also to elicit associations with the actual stranger. For example, Julia Kristeva's meditation on otherness, *Strangers to Ourselves* (1988), is premised on exactly this same idea, that the existence of an unconscious 'inside' each one of us means the haunting of the individual human subject by something else, strange, foreign, and yet real.

> With the Freudian notion of the unconscious the involution of the strange in the psyche loses its pathological aspect and integrates within the assumed unity of human beings an *otherness* that is both

biological *and* symbolic and becomes an integral part of the *same...*
[The] uncanny, foreignness is within us: we are our own foreigners,
we are divided.   (p. 181)

The use of the term 'uncanny' here is highly significant, not only
because it resonates with Freud's (1939) own terminology when describing circumcision: 'Further, among the customs by which the Jews
made themselves separate, that of circumcision has made a disagreeable, uncanny impression' (p. 91). The 'uncanny' as used by Kristeva
also refers to the same set of processes as Laplanche's admiration for
'possession' in the quotation given above. These terms are not meant
to suggest that there is a core of mysticism in the psychoanalytic
project, though some might argue that this is in fact the case, but
rather the opposite. Psychoanalysis claims that there is an unconscious
of a specifically *material* kind, acting from 'within' the subject but with
the phenomenology of something 'outside', and giving rise to precisely
those feelings of something non-materially 'uncanny', of 'possession',
which are so commonly drawn on to give voice to a sense of the mystical or even the sublime. To put it another way, the functioning of the
unconscious as an 'internal other', an 'it' speaking from within the personality, radically disturbs the rather homely sense that each of us is
'master' of himself or herself, and in doing so it opens the way to a
collapse of confidence in the self, to a sense that however robust it
might seem, it has already been infiltrated by something subjectively
inexplicable, something that the 'self' is not.

These references to the other that exists both on the inside and the
outside express the psychoanalytic perception of a subject whose
boundaries are constantly in flux, and they continue to problematise
the relationship between the 'other' found externally (for example,
the racialised other or the Jew) and the internal other of the unconscious. The notion of otherness is premised on something that is not
the same, hence something outside, yet what is being evoked here is an
interpenetration, a one-within-the-other, inescapably together yet
experienced as troubling and dangerous. In addition, the very alienness
of the other and the disturbing response this engenders can be seen
as a source for psychoanalysis' own difficulty in maintaining an
encounter with otherness without recourse to appeasement or even
colonialist ideology. Praising the Freudian decentring, Laplanche nevertheless argues that it is incomplete, that the 'Copernican revolution'
is 'unfinished': 'Certainly, the ego is not the master of its own house,
but it is, after all, nonetheless at home there' (1997, p. 659). Not for

the first time, psychoanalysis is accused of betraying its own radical vision, its capacity to roam with the tigers as they worry and tear at the fragile fabric of human egotism. Psychoanalysis shows us that we are 'not the master of [our] own house', but in its emancipatory and therapeutic move, it suggests that we *could* be, that what it takes is, as Freud (1917, p. 435) claims, merely that the patient should be repositioned so that he 'has rather less that is unconscious and rather more that is conscious in him than he had before.'

This, it seems, is similar to the disparaging contrast Philip Rieff (1966) made between the 'ecstatic attitude' characteristic of the therapeutic optimism of Jung, Reich, and others, and the unforgivingness – and the pessimism so attractive to the liberal consciousness – of the Freudian 'analytic attitude', which promises nothing by way of consolation, only more (and harder-to-bear) knowledge. For Laplanche, the relapse into the hope of mastery, the shift towards cure, perhaps, is a retreat from recognition of the essential alienness of human subjectivity. Moreover, it is not an accidental retreat, but inherent in the material. As John Fletcher (1999, p. 3) writes in his introduction to Laplanche's *Essays on Otherness*:

> To this dialectic between a decentring to which Freud officially aligns himself and a recurrent recentring, Laplanche joins the diagnostic notion of a wandering or going-astray of Freudian thought... The covering over and occlusion of the discovery of the radical otherness of the unconscious and sexuality in Freud's thought, Laplanche suggests, trace out the movements of just such a covering over in the human subject itself.

Awareness of the extent to which what is other dominates our existence is too painful, too terrifying, to be maintained; instead, both the individual and psychoanalysis itself 'wander' back from the momentary vision of this truth, to the fantasy of completeness, of narcissistic selfhood – not coincidentally referenced by several theorists as the driving dynamic behind anti-Semitism. There is something to be alert to here in reflecting on the impossibility of acceptance of the other, or at least on how painful such an acceptance can be; it is also possible that this is one source of psychoanalysis' historical 'wandering' away from its Jewish origins as well as from its commitment to critical thought.

Unlike some more abstract psychoanalytic theorists, Laplanche sees the other as a very specific figure: rather than being general and 'transindividual', it is the actual adult in the infant-adult relationship. This adult plays a 'seductive' role, where the term 'seduction' is employed because the adult's 'message' to the child is 'enigmatic', exciting yet also mystifying. That is, the child knows that she or he is in receipt of some kind of message from the other, but this message is opaque or 'enigmatic': it cannot be adequately translated. The child feels called, addressed, but does not know to what end; generalising the famous Freudian question about femininity, the subject asks, 'What does the other want?' For instance, the child knows of the breast as an object of desire, but also has a sneaking feeling that the breast wants something too. 'The maternal breast,' writes Fletcher (1999, p. 14), 'apart from satisfying the infant's needs and offering warmth and comfort, is itself an erogenous organ and agent of maternal fantasy.' 'Incorporating' this object, as contemporary psychoanalysis might have it, means taking in the unanswerable question of the other: 'What does it want (from me)?' That question is the one that plagues all who are put in the position of authority: the teacher, the lover, the parent, the political leader, the psychoanalyst; each of these 'impossible professions' is impossible in part because it is based on an enigmatic question, one not in any way formulated or capable of clear articulation, but nevertheless probing away, undermining the very claims that it seems to support. Freud himself, at the end of *Civilisation and its Discontents*, famously opined that what people seek is 'consolation', 'for at bottom that is what they are all demanding – the wildest revolutionaries no less passionately than the most virtuous believers' (Freud, 1930, p. 339); and he went on to argue that he could not give them any of that. Instead, psychoanalysis offers only the disruptive knowledge of something powerfully unmanageable operating at the core of the self. Selfhood is based on psychic integrity, but how can this be sustained when people have the feeling, always and everywhere, that something else is speaking within them – something over which they have no control (the defining feature of the unconscious), and the voice of which they cannot even properly hear?

Developmentally, what makes the message enigmatic, according to Laplanche, is not simply the child's limited conceptual understanding. It is, rather, the way desire operates within the adult. Bearing the traces of her or his own untranslatable residue, a kind of traumatic kernel of what was implanted in childhood, the adult speaks from her or his unconscious; so in the most important way, not only does the child not know what has been said, but the adult knows not what she or he is saying. As Laplanche himself puts it:

> To address someone with no shared interpretive system, in a mainly extraverbal manner… such is the function of adult messages, which I claim to be simultaneously and indissociably enigmatic and sexual – in so far as they are not transparent to themselves, but compromised (in the psychoanalytic sense of the term) by the adult's relation to his own unconscious, by unconscious sexual fantasies set in motion by his relation to the child.   (1997, p. 661)

The child is 'seduced' by enigmatic signifiers that arise from the external other and yet are constitutive of the child's own unconscious, in a never-ending cycle from generation to generation, laying a mystery, an alienness, at the centre of psychic life. This mystery is sexual, desiring, provoked by the same unconscious message implanted in the now-adult subject by the adult of her or his infancy; sexuality here, in the full Freudian sense, with all its disturbance and refusal to be reduced to something relational, is an alien anthem playing within each one of us. This is why the sexual can itself be experienced as 'other', as something that takes us over, as a 'not-me' that is at one and the same time the source of the subject's most intimate being.

Laplanche's theory has a range of connections with other psychoanalytic approaches and also links with assertions of the importance of the other in some very profound psychoanalytically-informed writing that has come out of the AIDs and '9/11' crises (e.g. Butler, 2003). But what Laplanche achieves most profoundly is to indicate that the other is not just a container or mirror, nor a purveyor of narcissistic fantasy, but is *causal* in the constitution of subjectivity, profoundly passionate yet utterly mysterious, and right there at the centre of psychic life. The parent no more 'intends' this seductive message than does the child invent it; both are ensnared by it, as a continuing disruption in the unconscious. Something passes between the other and the subject, a kind of code, glittering enigmatically, attractive and elusive, seductive and irreconcilably alien. In this passing between, it becomes clear just how much there can be no personal subject without the other; instead, it is *from the other* that the subject comes.

There is, however, a quandary here, arising out of the contrast between this assertion of the crucial presence of the other in constructing the subject – a presence that is psychological as well as ethical – and the hatred translated into anti-Semitic and other racist violence. If one assumes that there is a relationship between hatred and fear, that is, that the wish to obliterate the other arises out of the subject's own anxiety of dissolution, then what is it that makes the other so terrifying? Žižek (1994, p. 78) tracks the ways in which the very unreality of the denigrated other sustains it in the face of violence, making for an escalating phenomenon of hatred: 'This paradox, which has already emerged apropos the Jews in Nazi Germany... the more they were ruthlessly exterminated, the more horrifying were the dimensions acquired by those who remained.' Being unreal, being fantastic, the hated other cannot actually be eradicated; in a sense, the perfect enemy is the one who does not exist, who can be reinvented every time to face the subject's renewed wrath. But why? Why the fear and loathing?

Othering otherness

The argument in this chapter has focused on the centrality of the other in the construction of the subject. The reason why it makes no sense to insist on a clear boundary between self and other is that the latter is constantly involved in the former, not just being carried around as a set of memories and identifications, but absolutely implicated in and through its very being. The 'enigmatic signifier' faces us with a deeply mysterious yet absolutely concrete realization of the other's desire within us; this can be seen as *producing* the unconscious as a mode of 'outsideness' within. Taking this argument on, the search for recognition of and by the other, which some contemporary ('intersubjectivist') versions of psychoanalytic theory see as the central urge in people's lives, becomes a highly complex process in which what is being sought is a link with an other *who can embody this internal strangeness* and ease the subject out of it. 'Soliciting a becoming,' as Butler (2003, p. 25) puts it, is entwined with the other's difference because it is in this difference that the supposed answer to the subject's question might be found; *sameness*, after all, can do no more than confirm what is already known. Recognition of the outside other, in the strong sense of giving the other ascendancy, of tolerating the other's difference, is a key element in the maintenance of subjecthood because it brings the internal other to life, holding out the hope that something can be done with it, that the other can name it and give it shape.

In their work on early psychic life, Fonagy and Target (2000, pp. 854–5) offer the idea that the emergence of mentalising, the capacity 'to assume the existence of thoughts and feelings in oneself and in others, and to recognize these as connected to outer reality' is 'deeply embedded in the child's primary object relationships, principally in the "mirroring" relationship with the caregiver'. 'Understanding the nature of the mental world cannot be done alone,' they write; 'it requires discovery and recognition of the self in the eye of the other' (Target and Fonagy 1996, p. 461). This is but one example, attractive because of the detailed clinical and empirical grounding these analysts offer for their theories, of the view being taken here, that the creation of the mental life of the subject *depends upon* the existence and psychic capacities of the other. The infant feels emotions welling up, is psychically entangled in a sense of something passionate and material but horribly unknown that has its existence maybe 'inside', maybe 'outside'. Looking at the other who is also deeply present, and thus not at a distance but nevertheless 'different', the infant absorbs the message of what that fragmenting state may be. Something meaningful comes into existence, out of the other's mirroring of the subject's confusion.

In the light of Laplanche's theory, one can add to this the idea that the other also does not 'know' what she or he is reflecting 'back'; rather, her or his own unconscious desires are stirred up. This is the area of mystery arising from the untranslatable messages left through the previous generation's enigmatic signifiers. For the infant, then, the act of seeking the other's mind in order to give form to its own internal strangeness brings with it comfort and order ('mentalising'), but also produces further disturbance. This, perhaps, can be taken as a model for the subject-object encounter throughout life, not just in early infancy. We 'lean on' others to make sense of the unspeakable elements of our own subjectivities; in periods of loving intimacy, we do indeed find this, but we are also invaded by the other's mystery too, keeping the whole cycle going.

If we look to the other to bring us to life in this way, then his or her existence is an absolute necessity. But this dependence, this genuine psychological primacy of the other, is also what is hardest to bear: it threatens to make identities unsustainable, selfhood to collapse. The 'other' that is so intimate inside us – the unexplained message of the unconscious – 'calls out' to the other that is apparently outside, bypassing ego and self, desiring something without quite knowing what it is. To borrow the Kleinian terminology for a moment, what else could this bring up inside the subject but the most virulent paranoid-schizoid fantasies? The 'ex-centric' location of psychic life (in and of the other) is what most challenges and draws the subject, enriching it and moving it on ('instigating a transformation', as Butler (2003, p. 25) writes), but it also threatens to kill it completely, to make the subject irrelevant. Fighting for its continued existence, the subject seeks the other to give shape to its inner unknown message; but it might also turn on the other, as on that inner life, seeing in it not just the 'reflection' or repository of inner doubts projected outwards, but the *actual*, *material* source of those doubts. If the other is primary and one is torn apart by otherness within and without, then hatred for the other can become the overwhelming reality.

There is clearly a danger in this of reducing political issues to psychological ones, so it is worth reiterating the significance of social and historical conditions in the grounding and production of racist and other forms of hate. The argument in this chapter is in fact in line with this perception, with the additional claim that the intensity of the subjective charge with which anti-Semitic and racist hate is filled – the virulence with which the figure of the outside other is despised – derives from ways in which the psyche is structured around an encounter with otherness. Interpersonally and 'intersubjectively', people find themselves confronted with the splits around which society is organised; these splits are themselves coded in terms of the figures of the other and of otherness, so that they are laden with psychic meaning. This in turn becomes part of the psychological heritage as the mind forms, structured through processes of internalisation, differentiation and identification. In the contemporary psychoanalytic work described here, what is stressed is not just the connection between subject and other, but the 'originary' function of the other in forming the subject, and the continuing causal force of that other in psychic life. The other is marked by difference, otherwise it would not be genuinely 'other', but this difference is not just external to the subject; it is right there at its unconscious core. There are conditions of insecurity, oppression, and violence, so many of them it seems that they swamp the modern world, under which this internal otherness is not a source of solace and creativity so much as a disturbance, a reminder of the 'Real' described by Lacanian psychoanalysts, with its grimness and its continual threat of the abyss. When this happens, otherness is attacked. In turn, this diminishes the possibilities for transformation through recognition by and of the other, leading to a more isolated and poisonous 'internal' otherness, producing the weeds of doubt, the wilderness within. This is perhaps the way the racist lie, to which Rustin (1991) refers, grows. The individual subject becomes more and more dissipated in its own violence, more tempted to strike out, to hate for its own sake, to hate itself with all the world, to hate all difference, which it finds in everything because that is what difference is – to hate, that is, just to hate.

Anti-Semitism and racism in general are not, therefore simply convenient ways of dealing with split-off emotions. Instead, they are constructed from and in social divisions and given force by the founding role of the other in forming the psyche; this makes them full of the psychic intensity of the unconscious, it is true, but they reflect not some unchanging psychological fact – for example, that people will always fear and despise the other – but rather the derogation and disturbance around otherness in social life.

Conclusion

Jewish identity, anti-Semitism and psychoanalysis go together in powerful ways; each term makes some kind of sense of the others, and each has been implicated in the practices of the other. Psychoanalysis arose at a time in which Jewish identity was being forged in its modern form, and as such both expressed it and rebelled against it. Anti-Semitism was a significant force in impelling the creative burst that produced psychoanalysis and other Jewish contributions to the modernist revolution; but it could also be found in the concepts and practices of psychoanalysis itself, and specifically in the demise of German psychoanalysis when faced with Nazism. Turning things around, however, psychoanalysis as 'Jewish science' also offers productive concepts through which identity issues – including questions of Jewish identity – can be and have been explored; and it provides theories of anti-Semitism, albeit frequently muted ones. There is a great deal of what Laplanche might call 'wandering' in this history too: from Freud's own ambivalence about Jews and Jewish identity, through the abandonment of the 'Jewish science' amongst German psychoanalysts, to the failure to forcibly follow through the fruits of psychoanalytic thinking to encompass anti-Semitism and racism in general. In each case, there is a hint of psychoanalysts looking the truly difficult issues in the face, and then backing away in self-protective confusion. Just as it would have been easier to praise psychoanalysis if, 'At a certain stage of its development, "Aryan" psychoanalysts simply said "no"' (Chasseguet-Smirgel, 1988, p. 1061), so it would be more comfortable if the striking understanding of unconscious life so compellingly outlined by Freud and his followers, could be finally extended to a thorough encounter with the destructiveness of anti-Semitic and racist activity.

What seems to be both desired and feared is the 'other'. For psychoanalysts, this is primarily the other of the unconscious, but what is becoming increasingly clear from recent psychoanalytic theorising is that this inner other is itself an emblem of external otherness. To this point, this realisation seems mostly to be expressed in the form of an analogy (the unconscious is *like* the stranger, the alien), although this chapter has also outlined some recent thinking on how the sense of otherness can be implanted in the individual by the ministering activities of specific external others, nominally the parent. The key issue here is that the other is not some pragmatically constructed and convenient carrier of personal disturbance, but an absolutely central element in social life. Whether this has always to be the case is a moot point, but it is clear that historically and culturally, otherness and the sense of the alien is deeply embedded in Western society. Whilst there are several forms that this takes, including vicious modes of anti-Black and other colour racism, anti-Semitism has been and remains a potent signifier of the underside of Western culture. The Jew is a *principle* of otherness for the West, articulating (through contrast) what is safe and unitary by embodying difference. The two-thousand year history of Christian anti-Semitism has created a figure that is more than a symbol of the splits in Western society; the Jew is rather the kernel of otherness, that which is always found everywhere, yet is never to be allowed in. Inchoate fantasies of purity opposed by Jewish corruption, of secret societies and conspiracies, of trickery and poison ('poisoning the wells', as Grunberger (1964) remarks) show that the Jew is the materialisation of that otherness which is most feared and least understood. 'In' the unconscious, this means that otherness itself has a 'Jewish' feel to it; the hidden recesses of sex and aggression are easily identified with anti-Semitic paradigms. It is not, then, that the Jew is just a convenient scapegoat upon whom these inner urges can be projected; it is rather that just as psychoanalysis is 'Jewish' in important ways, so is the unconscious that it has discovered and invented. *All* otherness in the West is Jewish, including that inner otherness that is unconscious desire.

If this is an extreme formulation, then this is because what has to be thought about is an extreme phenomenon: the recurrent, never-ending, barely even cyclical reiteration of anti-Semitic ideology and practices. Freud offered some ways into understanding this, although these were undermined by his own cultural ambivalence about Jews and his powerfully motivated wish to sublimate the Jewish stereotype. Post-Freudian analysts have supplied only limited additional insights, though they have shown how anti-Semitism works to preserve psychic integrity in many people, and they have also offered some plausible accounts of what allows mass anti-Semitic movements to take hold. As psychoanalysis has often shown, however, in dealing with real irrational material, it is often necessary to push things to the limit, to embrace 'excessive' thoughts in order to counter 'excessive' emotional intensity. So despite it being easily shown that otherness in the West has many components – misogyny, for one crucial example, colonialist thought for another – I want to finish with the bald statement that anti-Semitism is precisely such a modality of excess, legitimised, institutionalised and naturalised over centuries and now deeply internalised in a coding of the Jew as both enticing and dangerous, both alluring and disgusting. This is not just a parallel phenomenon to how people feel about their unconscious desires – alluring and disgusting too; it is *the same thing*. The unconscious is the materialisation of otherness, and in a society historically constructed on the basis that the other is the Jew, then social otherness and psychological otherness entwine, feeding off each other and carrying anti-Semitism with them wherever they may go.

References

Abraham, K. and Freud, S. (1965) *A Psychoanalytic Dialogue: The Letters of Sigmund Freud and Karl Abraham 1907–1926*. New York: Basic Books.

Ackerman, N. and Jahoda, M. (1948) The Dynamic Basis of Anti-Semitic Attitudes. *The Psychoanalytic Quarterly, 17*, 240–260.

Ackerman, N. and Jahoda, M. (1950) *Antisemitism and Emotional Disorder: A psychoanalytic Interpretation*. NY: Harper.

Adorno, T., Frenkel-Brunswick, E., Levinson, D. and Sanford, R. (1950) *The Authoritarian Personality*. NY: Norton, 1982.

Adorno, T. and Horkheimer, M. (1947) *Dialectic of Enlightenment*. London: John Cumming, 1979.

Antonovsky, A. (1988) Aryan analysts in Nazi Germany: Questions of adaptation, desymbolization and betrayal. *Psychoanalysis and Contemporary Thought, 11*, 213–231.

Bair, D. (2004) *Jung: A Biography*. NY: Little, Brown.

Bauman, Z. (1989) *Modernity and the Holocaust*. Cambridge: Cambridge University Press.

Bergman, W. (1988) Approaches to Antisemitism Based on Psychodynamics and Personality Theory. In W. Bergman (ed.) (1988) *Error Without Trial: Psychological Research on Antisemitism*. Berlin and New York: Walter de Gruyter.

Bibring, G. (1952) Report on the Seventeenth International Psycho-Analytical Congress. *International Journal of Psycho-Analysis, 33*, 249–272.

Boyarin, D. (1997) *Unheroic Conduct*. Berkeley: University of California Press.

Brecht, K. (1995) In the Aftermath of Nazi-Germany: Alexander Mitscherlich and Psychoanalysis – Legend and Legacy. *American Imago, 52*, 291–312.

Brecht, K., Friedrioch, V., Hermanns, L., Kaminer, I. and Juelcih, D. (eds) (1985) *'Here Life Goes On in a Most Peculiar Way': Psychoanalysis before and after 1933*. Hamburg: Kellner Verlag/London: Goethe Institut.

Breuer, J. and Freud, S. (1895) *Studies on Hysteria*. London: Hogarth Press.

Brickman, C. (2003) *Aboriginal Populations in the Mind*. NY: Columbia University Press.

Bronner, S. and Kellner, D. (eds) (1989) *Critical Theory and Society: A Reader*. London: Routledge.

Butler, J. (2003) Violence, Mourning, Politics. *Studies in Gender and Sexuality, 4*, 9–37.

Chasseguet-Smirgel, J. (1987) 'Time's White Hair We Ruffle': Reflections on the Hamburg Congress. *International Review of Psycho-Analysis, 14*, 433–444.

Chasseguet-Smirgel, J. (1988) [Review of J-L Evard (ed.)] Les Années Brunes. 1. Psychoanalysis Under the Third Reich. *Journal of the American Psychoanalytic Association, 36*, 1059–1066.

Chasseguet-Smirgel, J. (1990) Reflections of a Psychoanalyst Upon the Nazi Biocracy and Genocide. *International Review of Psycho-Analysis, 17*, 167–176.

Chrzanowski, G. (1975) Psychoanalysis: Ideology and Practitioners. *Contemporary Psychoanalysis, 11*, 492–499.

217

Clarke, S. (2003) *Social Theory, Psychoanalysis and Racism*. London: Palgrave.

Cocks, G. (1997) *Psychotherapy in the Third Reich*. Oxford: Oxford University Press (second edition).

Cocks, G. (2001) The Devil and the Details. *Psychoanalytic Review, 88*, 225–244.

Derrida, J. (1995) *Archive fever: A Freudian Impression*. Chicago University of Chicago Press.

Diller, J. (1991) *Freud's Jewish Identity: A Case Study in the Impact of Ethnicity*. London: Associated University Press.

Eickhoff, F. (1995) The Formation of the German Psychoanalytical Association (DPV): Regaining the Psychoanalytical Orientation Lost in the Third Reich. *International Journal of Psycho-Analysis, 76*, 945–956.

Fanon, F. (1952) *Black Skin, White Masks*. London: Pluto, 1967.

Fenichel, O. (1946) Elements of a Psychoanalytic Theory of Anti-Semitism. In E. Simmel (ed.) *Anti-Semitism: A Social Disease*. NY: International Universities Press.

Fletcher, J. (1999) Psychoanalysis and the Question of the Other. Introduction to J. Laplanche (1999) *Essays on Otherness*. London: Routledge.

Fonagy, P. and Target, M. (2000) Playing with Reality: 3. The Persistence of Dual Psychic Reality in Borderline Patients. *International Journal of Psycho-Analysis, 8*, 853–73.

Freud, A. (1949) Report on the Sixteenth International Psycho-Analytical Congress. *Bulletin of the International Psychoanalytic Association, 30*, 178–208.

Freud, A. (1978) Inaugural Lecture for the Sigmund Freud Chair at the Hebrew University, Jerusalem. *International Journal of Psycho-Analysis, 59*, 125–148.

Freud, S. (1900) *The Interpretation of Dreams*. London: Hogarth Press (SE4, 1953).

Freud, S. (1905) *Jokes and their Relation to the Unconscious*. London: Hogarth Press (SE.8, 1960).

Freud, S. (1909) *Analysis of a Phobia in a Five-Year-Old Boy*. London: Hogarth (SE10, 1–145, 1955).

Freud, S. (1914) *Totem and Taboo*. London: Hogarth Press (SE13, 1–161, 1955).

Freud, S. (1917) *Introductory Lectures on Psychoanalysis*. London: Hogarth Press (SE15 and 16, 1963).

Freud, S. (1921) *Group Psychology and the Analysis of the Ego*. London: Hogarth Press (SE18, 65–143, 1955).

Freud, S. (1925) Resistances to Psycho-Analysis. London: Hogarth Press (SE19).

Freud, S. (1930a) Preface to the Hebrew Translation of *Totem and Taboo*. London: Hogarth Press (SE13, 1955).

Freud, S. (1930b) *Civilisation and its Discontents*. London: Hogarth Press (SE21, 57–145, 1961).

Freud, S. (1937) *Analysis Terminable and Interminable*. London: Hogarth Press (SE23, 209–53, 1964).

Freud, S. (1939) *Moses and Monotheism*. London: Hogarth Press (SE23, 1–137, 1964).

Freud, S. (1961) *Letters of Sigmund Freud 1873–1939* (edited by E. Freud). London: Hogarth Press.

Frosh, S. (1989) *Psychoanalysis and Psychology*. London: Macmillan.

Frosh, S. (1991) *Identity Crisis*. London: Macmillan.

Frosh, S. (1997) *For and Against Psychoanalysis*. London: Routledge.

Frosh, S. (1999) *The Politics of Psychoanalysis*. London: Macmillan.

Frosh, S. (2002) The Other *American Imago, 59,* 389–407.

Frosh, S. (2003) Psychoanalysis in Britain: The Rituals of Destruction. In D. Bradshaw (ed.) *A Concise Companion to Modernism.* Oxford: Blackwell.

Gay, P. (1988) *Freud: A Life for Our Time.* London: Dent.

Gilman, S. (1991) Reading Freud in English: Problems, Paradoxes, and a Solution. *International Review of Psycho-Analysis, 18,* 331–344.

Gilman, S. (1993) *Freud, Race and Gender.* Princeton: Princeton University Press.

Glenn, J. (1960) Circumcision and Anti-Semitism. *Psychoanalytic Quarterly, 29,* 395–399.

Glover, E. (1934) Report of the Thirteenth International Psycho-Analytical Congress. *Bul. Int. Psychoanal. Assn., 15,* 485–524.

Goggin, J. and Goggin, E. (2001) *Death of a 'Jewish Science': Psychoanalysis in the Third Reich.* West Lafayette: Purdue University Press.

Goldhagen, D. (1997) *Hitler's Willing Executioners.* London: Abacus.

Grossman, S. (1979) C.G. Jung and National Socialism. *Journal of European Studies, 9,* 231–259.

Grunberger, B. (1964) The Anti-Semite and the Oedipal Conflict. *International Journal of Psycho-Analysis, 45,* 380–385.

Grunberger, B. (1989) On Narcissism, Aggressivity and Anti-Semitism. In B. Grunberger *New Essays on Narcissism.* London: Free Association Books.

Halpern, J. (1999) Freud's Intrapsychic Use of the Jewish Culture and Religion. *J. Amer. Psychoanal. Assn., 47,* 1191–1212.

Hayman, R. (1999) *A Life of Jung.* London: Bloomsbury.

Horkheimer, M. (1938) The Jews and Europe. In S. Bronner, S. and D. Kellner, (eds) (1989) *Critical Theory and Society: A Reader.* London: Routledge.

Jacoby, R. (1975) *Social Amnesia.* Sussex: Harvester Press.

Jacoby, R. (1983) *The Repression of Psychoanalysis.* New York: Basic Books.

Jones, E. (1951) The Psychology of the Jewish Question. In E. Jones, *Essays in Applied Psycho-Analysis.* London: Hogarth Press.

Jung, C. (1918) The Role of the Unconscious. In C.G. Jung, *Collected Works.* London: Routledge, 1970 (Vol. 10, pp. 3–28).

Jung, C. (1933) Editorial to Zentralblatt für psychotherapie. In C.G. Jung, *Collected Works.* London: Routledge, 1970 (Vol. 10, pp. 533–4).

Jung, C. (1934a) The Development of Personality. In C.G. Jung, *Collected Works.* London: Routledge, 1970 (Vol. 10, pp. 167–186).

Jung, C. (1934b) The State of Psychotherapy Today. In C.G. Jung *Collected Works.* London: Routledge, 1970 (Vol. 10, pp. 157–173).

Jung, C. (1934c) A Rejoinder to Dr Bally. In C.G. Jung, *Collected Works.* London: Routledge, 1970 (Vol. 10, pp. 535–546).

Jung, C. (1936) Wotan. In C.G. Jung, *Collected Works.* London: Routledge, 1970 (Vol. 10, pp. 179–193).

Jung, C. (1946) After the Catastrophe. In C.G. Jung, *Collected Works.* London: Routledge, 1970 (Vol. 10, pp. 194–217).

Kijak, M. (1989) Further Discussions of Reactions of Psychoanalysts to the Nazi Persecution, and Lessons to be Learnt. *International Review of Psycho-Analysis, 16,* 213–222.

Klein, D. (1985) *Jewish Origins of the Psychoanalytic Movement.* Chicago: Chicago University Press.

Klein, M. (1946) Notes on Some Schizoid Mechanisms. In M. Klein, *Envy and Gratitude and Other Works*. New York: Delta, 1975.

Knafo, D. (1999) Anti-Semitism in the Clinical Setting. *Journal of the American Psychoanalytical Association, 47*, 35–63.

Knoepfmacher, H. (1979) Sigmund Freud and the B'Nai B'Rith. *Journal of the American Psychoanalytic Association, 27*, 441–449.

Kovel, J. (1984) *White Racism*. London: Free Association Books.

Kovel, J. (1995) On Racism and Psychoanalysis. In A. Elliott and S. Frosh (eds) *Psychoanalysis in Contexts*. London: Routledge.

Kreuzer-Haustein, U. (2002) Psychoanalysis and Psychoanalysts in Germany after the Shoa: Points for Discussion by the Panel. *European Psychoanalytic Federation Bulletin, 56*, (16).

Kristeva, J. (1988) *Strangers to Ourselves*. London: Harvester Wheatsheaf, 1991.

Lacan, J. (1972–3) Seminar XX: Encore. In J. Mitchell and J. Rose (eds) *Feminine Sexuality*. London: Macmillan, 1982.

Laplanche, J. (1997) The Theory of Seduction and the Problem of the Other. *International Journal of Psycho-Analysis, 78*, 653–66.

Léon, M. (1946) The Case of Dr Carl Gustav Jung: Pseudo-scientist Nazi Auxiliary. *Report to U.S. Department of State and Nuremberg Tribunal*.

Levinas, E. (1991) *Entre Nous: On Thinking of the Other*. London: Athlone, 1998.

Loeblowitz-Lennard, H. (1947) The Jew as Symbol. *Psychoanalytic Quarterly, 16*, 33–38.

Loewenstein, R. (1947) Review of E. Simmel (ed.) *Anti-Semitism: A Social Disease*. NY: International Universities Press, 1946 *The Psychoanalytic Quarterly, 16*, 409–413.

Lowenstein, R. (1952) Anti-Semites in Psychoanalysis. In W. Bergman (ed.) (1988) *Error Without Trial: Psychological Research on Anti-Semitism*. Berlin and New York: Walter de Gruyler.

Marcuse, H. (1955) *Eros and Civilisation*. Boston: Beacon Press, 1966.

McLaughlin, F. (1978) Report of the 30th International Psycho-Analytical Congress. *Bull Int Psyan Assn, 59*, 64–130.

Mitscherlich, A. and Mitscherlich, M. (1967) *Inability to Mourn*. NY: Grove Press, 1984.

Moses, R. and Hrushovski-Moses, R. (1986) A Form of Group Denial at the Hamburg Congress. *International Review of Psycho-Analysis, 13*, 175–180.

Müller-Braunschweig, C. (1938) German Psycho-Analytical Society. *Bul. Int. Psychoanal. Assn, 19*, 163–164.

Nitzschke, B. (1999) Psychoanalysis during National Socialism: Present-Day Consequences of a Historical Controversy in the 'Case' of Wilhelm Reich. *Psychoanalytic Review, 86*, 349–366.

Ostow, M. (1986) The Psychodynamics of Apocalyptic: Discussion of Papers on Identification and the Nazi Phenomenon. *International Journal of Psycho-Analysis, 67*, 277–285.

Ostow, M. (1996a) *Myth and Madness: The Psychodynamics of Antisemitism*. New Brunswick: Transaction.

Ostow, M. (1996b) Myth and Madness: A Report of a Psychoanalytic Study of Antisemitism. *International Journal of Psycho-Analysis, 77*, 15–31.

Rappaport, R. (1975) *Anti-Judaism: A Psychohistory*. Chicago: Perspective Press.

Reich, W. (1933) *Character Analysis*. NY:OIP, 1949.

Reich, W. (1948) *The Mass Psychology of Fascism*. Harmondsworth: Penguin.

Rickels, L. (2002) *Nazi Psychoanalysis: Volume 1, Only Psychoanalysis Won the War*. Minneapolis: University of Minnesota Press.

Rieff, P. (1959) *Freud: The Mind of the Moralist*. Chicago: University of Chicago Press, 1979.

Rieff, P. (1966) *The Triumph of the Therapeutic*. Harmondsworth: Penguin.

Rittmeister, J. (1939) Letter to Alfred and Edith Storch, Münsingen, 15.10.1939.

Rose, J. (2003)) Response to Edward Said. In Said, E. *Freud and the Non-European*. London: Verso.

Roudinesco, E. (1986) *Jacques Lacan and Co.: A History of Psychoanalysis in France 1925–1985*. London: Free Association Books, 1990.

Rustin, M. (1991) *The Good Society and the Inner World*. London: Verson.

Said, E. (2003) *Freud and the Non-European*. London: Verso.

Samuels, A. (1993) *The Political Psyche*. London: Routledge.

Sharaf, M. (1983) *Fury on Earth: A Biography of Wilhelm Reich*. London: Hutchinson.

Simmel, E. (1946a) Introduction. In E. Simmel (ed.) *Anti-Semitism: A Social Disease*. NY: International Universities Press.

Simmel, E. (1946b) Anti-Semitism and Mass Psychopathology. In E. Simmel (ed.) *Anti-Semitism: A Social Disease*. NY: International Universities Press.

Spiegel, R. (1975) Survival of Psychoanalysis in Nazi Germany. *Contemporary Psychoanalysis*, 11, 479–491.

Steiner, R. (2000) '*It is a New Kind of Diaspora*': *Explorations in the Sociopolitical and Cultural Context of Psychoanalysis*. London: Karnac.

Target, M. and Fonagy, P. (1996) Playing with Reality: 2. The Development of Psychic Reality from a Theoretical Perspective. *International Journal of Psycho-Analysis*, 77, 459–79.

Theweleit, K. (1977) *Male Fantasies*. Cambridge: Polity, 1987.

Thomä, H. (1969) Some Remarks on Psychoanalysis in Germany, Past and Present. *International Journal of Psycho-Analysis*, 50, 683–692.

Von Dohnyani, K. (1986) Opening Ceremony, 34th IPA Congress. *International Journal of Psychoanalysis*, 67, 2–4.

Wangh, M. (1964) National Socialism and the Genocide of the Jews – A Psychoanalytic Study of a Historical Event. *International Journal of Psycho-Analysis*, 45, 386–395.

Weinshel, E. (1986) Report of the 34th International Psycho-Analytic Congress. *Bull. Int. Psychan. Assn*, 67, 87–130.

Wiggershaus, R. (1986) *The Frankfurt School*. Cambridge: Polity, 1995.

Winnicott, D. (1965) *The Maturational Process and the Facilitating Environment*. London: Hogarth Press.

Yerushalmi, Y. (1991) *Freud's Moses*. New Haven: Yale University Press.

Žižek, S. (1991) *Looking Awry: an Introduction to Jacques Lacan through Popular Culture*. Cambridge, Mass.: MIT Press.

Žižek, S. (1993) *Tarrying with the Negative*. Durham: Duke University Press.

Žižek, S. (1994) *The Metastases of Enjoyment: Six Essays on Woman and Causality*. London: Verso.

Žižek, S. (1997) *The Plague of Fantasies*. London: Verso.

Index